CUYAHOGA VALLEY
SCENIC RAILROAD

CRAIG SANDERS

FONTHILL

Fonthill Media Inc.
www.fonthillmedia.com
office@fonthillmedia.com

First published 2017

ISBN 978-1-63499-032-5

Typeset in Mrs Eaves XL Serif Narrow
Printed and bound in England

CONTENTS

ACKNOWLEDGEMENTS

Many people played a role in helping bring this book to fruition, but I particularly want to acknowledge the members of the Akron Railroad Club who generously allowed me to use their photographs. They include Peter Bowler, Marty Surdyk, Robert Farkas, Paul Woodring, Mark Demaline, Edward Ribinskas, Jim Mastromatteo and Tom Fritsch. Others who provided photographs include Jim Semon, Jerry Jordak and Robert Todten.

The staff of the Akron Public Library and the Peninsula Library & Historical Society were helpful in directing me to historical information about the Cuyahoga Valley Scenic Railroad.

Finally, I want to thank my wife, Mary Ann Whitley, for copyediting the manuscript and providing encouragement throughout the project.

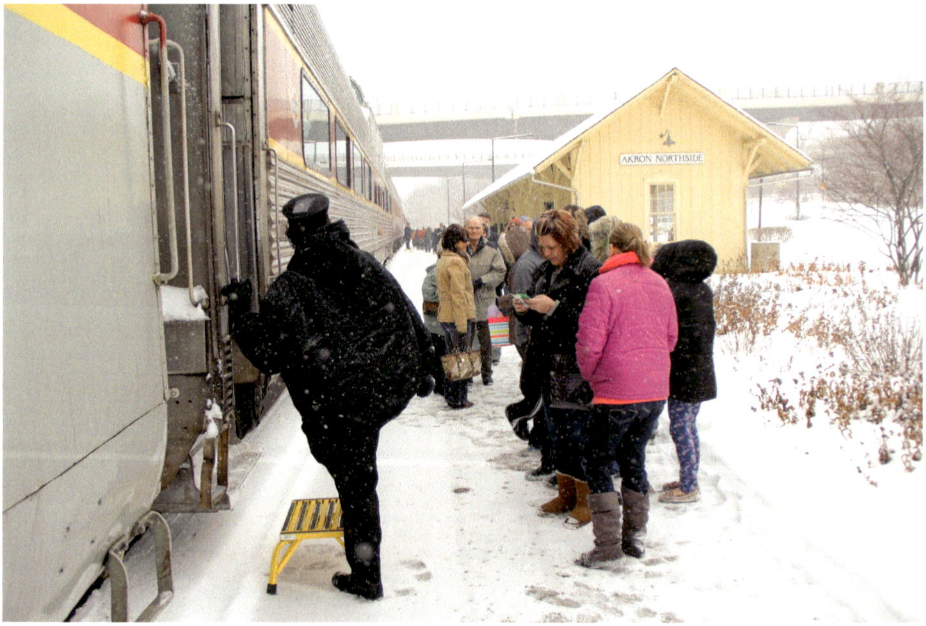

ALL ABOARD IN AKRON: Passengers line up in the snow and cold at Akron Northside Station to board their train on February 9, 2014. The CVSR has a free app that passengers can download onto their smartphones that enables them to follow the train's location, heading and speed on a map as it makes its way through the Cuyahoga Valley National Park. The app also provides access to the audio tour with stories about the history of the Cuyahoga Valley and points of interest within the CVNP. (*Craig Sanders photo*)

INTRODUCTION

The Cuyahoga Valley Scenic Railroad provides transportation to and within the Cuyahoga Valley National Park, a 33,000-acre preserve located between Cleveland and Akron in Northeast Ohio. Named for the Cuyahoga River, Ohio's only national park averages 2.8 million annual visitors, placing it among the country's fifteen most-visited national parks.

Since operations began in August 1975 on weekends during the summer and autumn, the CVSR has grown into a year-round operation running 50 weeks a year that in 2016 carried 214,063 passengers. Fifty-four percent of them rode the *National Park Scenic*, which operates Tuesday through Sunday during the summer and mostly on weekends the remainder of the year between Independence in suburban Cleveland and Akron.

Other CVSR ridership is divided among theme trains, including the *Polar Express*, wine and beer tasting, fine dining, educational programs, and children-oriented events.

CVSR trains use 25 miles of a former Baltimore & Ohio Railroad branch line now owned by the National Park Service, which purchased it on September 29, 1987, for $2.5 million after CSX Transportation won regulatory approval to abandon the route.

The CVSR is named after the Cuyahoga River Valley, which has served as a transportation artery throughout the 12,000 years that humans have lived there. Native Americans deemed the Cuyahoga—thought to be an Indian word meaning crooked river—to be neutral territory for tribes traveling between Lake Erie and the Ohio River.

Inspired by the success of New York's Erie Canal, the State of Ohio in the 1820s established the Ohio & Erie Canal to link Cleveland and Portsmouth. Built in part through the Cuyahoga Valley, the canal's first section (Akron-Cleveland) opened July 4, 1827.

The 1880 coming of the Valley Railway—later acquired by the B&O—between Cleveland and Canton via Akron dealt a devastating blow to the O&E Canal's freight and passenger business. The canal ceased operating in the Cuyahoga Valley after a 1913 flood badly damaged its infrastructure.

For decades, the Cuyahoga Valley remained a tranquil rural area that the Valley Railway and its successors promoted as a place to escape the pressures of urban life. Land donations led to the development of privately owned recreation venues, and portions of the Valley were incorporated into metropolitan park districts of Cleveland and Akron.

By the mid-1960s, some feared that encroaching urban sprawl might swallow the Cuyahoga Valley and spoil, if not ruin, its natural beauty. The National Park Service began establishing urban recreation areas in 1972, but resisted designating the Cuyahoga Valley as a national recreation area, insisting it would be better served as a state park. Congressmen John Seiberling of Akron and Ralph Regula of Navarre joined with other Ohio leaders to push legislation through Congress to establish the Cuyahoga Valley National Recreation Area. A reluctant President Gerald Ford on December 27, 1974, signed the bill that established the CVNRA. It was renamed Cuyahoga Valley National Park on October 11, 2000.

The genesis of the CVSR dates to about 1967 when Henry Lucas, a Cleveland attorney and director of the Cuyahoga County Fair, and Siegfried Buerling of the Western Reserve Historical Society, which owned Hale Farm and Village in Bath Township in Summit County, asked the B&O to operate a steam-powered passenger train to Hale Farm. The B&O turned them down, but Lucas and Buerling later joined with Cleveland businessman Nick Mileti to continue pressing for rail excursion service in the Valley, forming the nonprofit Cuyahoga Valley Preservation and Scenic Railway Association on February 16, 1972.

On June 15, 1973, the B&O became part of the Chessie System, which was headquartered in Cleveland. Chessie Chairman Cyrus S. Eaton took an interest in the Valley excursion train proposal and a railroad vice president served on the CVP&SRA board of directors. Thirty people rode a demonstration run in June 1972, but it would be another three years before the excursion service began.

The CVP&SRA reached an agreement with the Cleveland-based Midwest Railway Historical Foundation to provide a steam locomotive and passenger cars. The Midwest Chapter of the National Railway Historical Society, also based in Cleveland, provided volunteers to serve as car hosts and operating personnel. The CVL sold tickets, did marketing and performed administrative duties of the then-named Cuyahoga Valley Line. This arrangement lasted until 1991 when the CVL began operating its own equipment with its own personnel.

Changing its name to the Cuyahoga Valley Scenic Railroad in April 1994, operations grew from 32 trips a year in 1990 to more than 1,000 in 2000 as the railroad's focus shifted to serving the park. CVSR trains began running to Canton in July 2003, but that service ended in 2013.

The CVSR has a fourteen-member board of trustees, a professional staff of fifteen to twenty and more than 1,200 volunteers. The fleet includes eight locomotives and 30 passenger cars.

Aside from ticket revenue, the CVSR is funded by donations, grants, financial support from foundations, partnerships and government funding. The federal government has poured more than $20 million into infrastructure development and track maintenance, and provides financial assistance for the CVSR to maintain its facilities and equipment.

1 A RAILROAD IN THE VALLEY

The railroad line used by the Cuyahoga Valley Scenic Railroad began as the Valley Railway. Organized on August 21, 1871, to build a rail line between Cleveland and the Southeast Ohio coal fields, construction started in March 1873, but halted a year later due to financial difficulties. A ceremonial spike was driven near Old Forge in Akron on October 30, 1878, to mark the resumption of construction.

More than 200 boarded an excursion train on August 15, 1879, to ride 15.5 miles to Boston aboard four flatcars pushed by locomotive No.1 so that the passengers would not be showered with sparks. The train trip left at 6:18 a.m. and took nearly two hours.

The Valley opened between Cleveland and Canton on February 4, 1880, with an initial schedule of two daily mixed trains. On April 1, 1880, service expanded to three roundtrips, two of which were billed as "express trains."

The Valley was extended in 1882 from Canton to Valley Junction, Ohio, connecting with the Wheeling & Lake Erie Railroad and the Cleveland & Marietta Railway. The latter began hosting a Cleveland-Marietta through train and through car service also was established between Cleveland and Wheeling, West Virginia, via the W&LE.

Valley passenger service in the late 1880s was four roundtrips between Cleveland and Valley Junction and one Cleveland-Akron roundtrip. Most of this business was local and it began slipping after the Connotton Valley Railway began passenger service between Cleveland and Canton in February 1882. Further eroding Valley passenger traffic was the November 10, 1895, opening of the Akron, Bedford & Cleveland Railway, a high-speed interurban railway.

The Valley entered receivership in 1894 and emerged on October 5, 1895, as the Cleveland, Terminal & Valley Railway.

The Baltimore & Ohio Railroad viewed the Valley as a link between Cleveland and Baltimore. In 1890, the B&O gained control of a majority of the Valley's stock and on February 1, 1902, the B&O integrated the CT&V into its system although the CT&V continued to exist on paper until November 1915.

The B&O established through passenger service between Cleveland and Pittsburgh, which was later extended to Baltimore and Washington, D.C. Connections were offered at Akron Union Depot with other B&O Chicago-Baltimore/Washington trains.

By the end of World War II, the only passenger service left on the Valley was a Cleveland-Washington train and a Cleveland-Wheeling train. Only the latter served any stations between Cleveland and Akron. The Cleveland-Washington trains lasted as long as they did because they offered the fastest route between the two cities.

By the early 1960s, patronage was low and the trains began their last trips on January 3, 1963. The last scheduled passenger train through the Valley was Cleveland-bound No. 17 the next morning.

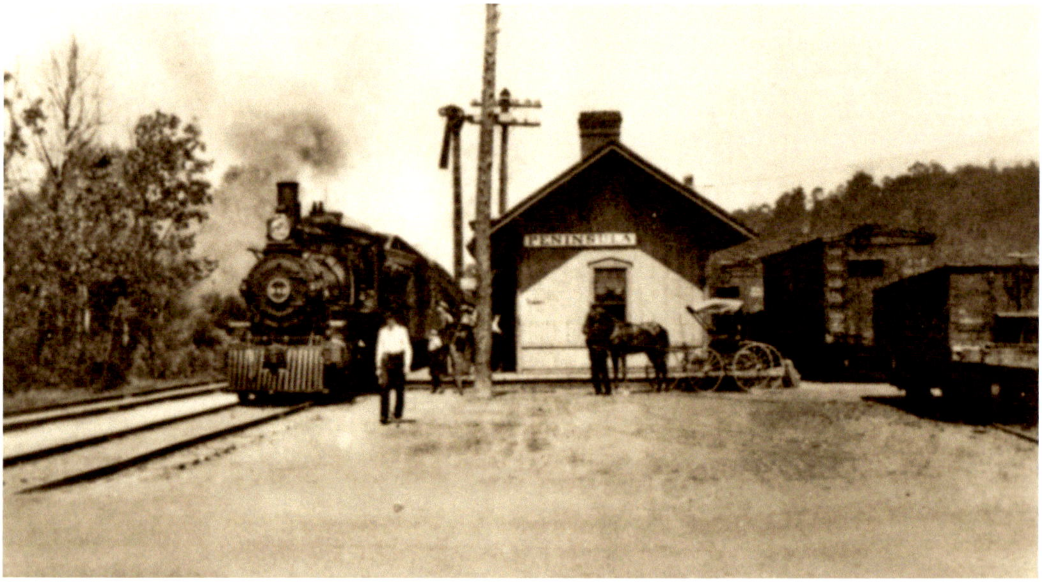

VALLEY PASSENGER SERVICE: Scheduled Valley Line passenger service began February 4, 1880, with two roundtrip Cleveland-Canton mixed trains. Service was upgraded to three roundtrip express trains on April 1, 1880, serving Cleveland at Seneca Street station. One pair of trains would later operate between Cleveland and Marietta, Ohio, using a Pennsylvania Railroad branch south of Valley Junction. Cleveland-Marietta service ended July 18, 1933, and the last service through Canton, a Rail Diesel Car to Valley Junction, continued until September 30, 1934. Passenger service at Peninsula, Jaite and South Park ended on September 30, 1951. The last B&O passenger trains on the Valley Line, Cleveland-Washington, D.C. Nos. 17/18, did not pick up or discharge passengers between Cleveland and Akron.

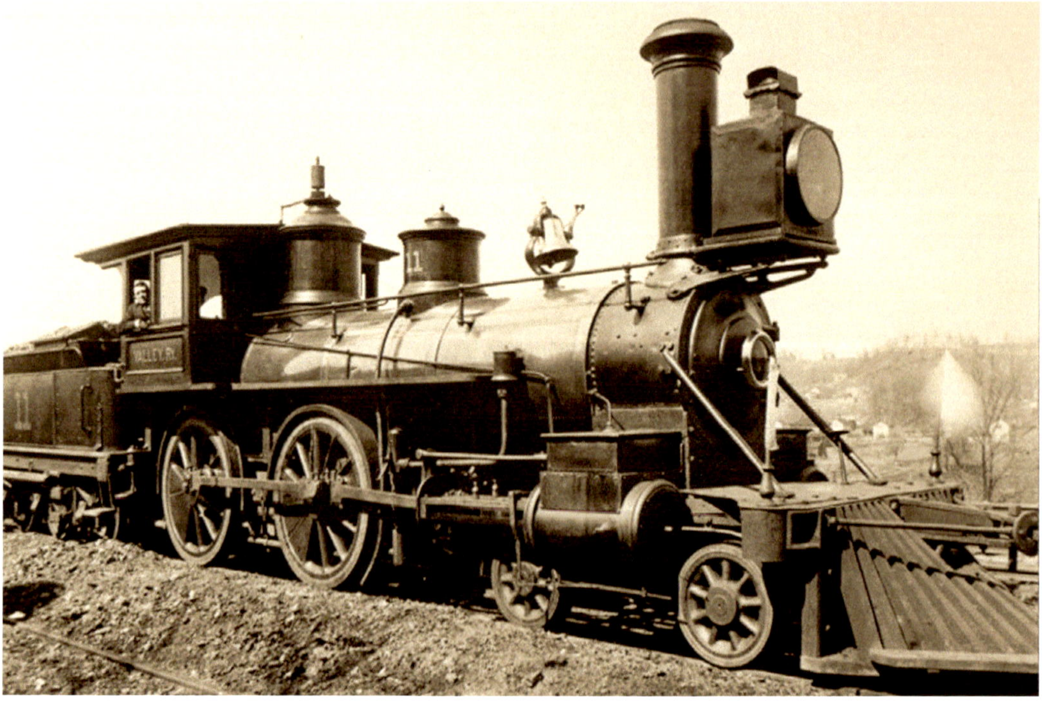

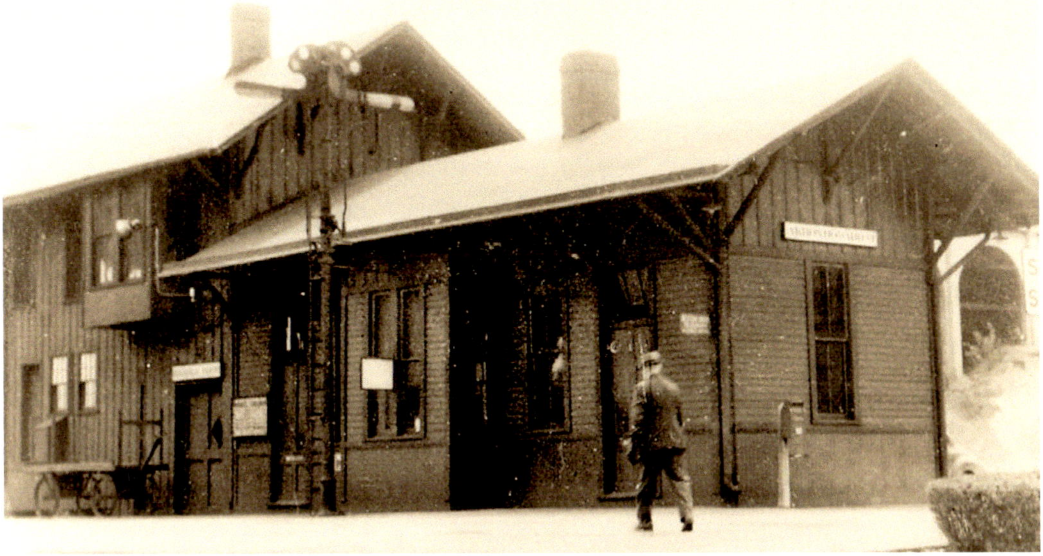

PASSENGER DEPOTS: Above, The Valley Railway's Akron station was at Ridge and Howard streets. Between June 1888 and April 3, 1892, the Valley used a station it built at West Market and Canal streets on the Akron Belt Line. After abandoning the Market Street station, Valley trains used Akron Union Depot, Howard Street station and a station in East Akron that opened on May 5, 1880. Below, the CT&V built this station in Cleveland on Canal Street in 1898. The B&O shifted its passenger trains to Cleveland Union Terminal in June 1934. The depot, shown on June 26, 1976, when it was still used as railroad offices, is today owned by Sherwin-Williams Company. *(Below, Mark Demaline photo)*

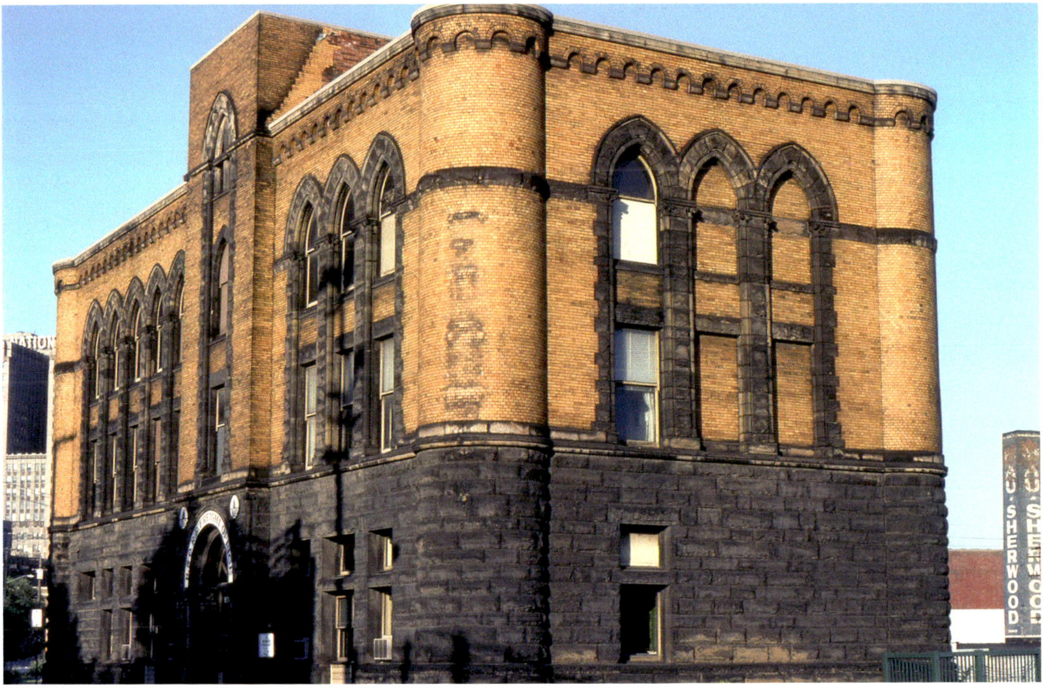

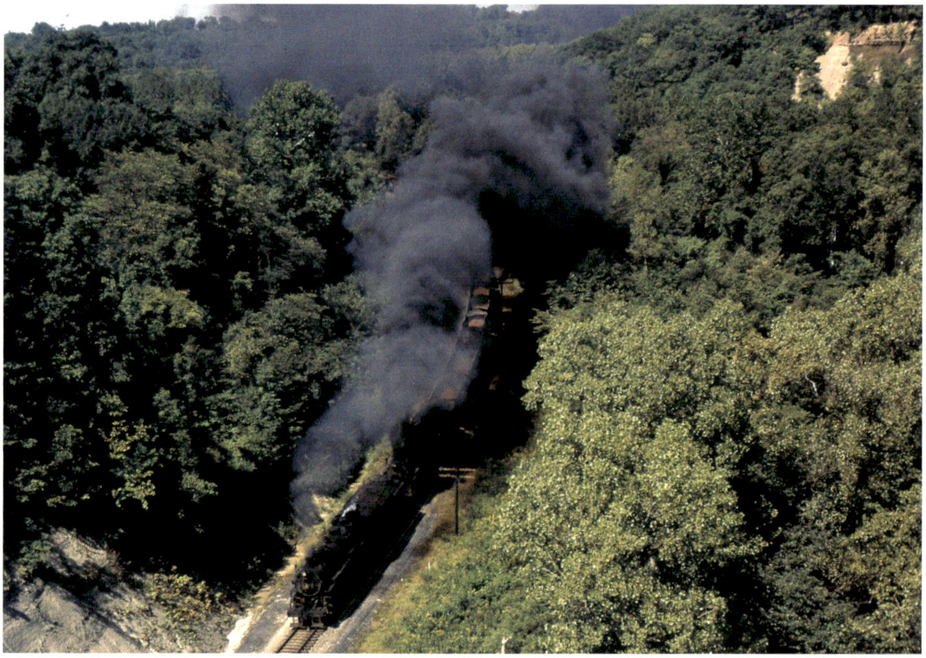

TWILIGHT FOR B&O STEAM: Northeast Ohio was among the last bastions of B&O steam locomotive power. It was common for Valley Line trains to have two steam locomotives pulling up front and another pushing on the rear to climb the ascending grade from Cleveland to Akron. Above, in September 1957, Q-4 No. 481 leads a steam double-header pulling a hopper train beneath the Ohio Route 82 bridge. Below, the same train is shown along Riverview Road just beyond the diagonal crossing of Riverview south of Peninsula. The 2-8-2 Q-class locomotives were known as Mikados. A traffic slump in early 1958 enabled the B&O to remove its last steam locomotives from service. *(William Surdyk photos)*

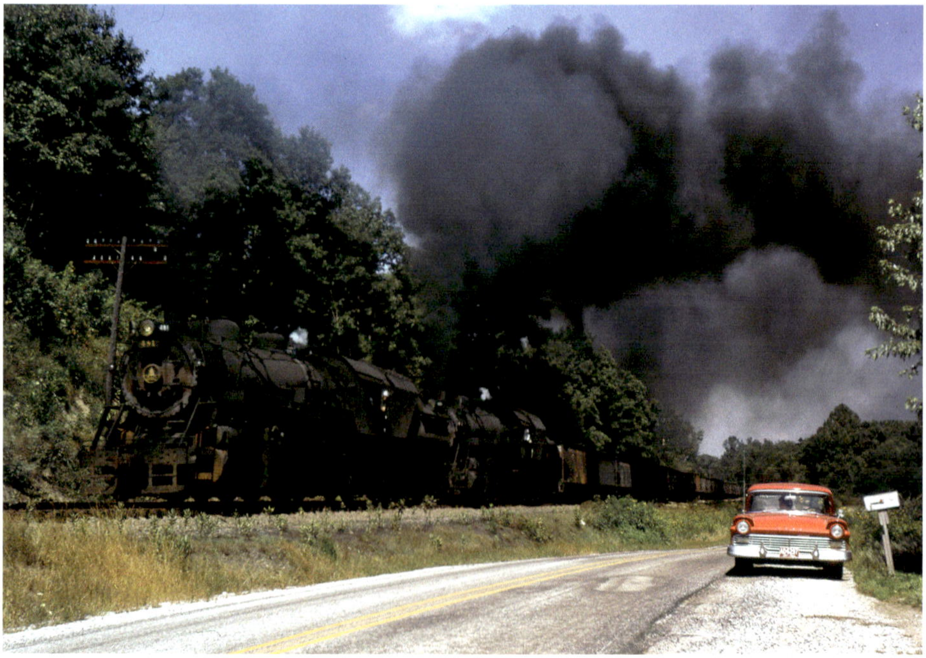

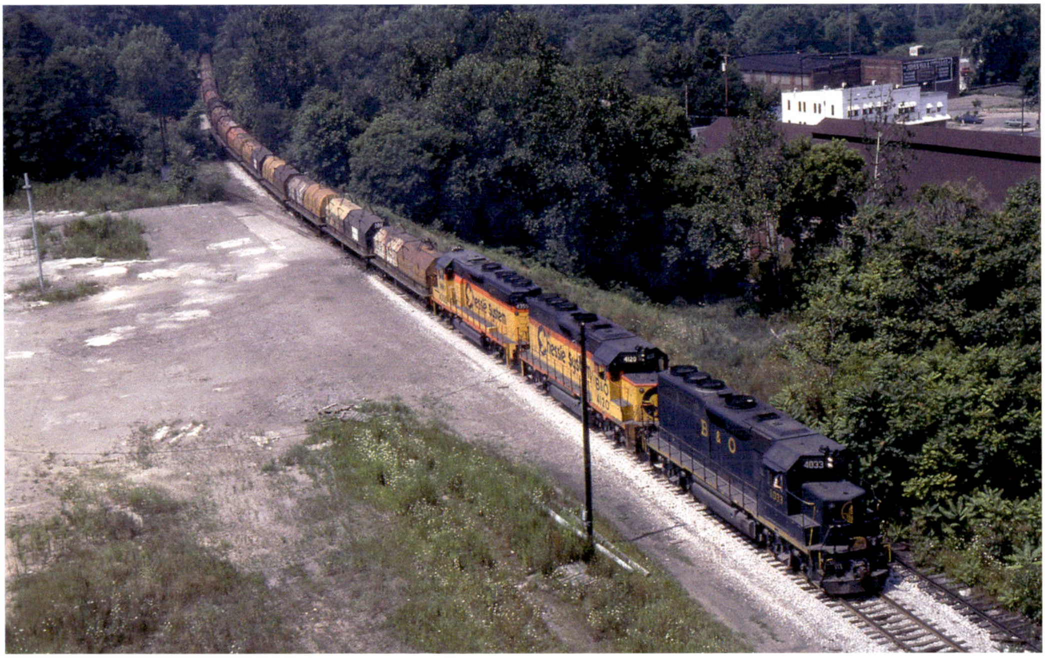

MODEST FREIGHT TRAFFIC: Freight traffic during the last decade of Valley Line freight service consisted of coke originating in Aliquippa, Pennsylvania, for a Cleveland steel mill, and iron ore moving from Cleveland to steel mills in Youngstown, Ohio. These trains did not operate daily. As Chessie looked for routes to cut in the middle 1980s, the Valley Line became expendable because its traffic could be shifted to another route between Cleveland and Sterling, Ohio. Above, a Chessie train passes the former B&O station site in Akron on August 15, 1982. Below, a southbound hopper train rumbles along Riverview Road in August 1983. (*Above, Mark Demaline photo; below, Marty Surdyk photo*)

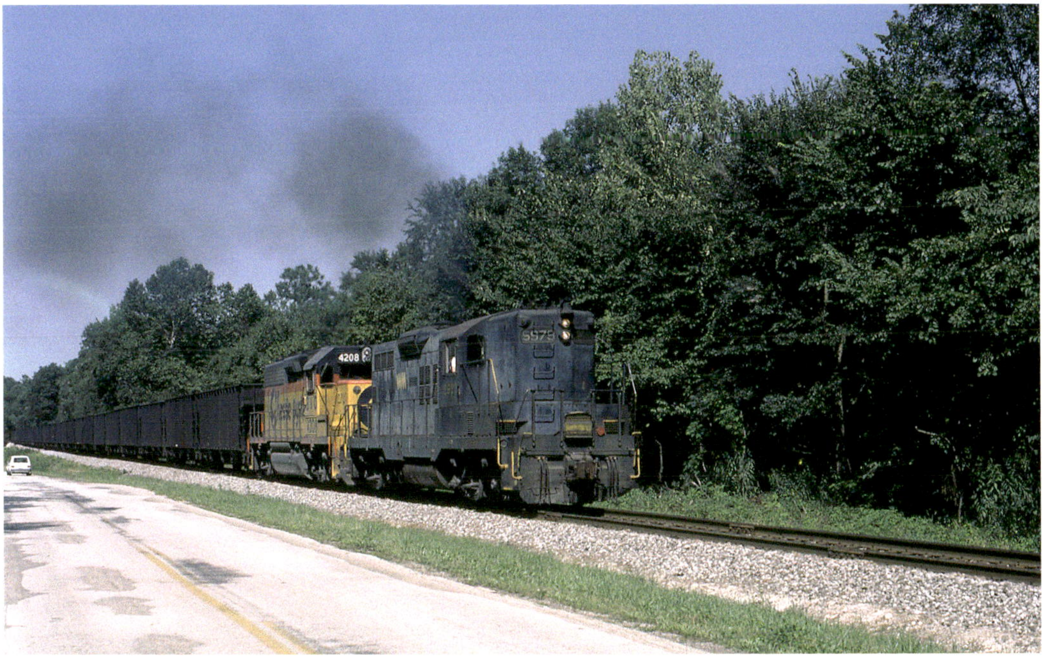

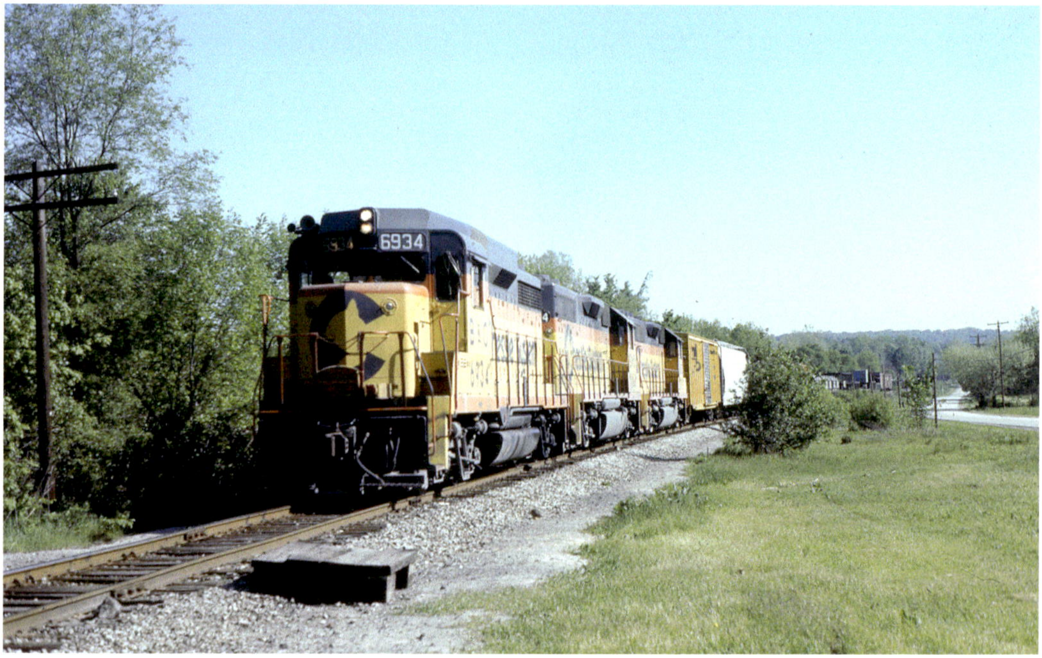

B&O OPERATIONS: In the mid-1950s, the B&O served 25 freight customers on the Valley Line between Cleveland and Akron Junction and another 14 on the Akron Belt Line that diverged from the Valley Line at Howard Street. In the 1970s, a pair of manifest freights between Akron and Cleveland interchanged cars with Chicago-Pittsburgh mainline trains in Akron. Above, a southbound B&O manifest freight nears Ira Road in June 1977. Below, the B&O had a five-stall engine house in Akron, which was between the Valley Line and Eastwood Avenue and adjacent to the Chicago Line and Hill Yard. *(Above, Paul Woodring photo; below, Marty Surdyk photo)*

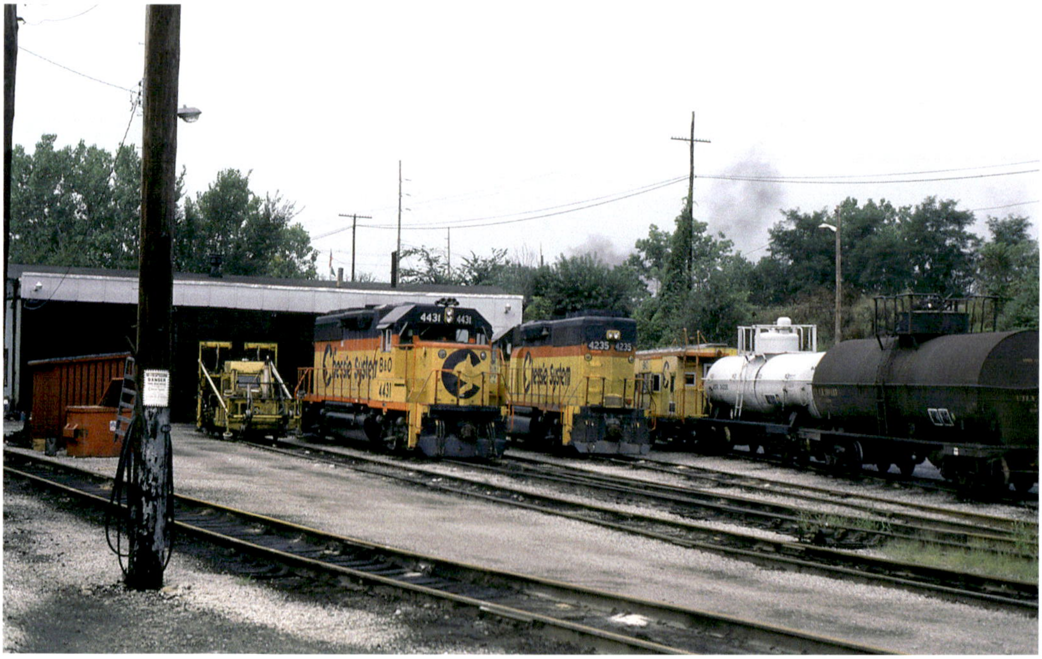

2 THE CUYAHOGA VALLEY LINE EMERGES

The Cuyahoga Valley Line began regular service in August 1975 between the Cleveland Zoo and Hale Farm and Village. Passengers disembarked at Ira Road and went to Hale Farm by bus. Trains ran on weekends between early June and late October, pulled by former Grand Trunk Western steam locomotive No. 4070.

CVL shared the track with the Chessie System's two daily freight trains, which operated on varying schedules. Tickets were sold by mail and at Furniture Land stores. Patronage in the first year averaged 200 to 300 per weekend.

In 1976, the CVL began offering trips to Akron. Passengers later had the option of disembarking near Howard Street and going to Quaker Square by bus. The best single-day patronage in the early CVL years occurred in August 1979 when 855 rode the train.

The CVL carried more than 90,000 passengers during its first five years of operation but lost $30,000 to $37,000 a year. Fares covered half of the operating costs and donations and grants kept the CVL afloat.

When Chessie raised its fees to $3,000 per trip in 1980, the CVL said that would cost $62,000 more than what it had paid in 1979 when costs had ranged between $1,600 and $1,780 per trip. Facing a $94,000 deficit, the CVL threatened to cancel the 1980 season. It was saved by a $28,000 aid package put together by the City of Akron, the developer of Quaker Square and other government entities in Summit and Cuyahoga counties.

As part of a route reduction program, Chessie said in late July 1984 that it was considering abandoning the Valley Line between Akron and Independence. The last freight train to use the route was a coke train from Aliquippa, Pennsylvania, to a Cleveland steel mill that did not operate daily. Iron ore trains that had originated in Cleveland now originated in Lorain and used a different route. Chessie stopped using the Valley Line in December 1984 and the abandonment became official in 1985. The CVL did not operate in 1986 or 1987.

A National Park Service bid to purchase the line stalled when Chessie could not produce clear title for all of the land used by the rail line. The stalemate was broken during a meeting in Congressman Seiberling's office in September 1987 that resulted in the Park Service buying the line. The CVL resumed service on June 18, 1988.

In July 1988 the CVL acquired its first diesel locomotive, using it to pull its first weekday excursion on September 27, 1989.

The CVL said in March 1991 it had not renewed the contract with the Midwest Railway Historical Foundation, which owned No. 4070 and the passenger cars used on CVL trains.

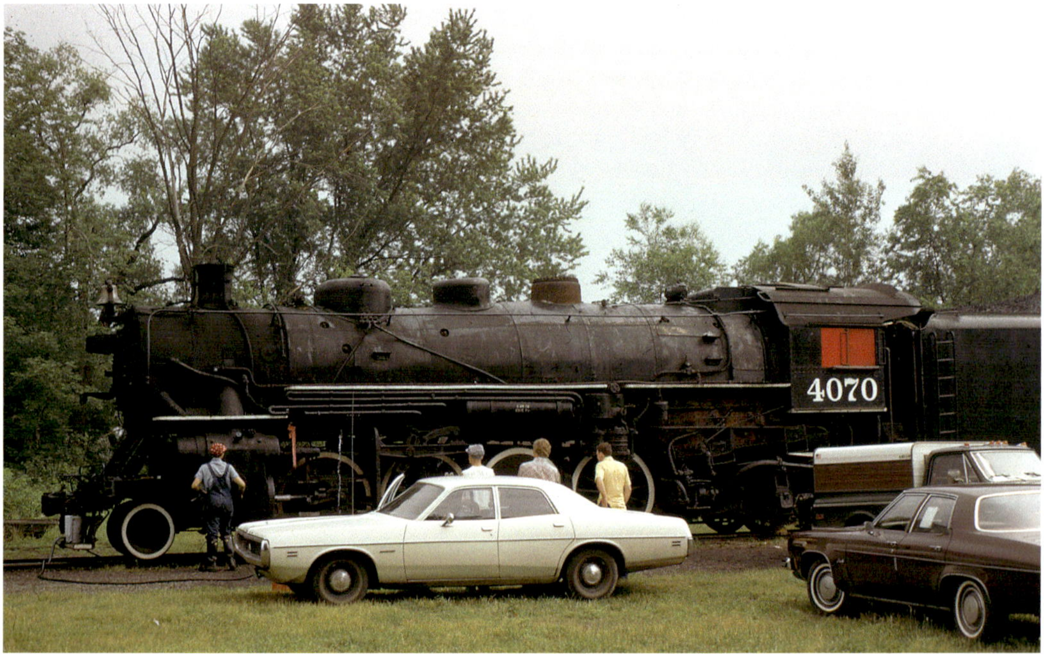

STEAMER FOR THE VALLEY: Grand Trunk Western No. 4070 was built by the American Locomotive Company in December 1918 to a United States Railroad Administration design. The 2-8-2 light Mikado handled freight and passenger trains in Michigan before GTW retired it in 1960. No. 4070 then pulled excursions in Chicago before the Midwest Railway Historical Foundation brought it to Cleveland in 1966. Above, No. 4070 is shown in April 1973 at Conneaut Lake, Pennsylvania, where it pulled excursions for two years. Below, two Newburgh & South Shore diesels pull No. 4070 on August 24, 1974, to the B&O's Cleveland roundhouse. The steam engine is arriving from Conneaut Lake. *(Above, Paul Woodring photo; below, Mark Demaline photo)*

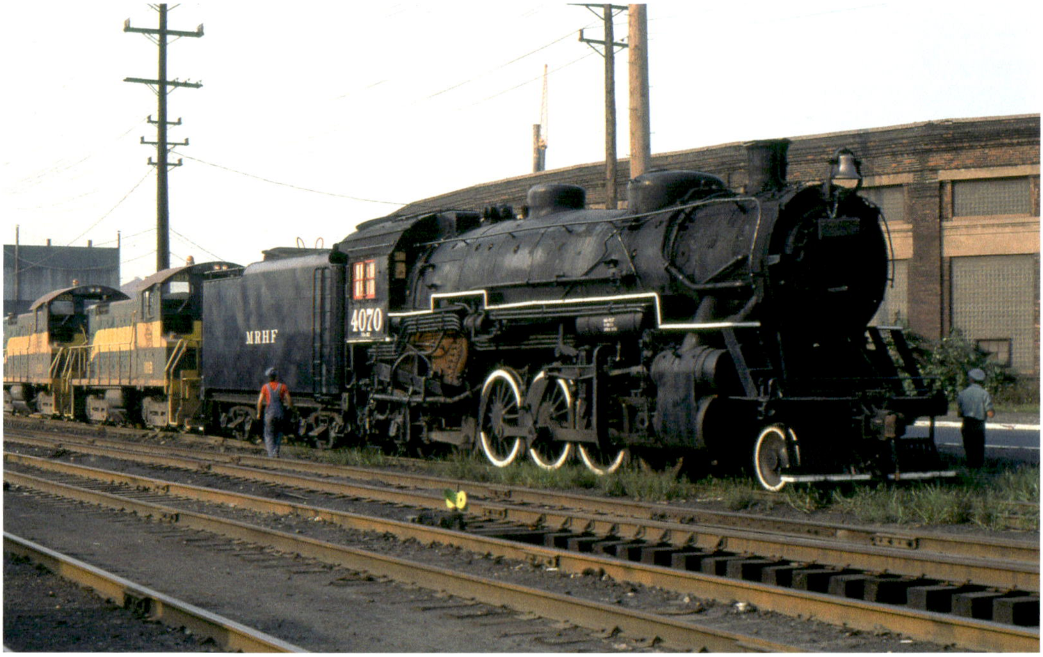

INAUGURAL RUN: The CVL's maiden excursion was a June 28, 1975, fundraiser called the Choo Choo Caper. The $100 tickets included onboard cocktails and dinner at Hale Farm. A labor dispute delayed the scheduled 7 p.m. Cleveland departure by 45 minutes when the United Transportation Union refused to allow its members to work as volunteers. The union subsequently relented for this trip. Hundreds, some on horseback, turned out to watch, backing up traffic on Riverview Road. No. 4070 suffered an overheated axle bearing and was set out at Ira Road. The more than 100 passengers returned to Cleveland after midnight behind a diesel locomotive. The first trip is shown at Clark Avenue in Cleveland. *(Mark Demaline photos)*

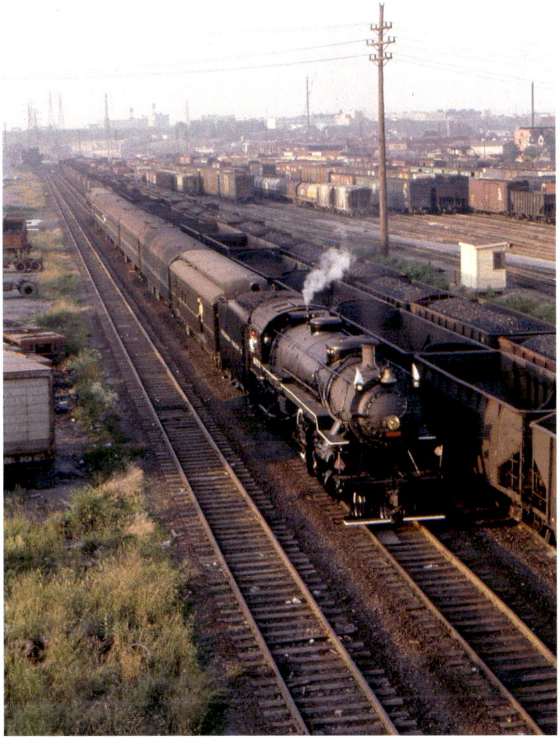

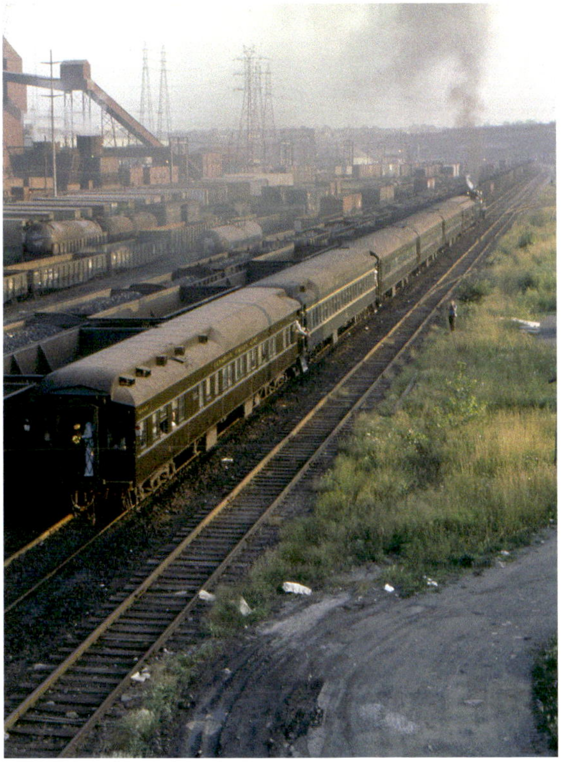

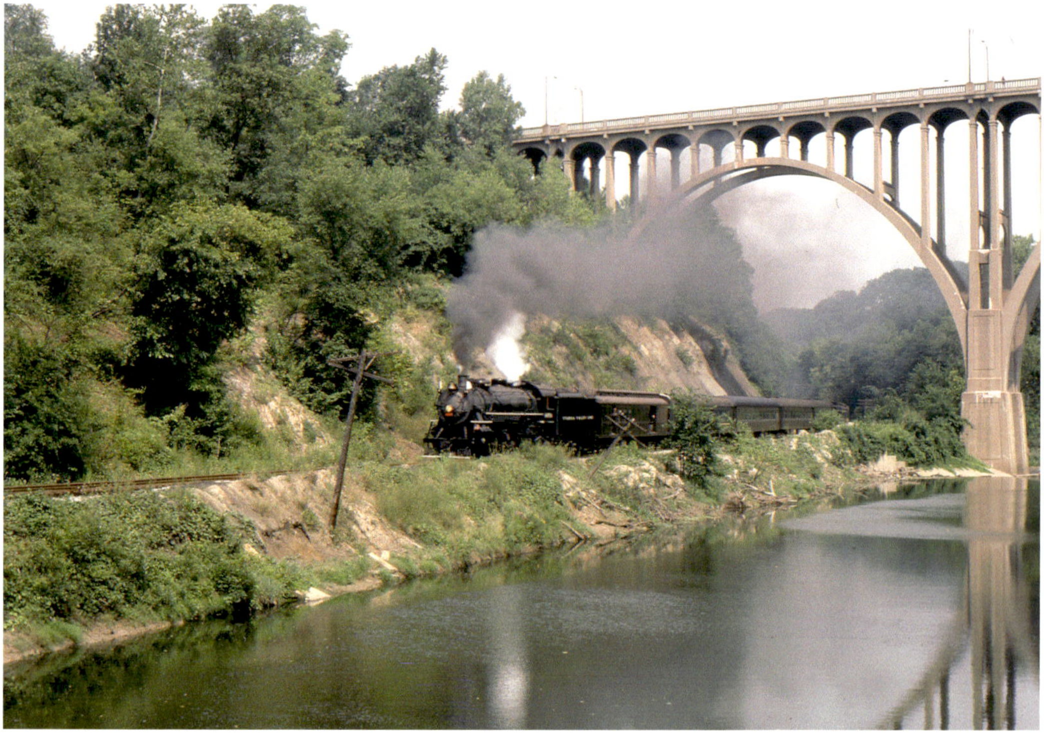

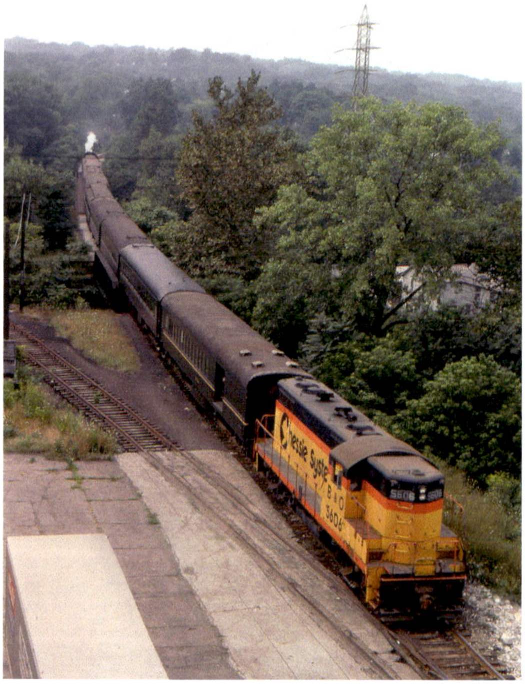

GETTING UNDERWAY: The CVL sold more than 200 tickets for it first regular trip, which was to run on July 26, 1975, but was canceled when the UTU continued to balk at allowing its members to work as volunteers. Some union members agreed to volunteer, but the conductors would not. The CVL said paying Chessie operating employees union scale wages would cost $1,500 per trip for a full crew. The CVL eventually agreed to pay that and the first trip ran on August 17, 1975. It is shown above at Brecksville and below in Akron after being turned for the return to the Cleveland Zoo. Tickets were $7.50 for adults and $4 for children. *(Mark Demaline photos)*

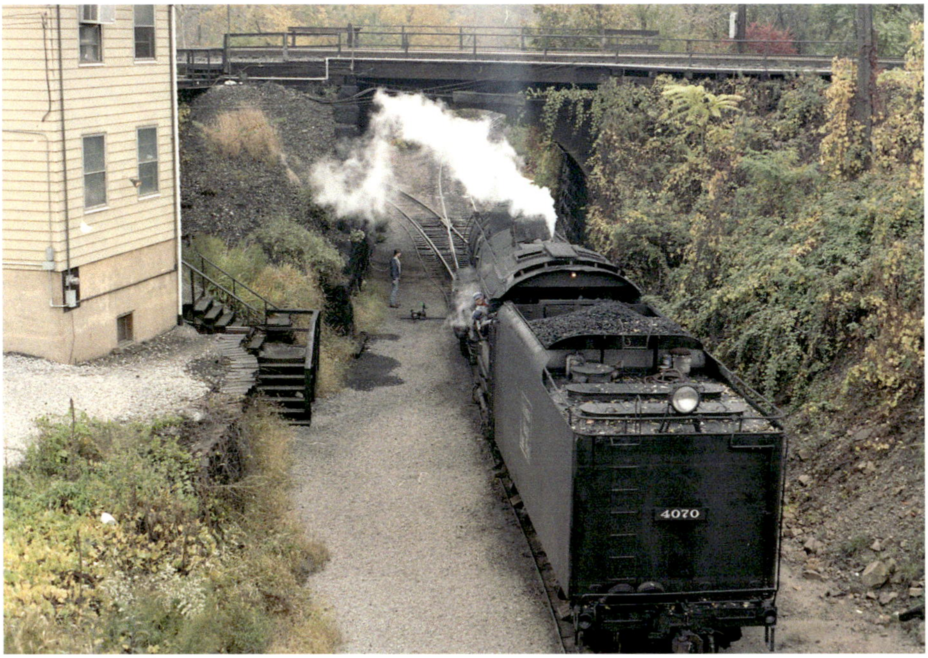

TURNING AT AKRON JUNCTION: After discharging passengers at Ira Road for Hale Farm, CVL trains ran empty to Akron Junction, where No. 4070 was turned. No. 4070 was cut away as shown above and moved onto the Pittsburgh, Cleveland & Toledo connection track to the left of the locomotive nose. After a diesel on the rear pushed the train southward on the Valley Line, No. 4070 would be turned and backed onto the train as shown below. The diesel and last car were added to the rear after the train pulled forward. In later years the passenger cars were left in Valley Yard west of Arlington Street while No. 4070 was turned. *(Above, Edward Ribinskas photo; below, Robert Todten photo)*

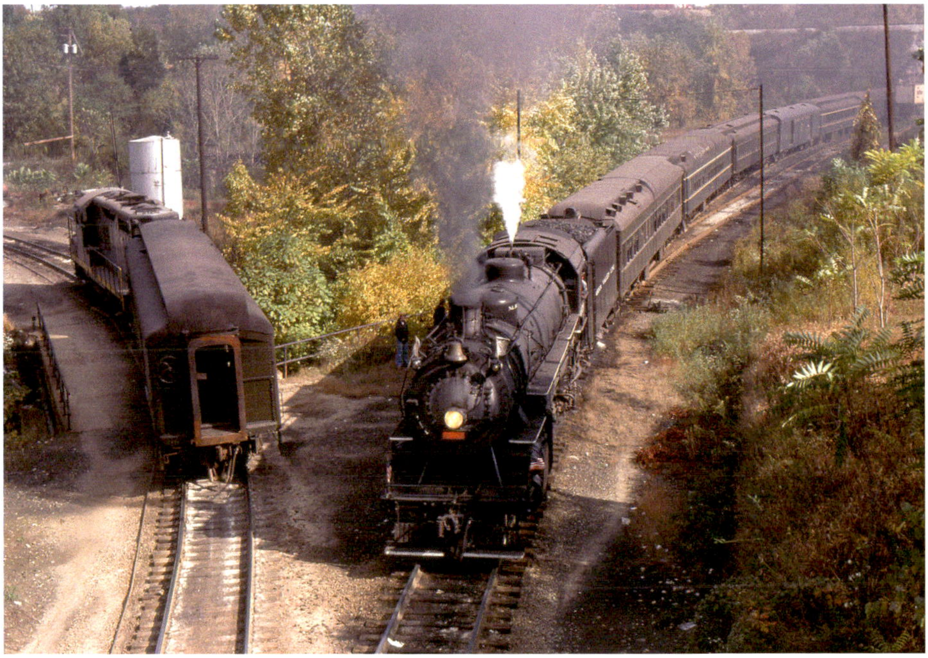

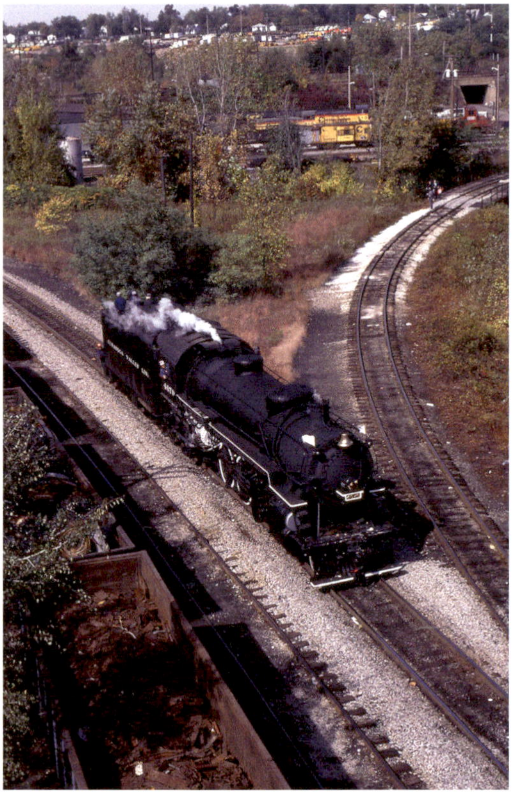

PHOTOGRAPHER'S DELIGHT: No. 4070 was serviced at Akron Junction, which made it a popular spot for photographers and railfans to watch the crews at work. Above, the photographer was standing on the bridge carrying the Erie Lackawanna Railroad over the B&O Valley Line to get this fall 1981 image. No. 4070 will back up on the East Wye Track, shown diverging to the right. Near the Eastwood Avenue crossing of the PC&T connection track, the crews will attach a hose to a fire hydrant to put water into the tender. Below, No. 4070 cruises along Riverview Road in September 1983. (*Above, Paul Woodring photo; below Marty Surdyk photo*)

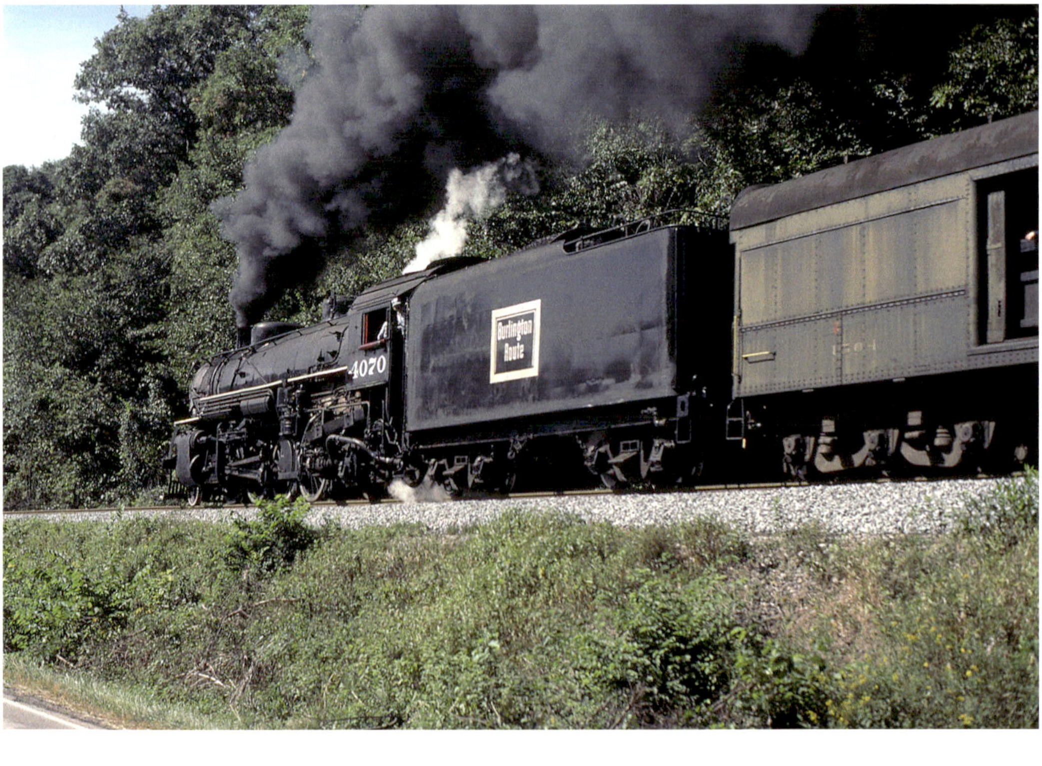

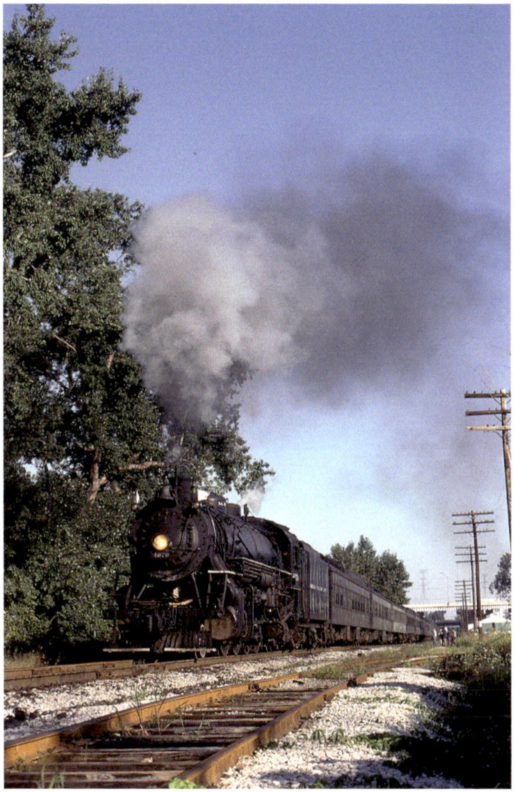

CVL IN CLEVELAND: In 1975 and 1976, CVL trains boarded at the Cleveland Zoo on the B&O's Cleveland-Lester branch. Trains ran empty from West Third Street roundhouse to the zoo. After boarding, a diesel pulled the train to RD Tower near Dennison Avenue to get onto the Valley Line. CVL trains were subject to being delayed by Chessie and Norfolk & Western freight traffic. The Cleveland station moved in 1977 to behind a Value City Furniture store on Granger Road in Independence, near where the top photograph was made in October 1979. Below, the train returns to Cleveland on September 6, 1975, as seen from Conrail's Cleveland Short Line bridge. (*Above, Jim Semon photo; below Mark Demaline photo*)

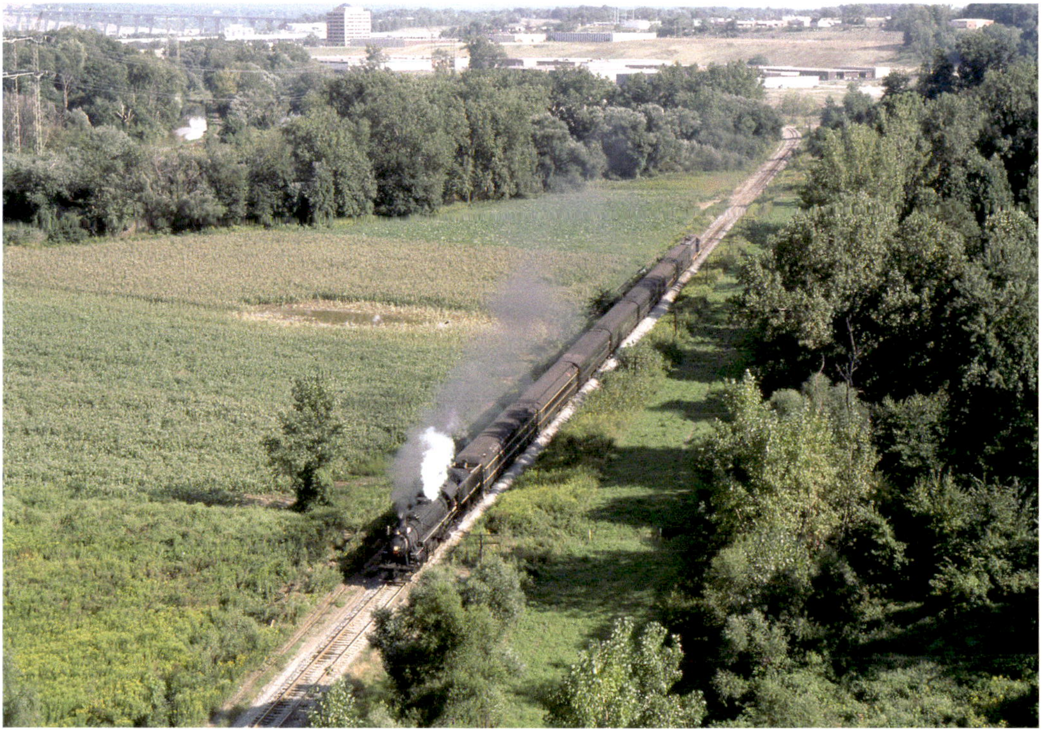

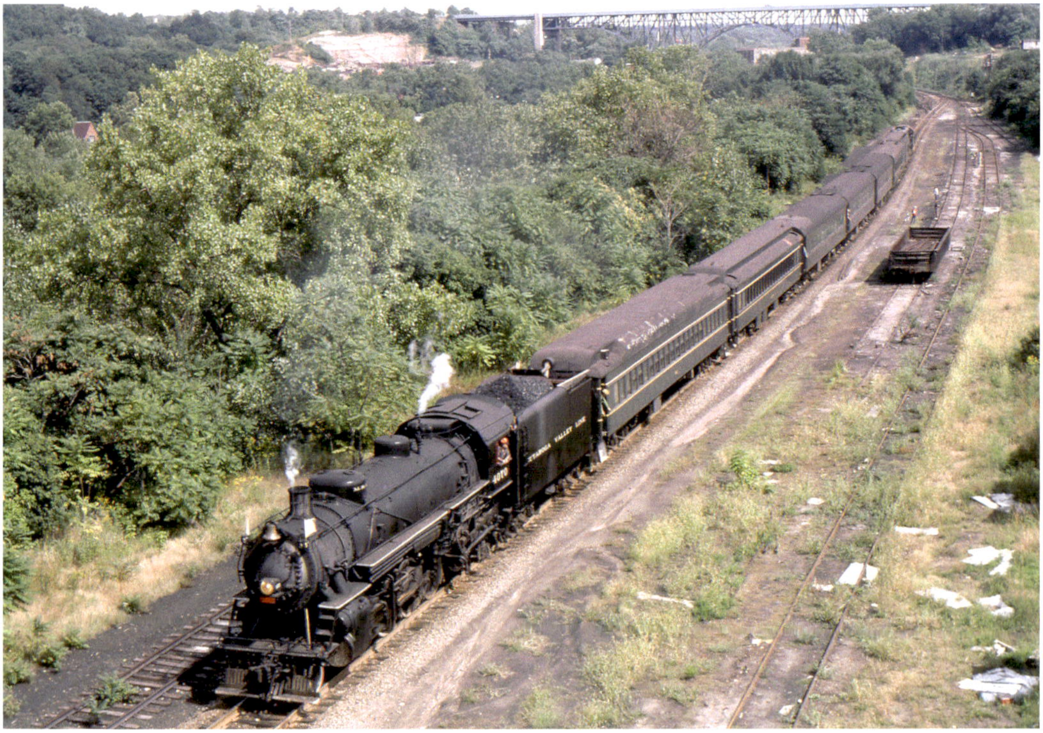

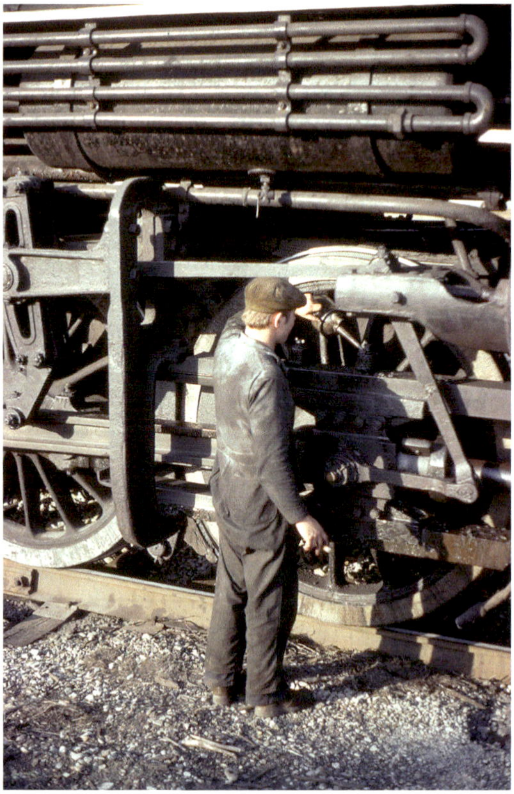

CVL IN AKRON: The CVL began offering rides between Ira Road and Akron on May 15, 1976. Fares were half of the Cleveland-Hale Farm prices of $8 for adults and $4 for children. Akron passengers later were given the option to visit Quaker Square, a shopping center and hotel in a former Quaker Oats factory that helped pay for the shuttle bus service. Above, a CVL train approaches the Akron boarding site at Ridge and Howard streets, where the B&O once had a passenger station. The view is from the North Hill Viaduct. Below, Russ Jaite lubricates No. 4070 during the service stop at Akron Junction in May 1977. (*Above, Mark Demaline photo; below, Paul Woodring photo*)

3 STEAM TO DIESEL

The early 1990s presented numerous challenges for the Cuyahoga Valley Line. The 1990 season didn't begin until July 21 because mechanical problems had sidelined steam locomotive No. 4020. The trains could not go into Akron because the Howard Street Bridge had been condemned. The loss of service to Akron sent ridership plummeting. Two fall foliage trips in late October were canceled due to poor ticket sales. However, trains began stopping at the Canal Visitor's Center at Lock 38 and service increased to twice a day.

In 1991, the CVL acquired five passenger cars and a baggage car from an Indiana railroad equipment dealer. The season began on May 25, operating on Wednesday, Saturday and Sunday and expanded to 81 trips, compared with 32 trips in 1990.

In June 1991, the National Park Service announced plans to build a 22-mile hiking and biking trail on the old towpath of the Ohio & Erie Canal. The $6 million project would change the nature of the Cuyahoga Valley National Recreation Area and, in turn, the focus of the CVL as it became more oriented to serving the park and not just taking passengers to Hale Farm and Akron cultural and commercial institutions.

The Park Service budgeted $300,000 in 1991 for tie replacement and rail rehabilitation. It also gave the CVL a $50,000 grant to help get the 1991 season started.

The CVL began launching theme trains, starting with nature trains in November 1991 and a Christmas-themed train for children in December 1992. It eyed starting a ski train to the Boston Mills ski resort. In 1992 trains ran to the Merriman Valley business district on the north edge of Akron. October fall foliage trains operated on Fridays. The CVL also began carrying bicycles in a baggage car. The 1992 Park Service budget contained $500,000 for track work.

Service was a single roundtrip that left Independence at 11 a.m. and arrived at Merriman Valley at 12:25 p.m. It departed the latter at 3:25 p.m. and arrived in Independence at 5:10 p.m. Intermediate stops were made at Ira Road (Hale Farm) and Canal Visitor's Center.

Service to downtown Akron resumed on August 1, 1993. The CVL said that Akron was its No. 1 destination, with most passengers visiting Quaker Square and the Akron Art Museum.

In April 1994 the CVL announced that it had a new name, Cuyahoga Valley Scenic Railroad, and a new look. Passenger cars and locomotives would be painted red, gold and black. The railroad adopted the winged logo that it continues to use today. The 1994 season began on May 1 and the CVSR launched a $10.4 million fundraising campaign to pay for additional locomotives and passenger cars.

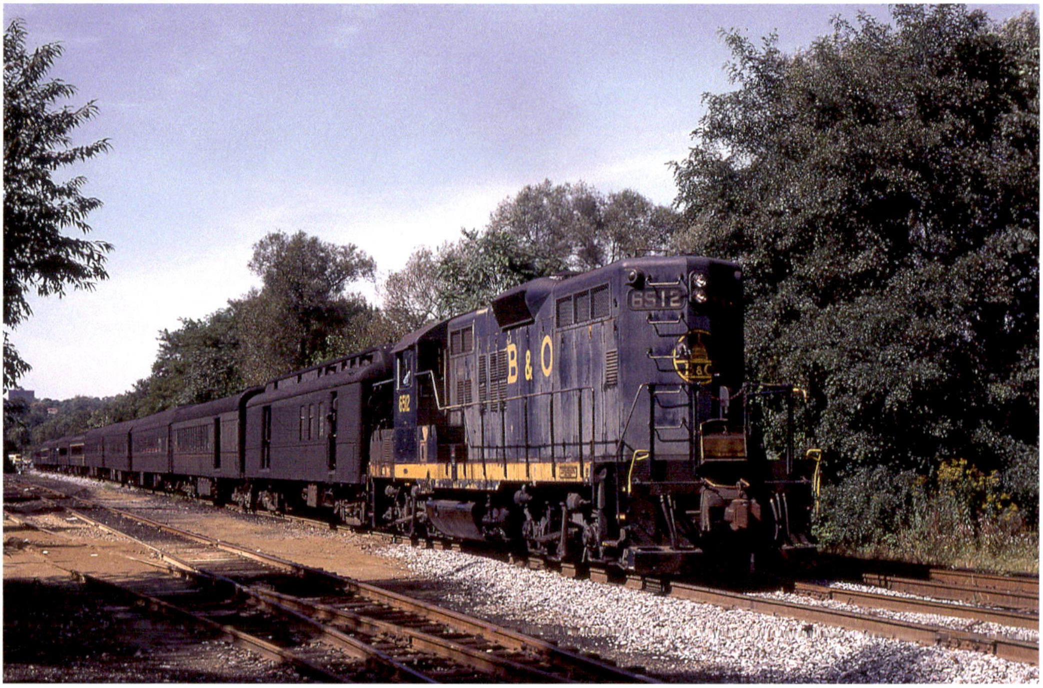

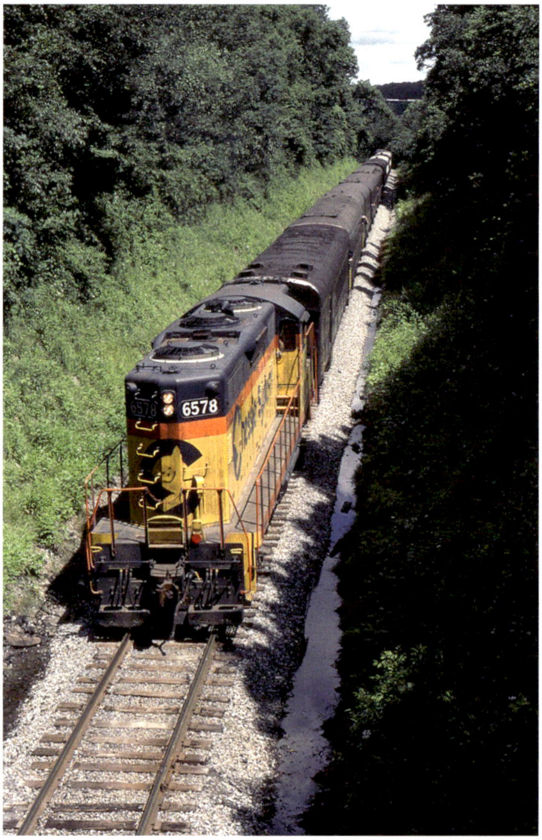

DIESELS TO THE RESCUE: When No. 4070 was unable to operate because it was being repaired or was unavailable, Chessie diesels, usually GP9s built by the Electro-Motive Division of General Motors, pulled CVL trains. Above, B&O GP9 No. 6512 is shown substituting for No. 4070 in Akron on September 27, 1990. Below, Chessie GP9 No. 6578 pulls a southbound CVL train at Peninsula in July 1984, in a view from a wood bridge that has since been removed. No. 6578 was built for the B&O. Diesels often were placed on trains pulled by No. 4070 to push or pull the train if No. 4070 failed en route. *(Above, Robert Farkas photo; below, Paul Woodring photo)*

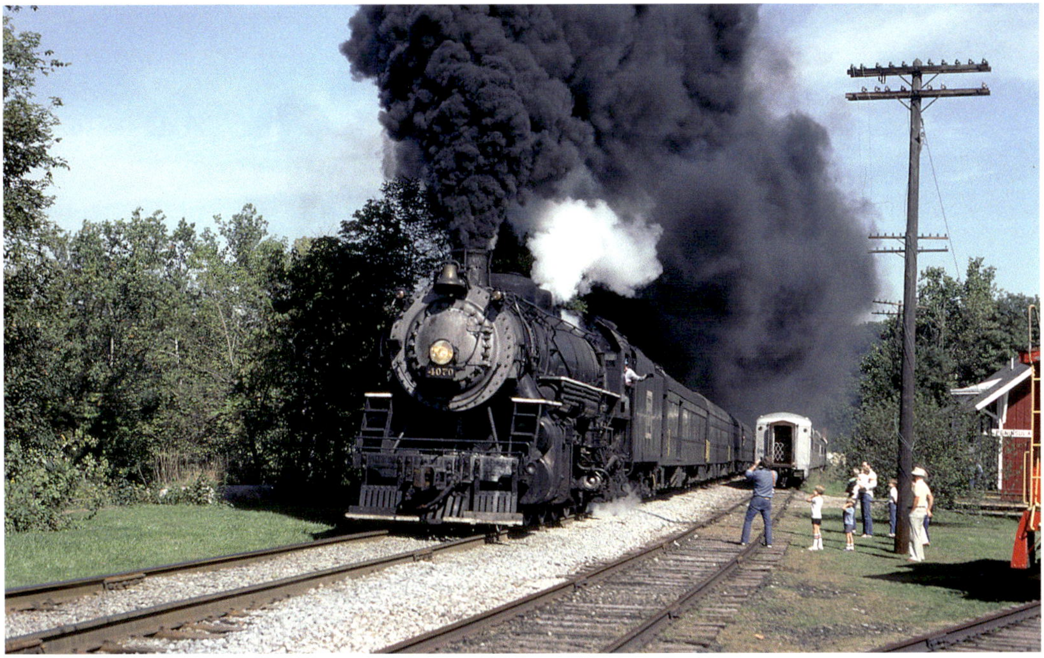

PASS BUT DO NOT STOP: The CVL in 1978 proposed establishing a stop in Peninsula, but the village balked, saying it lacked adequate sanitary facilities to accommodate an influx of passengers, and was already congested on weekends. At the time, CVL trains averaged 200 to 300 passengers per trip. Some local merchants objected to the ban, but the CVL did not begin stopping in Peninsula until 1992. Above, a southbound train passes through Peninsula in September 1983 as trackside observers keep watch. Below, No. 4070 leaves a trail of smoke as it rumbles south of Everett near the site of Szalay's Farm and Market. (*Above, Marty Surdyk photo; below, Robert Farkas photo*)

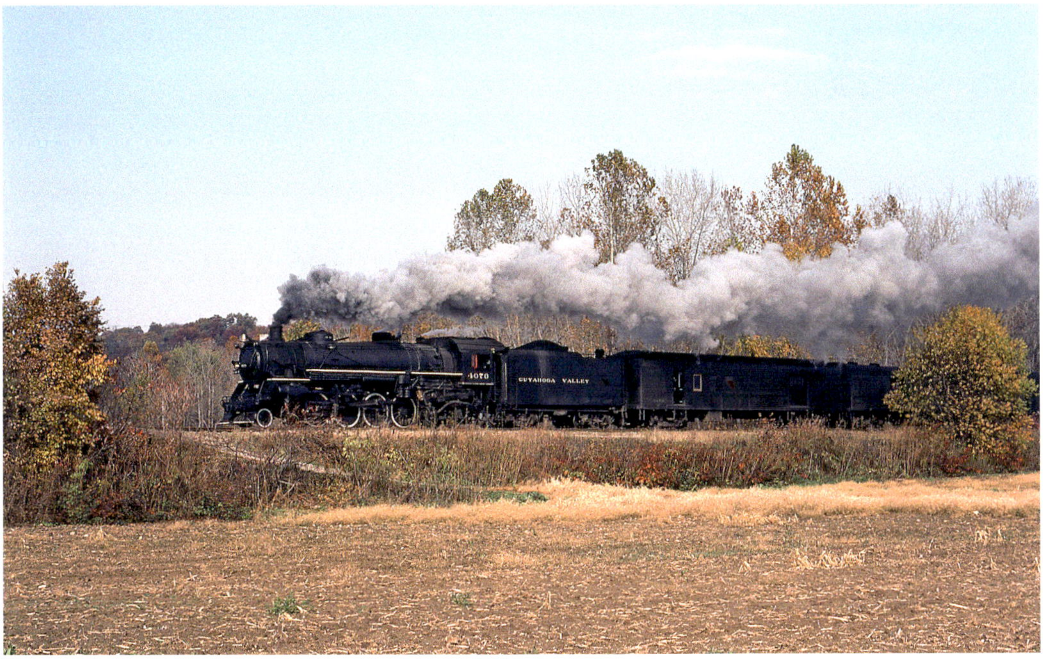

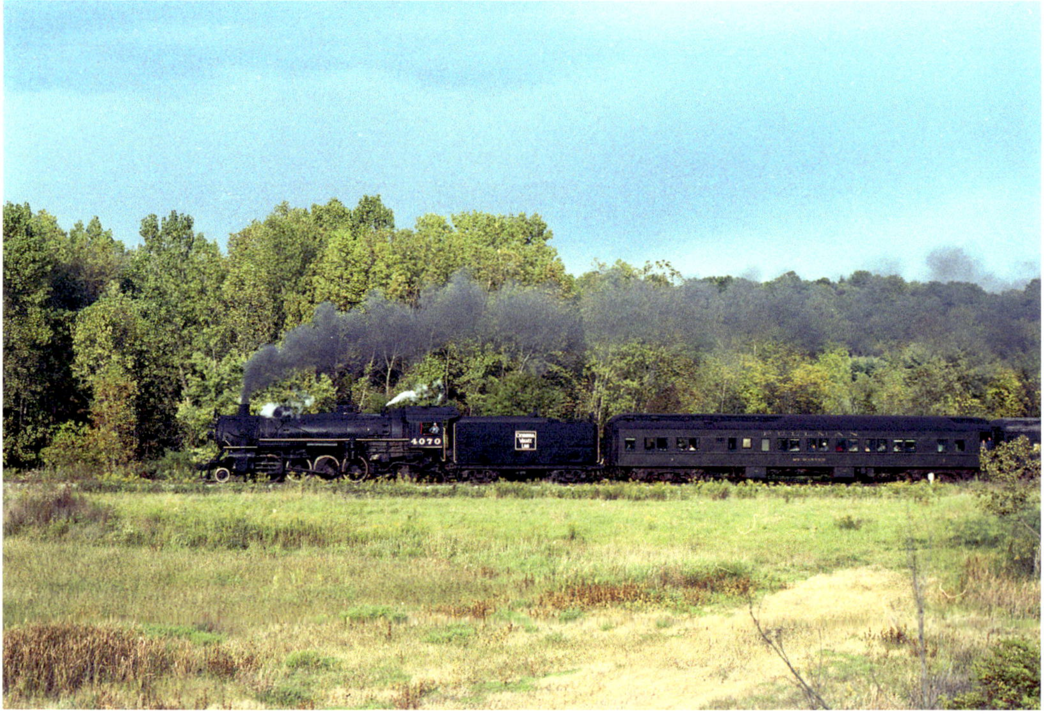

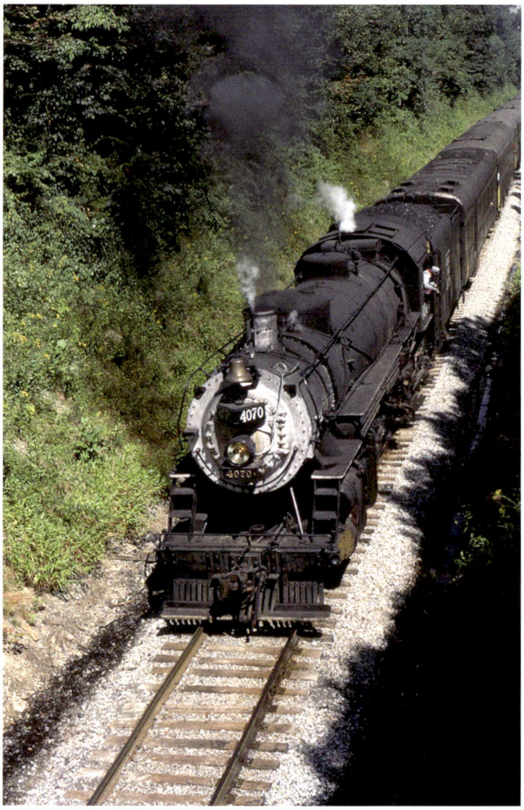

CHANGES IN APPEARANCE: No. 4070 underwent a few appearance changes during its time on the CVL. At times it had a silver smoke box and white accent stripes on its wheels, walkway sides and front. The tender ran with five variations, including the names "Midwest Railway Historical Foundation," "Cuyahoga Valley Line Rwy" and "Cuyahoga Valley Line." It also ran painted solid black. After No. 4070 appeared in the 1983 filming of *The Natural,* the logo of the Chicago, Burlington & Quincy Railroad appeared on the tender on the fireman's side. Above, No. 4070 travels northbound near Jaite. Below, No. 4070 nears Peninsula in October 1984 with the silver smokebox. (*Above, Edward Ribinskas photo; below, Paul Woodring photo*)

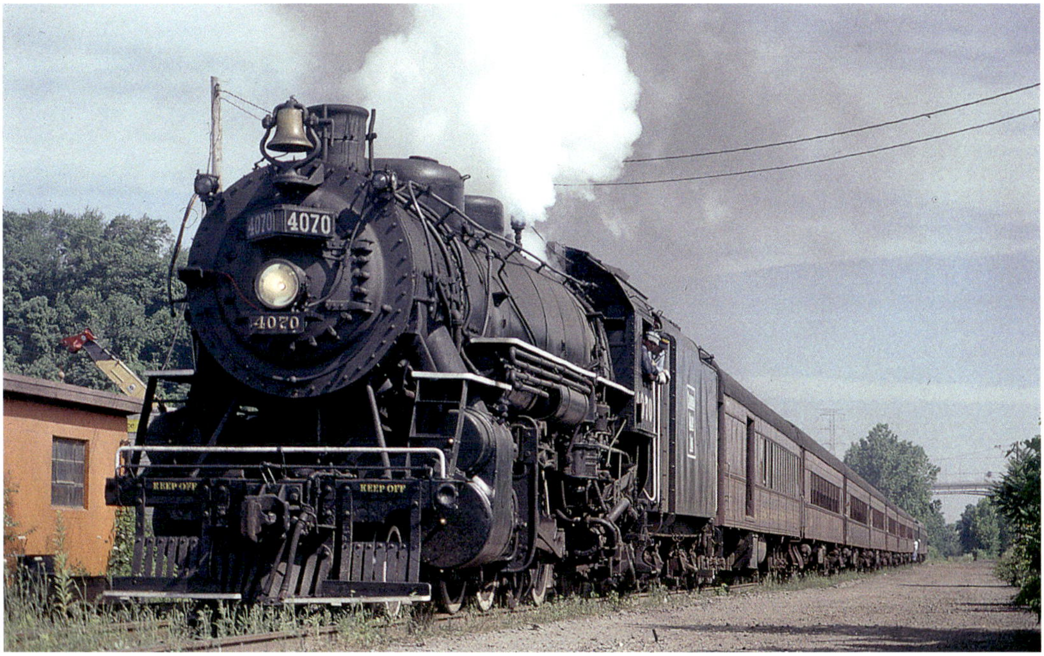

CHANGES IN INDEPENDENCE: In the 1985 season, the CVL began boarding Cleveland passengers near Old Rockside Road in Independence just north of the present day Rockside Road station. The CVL continued to drop passengers off at Ira Road to visit Hale Farm, but an increasing number of passengers were continuing to Akron to board shuttle buses to visit Quaker Square, the Akron Art Museum, Stan Hywet Hall and Gardens, and the Akron Zoological Park. In the early 1980s, most of the passenger cars used on the CVL were replaced by former Pennsylvania Railroad P70 commuter coaches. Both photos show No. 4070 and its train leaving Independence. (*Above, Marty Surdyk photo; below, Robert Farkas photo*)

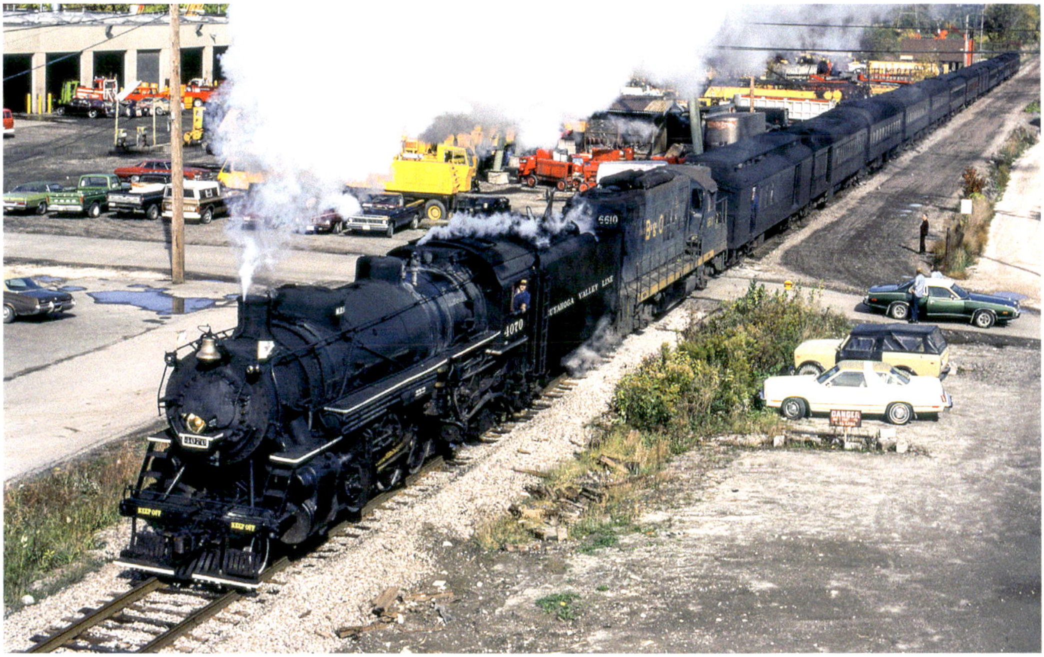

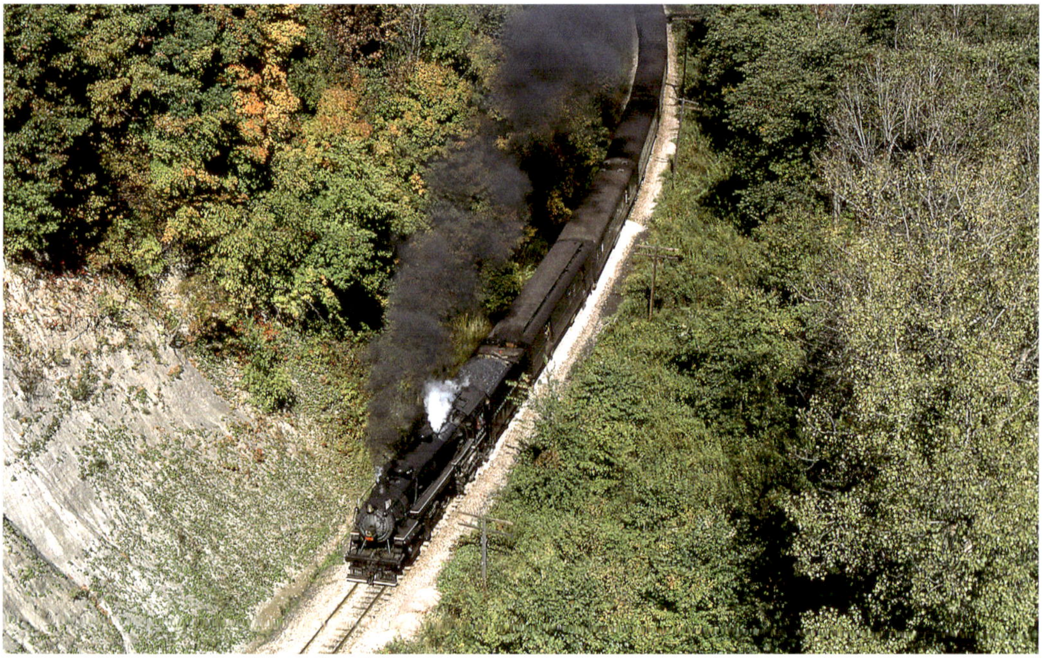

HIGH PERCH: Built in 1931, the Brecksville-Northfield High Level Bridge soars 145 feet above the Cuyahoga River Valley at Brecksville. More commonly known as the Ohio Route 82 Bridge, it has been a favorite location for photographers to make images of trains on the Valley Line as they pass through an area known as the narrows, as seen in the photograph above made in October 1975. In the photograph below, No. 4070 leads a northbound train in August 1985 past Old Station Road Bridge over the Cuyahoga River in an area that is now the Brecksville station of the CVSR. (*Above, Robert Farkas photo; below, Marty Surdyk photo*)

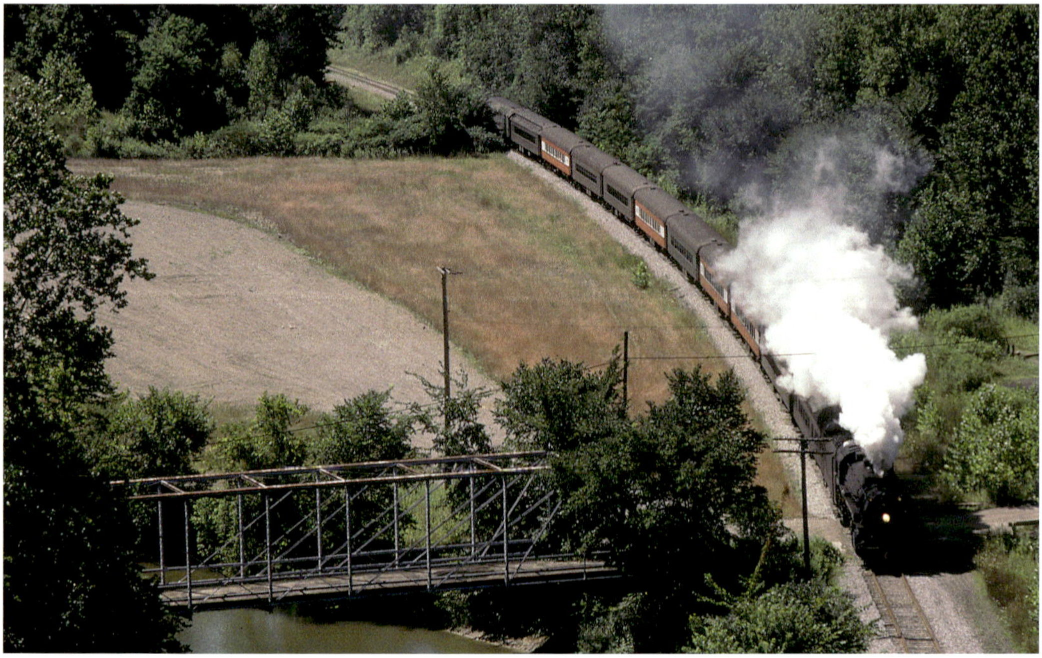

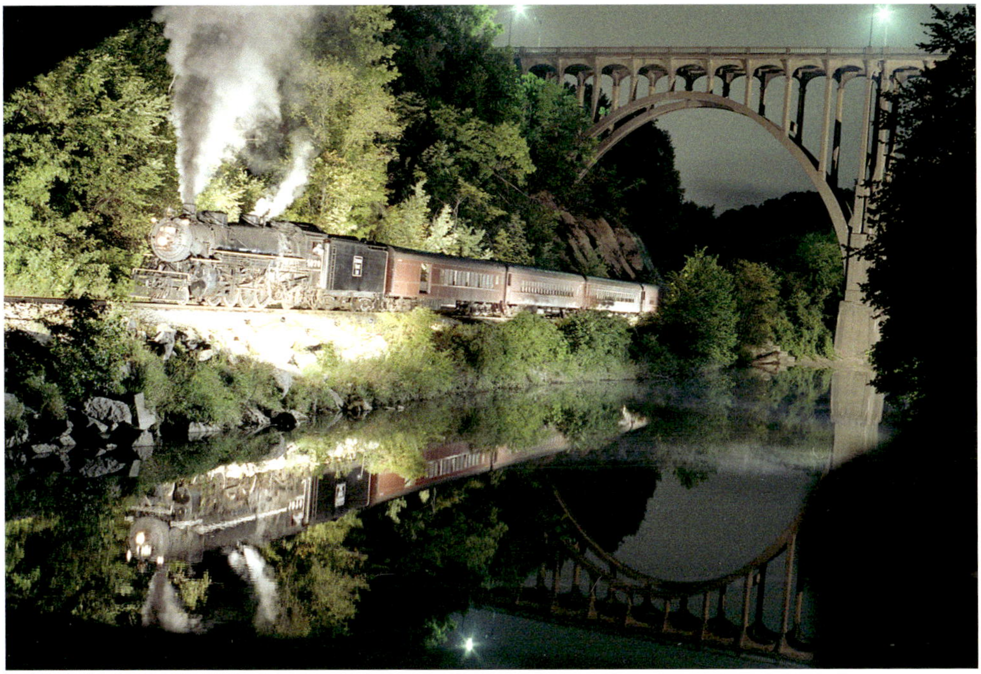

ROUTE 82 BRIDGE: Countless photographs have been made of trains alongside the Cuyahoga River in Brecksville against the backdrop of the majestic concrete arches of the Brecksville-Northfield High Level Bridge carrying Ohio Route 82 over the Cuyahoga River Valley. For a railfan day on September 10, 1988, the CVL arranged for a night photo shoot of No. 4070 and its train beneath the bridge. Artificial lighting was provided. Below, the autumn foliage is at its peak as No. 4070 puts on a smoke show as it roars southbound in October 1978. *(Above, Edward Ribinskas photo; below, Robert Farkas photo)*

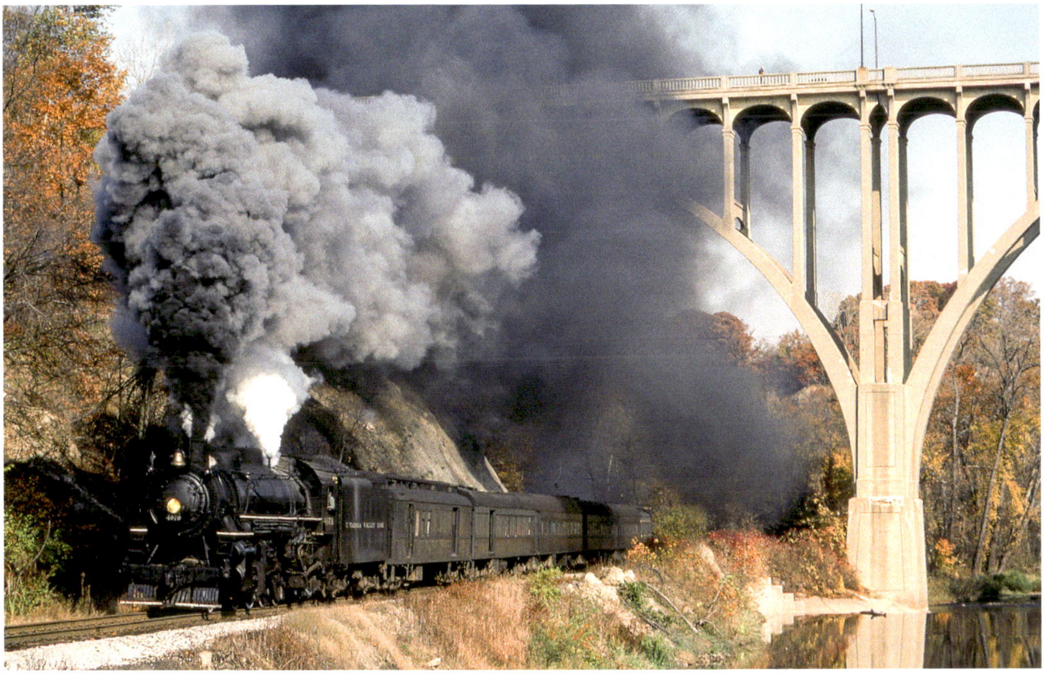

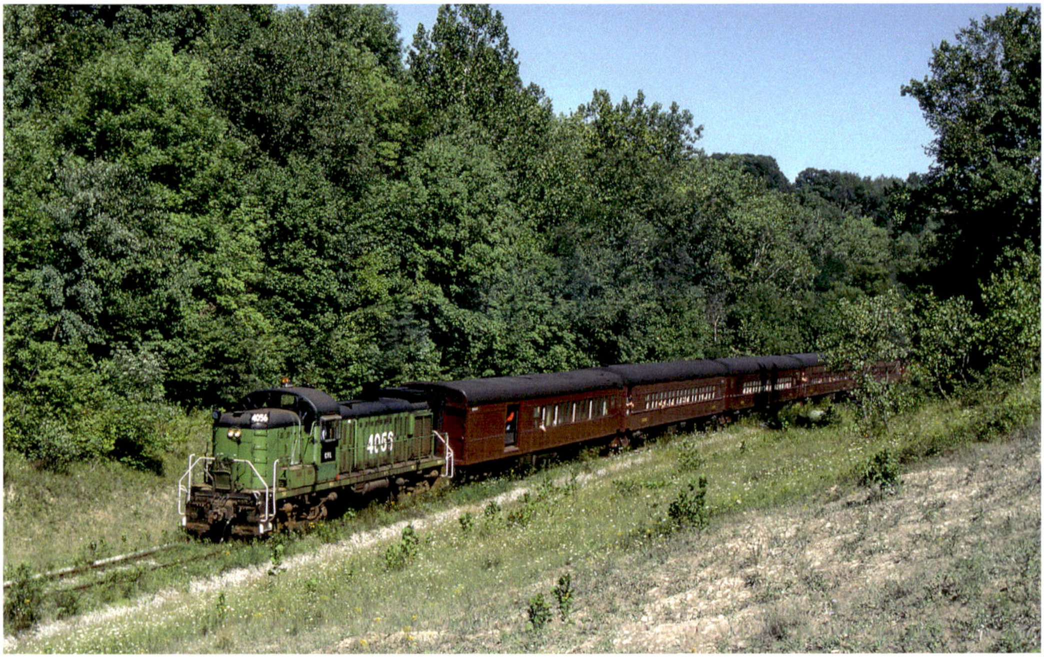

FIRST CVL DIESEL: The CVL acquired its first diesel, an Alco RS-3, in July 1988. Built in January 1952 for the Spokane, Portland & Seattle Railway, it never wore CVL colors. No. 4056 usually pulled trains northward while No. 4070 took them southward. No. 4056 blew a crankshaft near Ira Road on October 18, 1989, during a diesel-only Wednesday trip, stranding 260 passengers for two hours in cold and rainy conditions until buses arrived. No. 4056 was never repaired and instead cannibalized for parts before being scrapped in September 1996. It is shown above at Brecksville on August 20, 1988, and near Akron in 1988. *(Above, Robert Farkas photo; below, Tom Fritsch photo)*

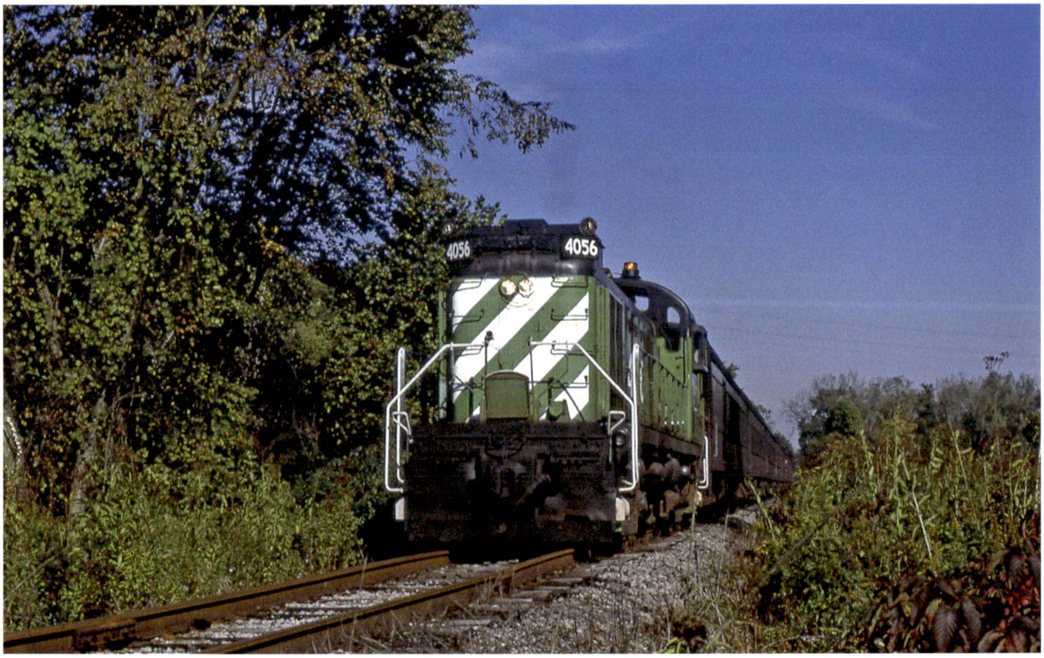

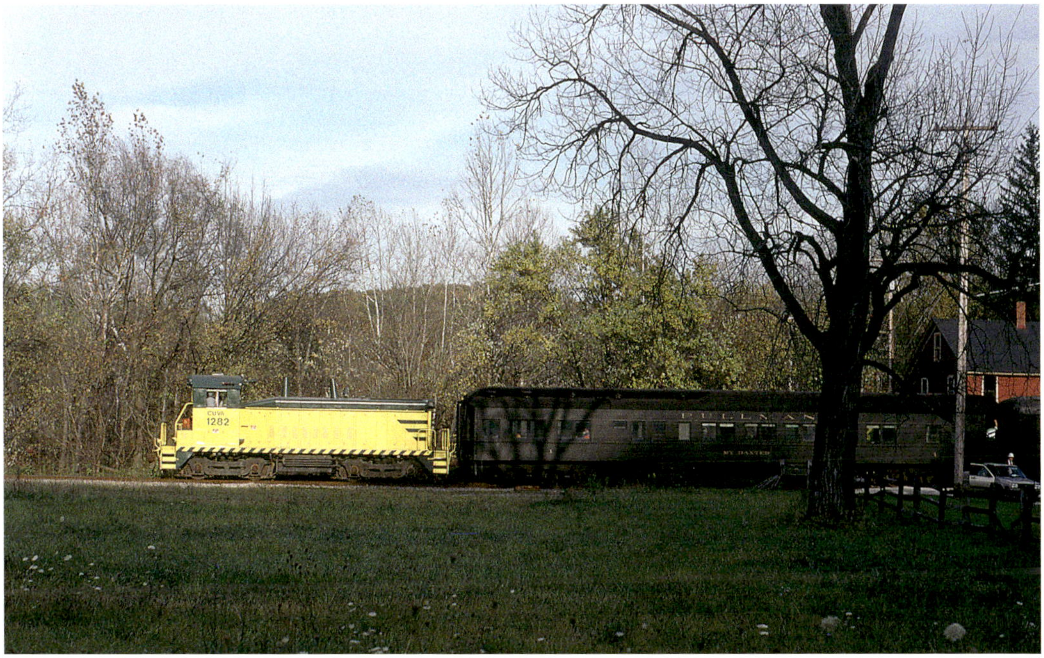

SWITCHERS IN ACTION: The CVL borrowed or acquired diesel motive power as needed, including a pair of EMD switch engines that briefly pulled CVL trains. SW1200 No. 1282 (above) was borrowed from the Cuyahoga Valley Railway (later renamed ISG Cleveland Works Railway), a Cleveland steel mill railroad, in summer 1990. Below, SW8 No. 2014 was acquired from the U.S. Army, which had used it at an arsenal near Ravenna, Ohio. It ran on the Cuyahoga Valley Scenic Railroad in 1995 and 1996 and is shown in Brecksville in July 1995 with observation-lounge car *Saint Lucie Sound*, which still has its Florida East Coast lettering. *(Marty Surdyk photos)*

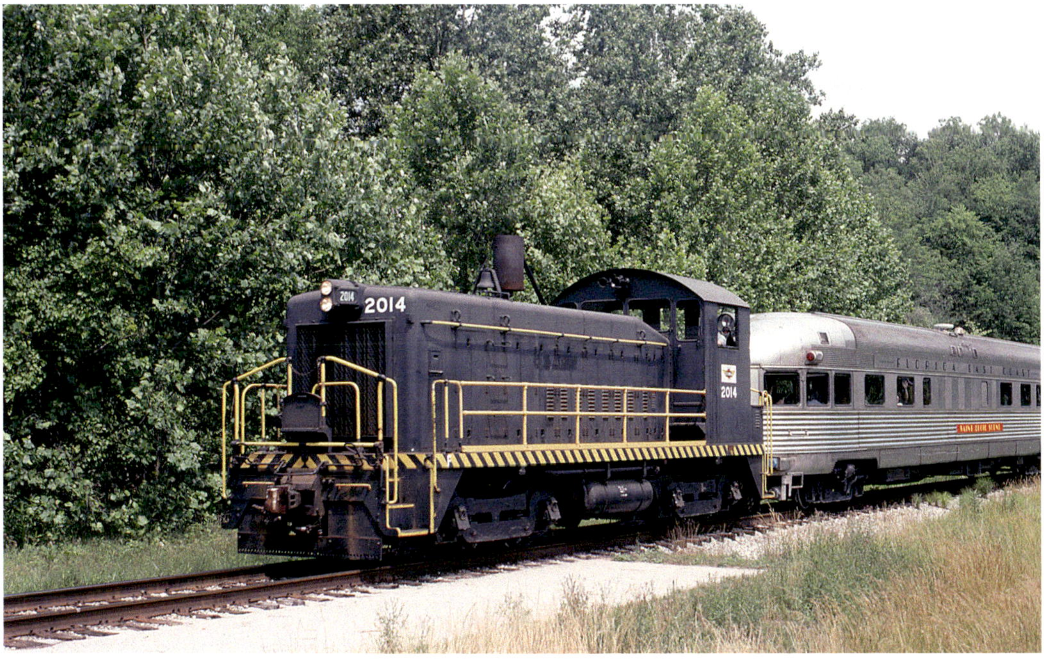

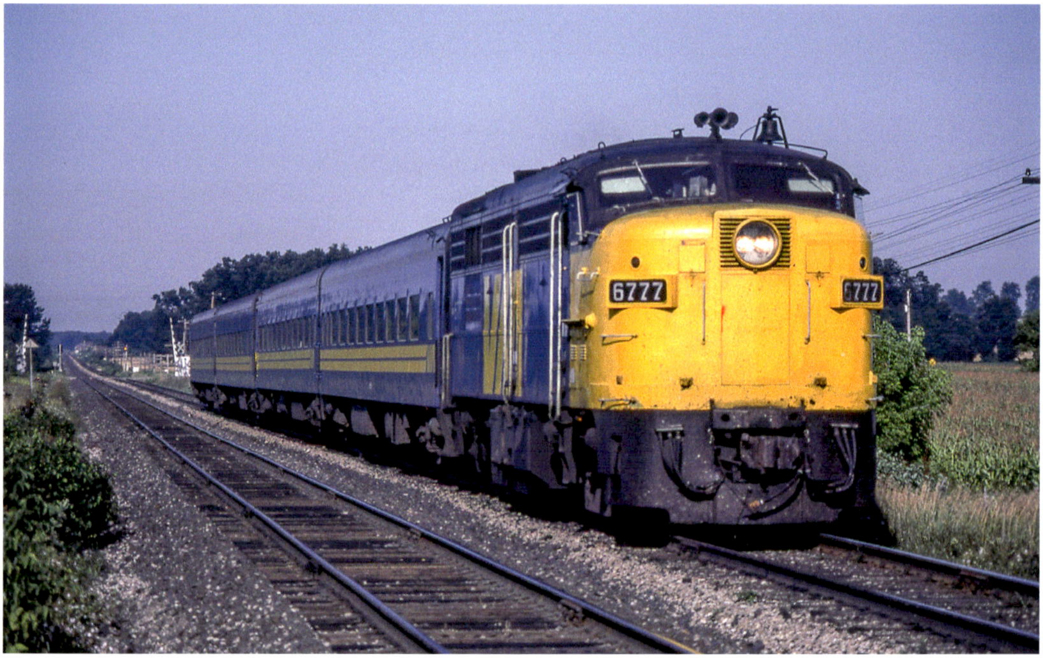

ORIGINAL LIVERIES: The CVSR has operated four FPA-4 diesels, all of them built in 1959 by Montreal Locomotive Works for Canadian National. All served VIA Rail Canada before coming to the CVSR. Above, No. 6777 leads a VIA train at Komoka, Ontario, on August 13, 1982. The CVSR has preserved the CN/VIA roster numbers on three of the four FPA-4s. Some locomotives arrived on the CVSR wearing their original livery and operated with that appearance for a short time. Below, this FPA-4 arrived as Western Maryland Scenic Railroad No. 305 before it became CVL 15 and then CVSR 6771. *(Above, Robert Farkas photo; below, Jim Mastromatteo photo)*

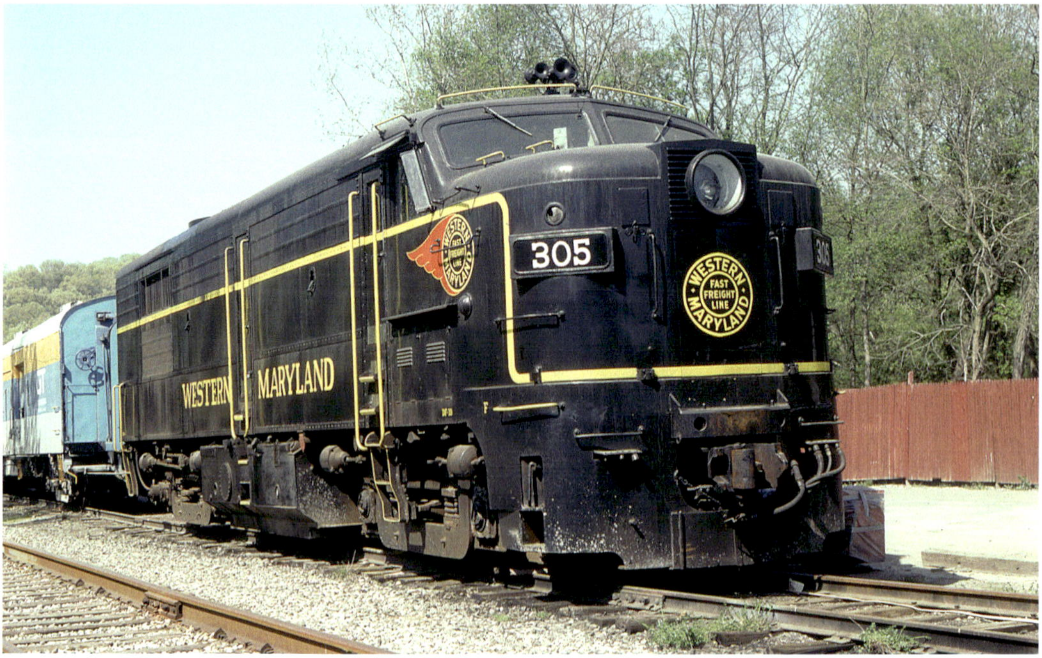

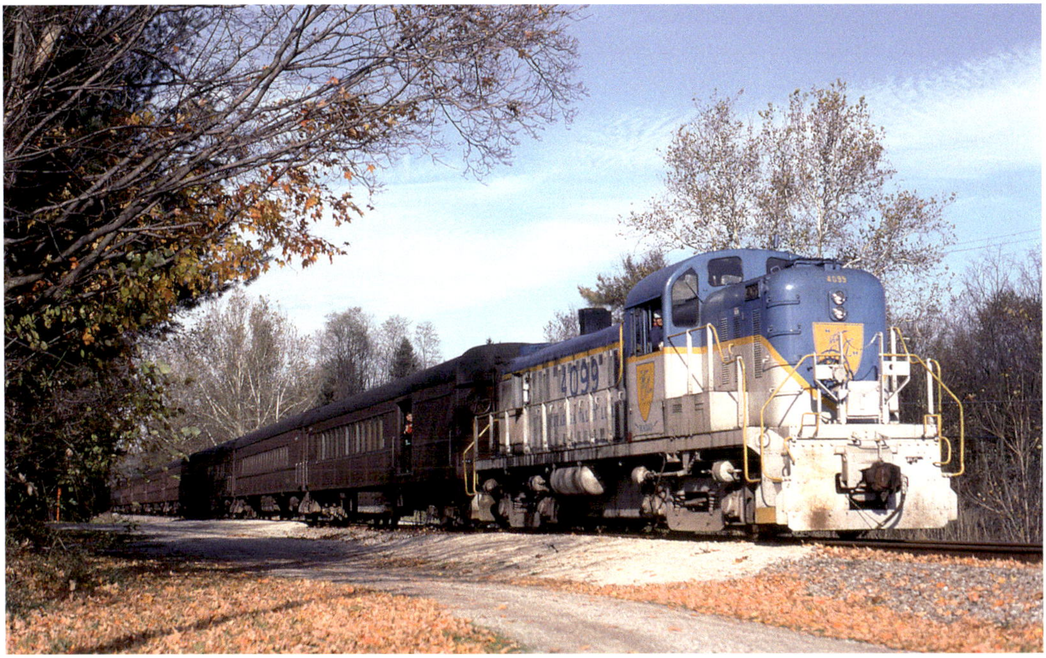

ANOTHER ALCO FOR THE CVL: The CVL acquired former Delaware & Hudson Alco RS-3 No. 4099 in summer 1989. The CVL retained the engine's D&H livery of blue and gray with gold stripes. Paired with No. 4070 for the 1990 season, No. 4099 usually operated on the north end of the train. That season CVL trains went no farther than Ira Road after a bridge over Howard Street in Akron was condemned by the Federal Railroad Administration in late 1989. In these 1990s photos, No. 4099 leads the train southbound at Howe Meadow in October 1990 (above) and along Riverview Road in summer 1990 (below) due to No. 4070 being out of service. *(Marty Surdyk photos)*

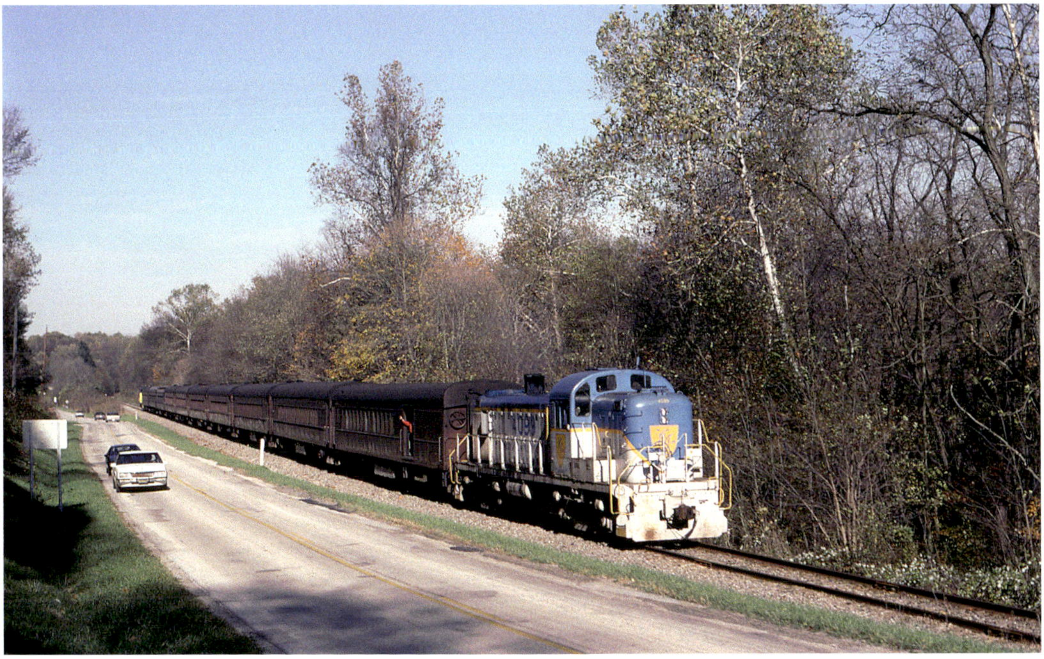

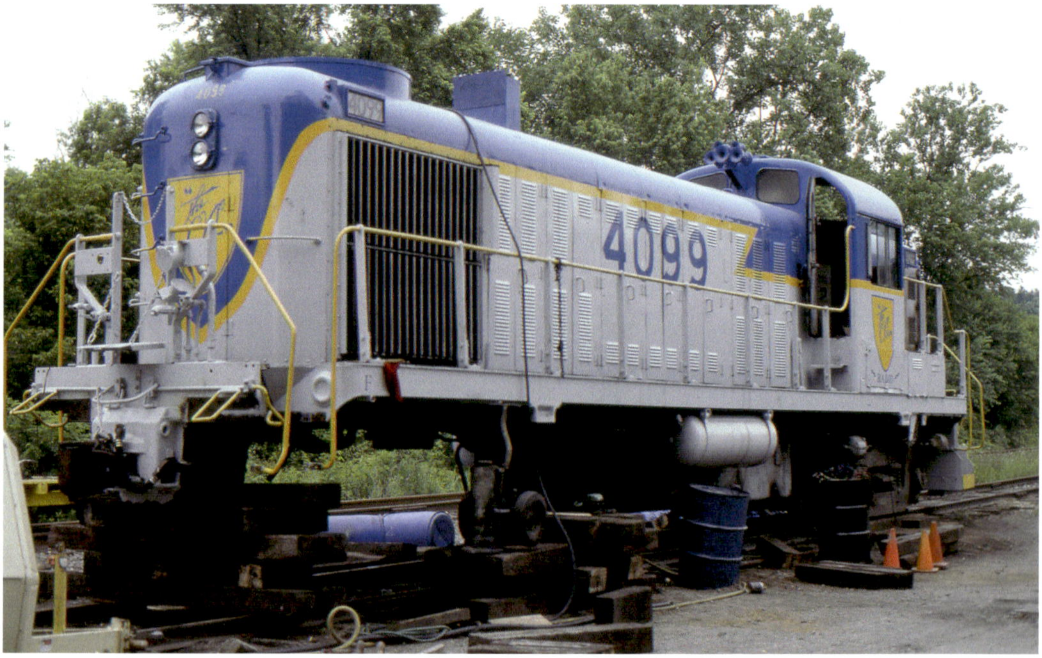

CVL IN PENINSULA: Peninsula was the business headquarters for the CVL and became its maintenance base after the railroad began acquiring its own locomotives and rolling stock. Above, maintenance was done outdoors on a siding track with supplies stored in a boxcar. Below, some cars and locomotives were stored on a stub-end track near the depot. By 1992, CVL fares had increased to $14.95 for adults and $9.95 for children. Nature trips were added in November 1991 and featured a park naturalist discussing the flora and fauna of the park. Passengers could disembark near Deep Lock quarry for a 45-minute guided tour. (*Above, Mark Demaline photo; below, Paul Woodring photo*)

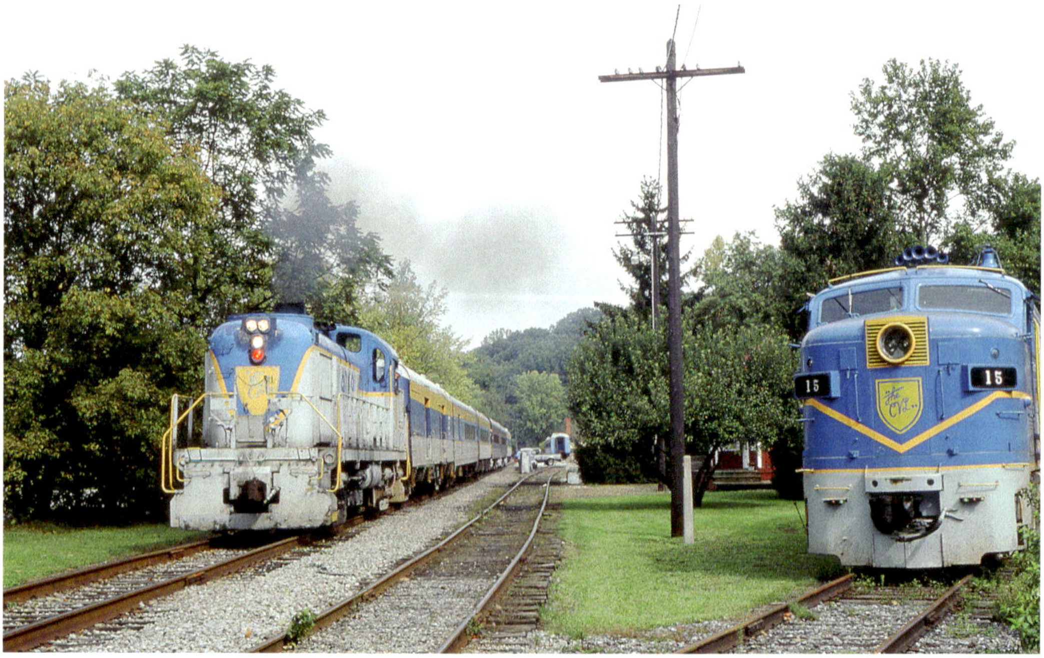

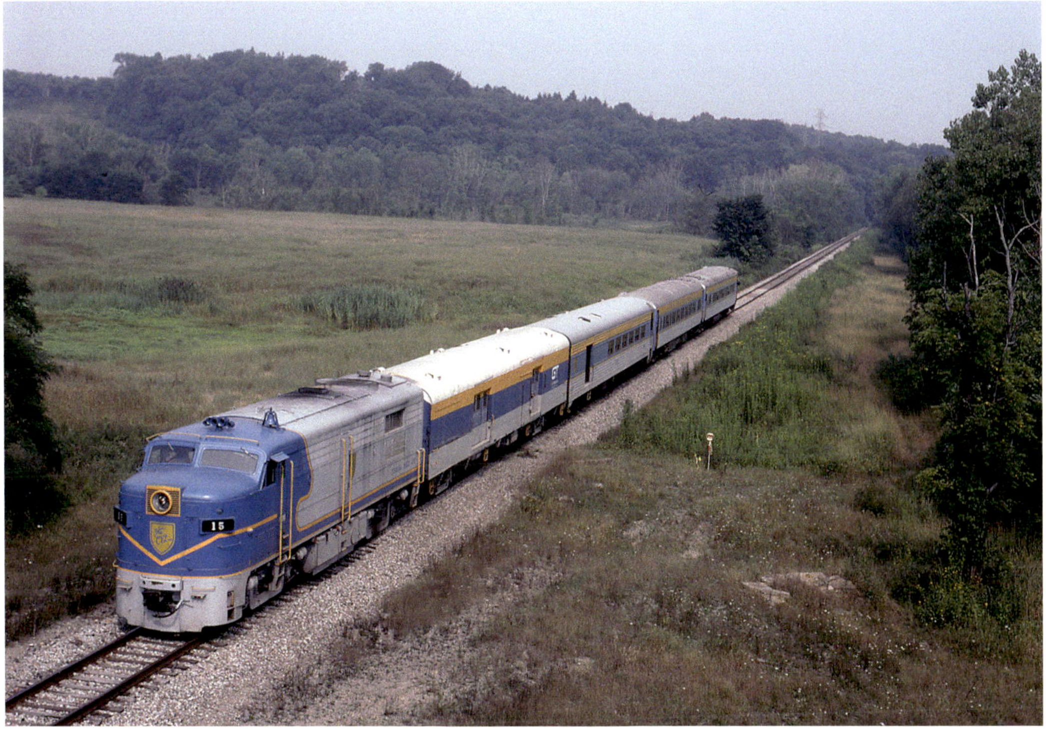

BACK IN AKRON: The National Park Service 1991 budget of $12 million for the Cuyahoga Valley National Recreation Area included money for track rehabilitation, including $500,000 to replace the bridge over Howard Street in Akron. The bridge project began in March 1993 and CVL trains resumed running into downtown Akron on August 1. As had been the case with No. 4070, CVL diesel locomotives were turned at Akron Junction. Above, a southbound train nears East Pleasant Valley Road in June 1991. Below, CVL No. 15 turns in October 1983 at Akron Junction with the unused B&O coaling tower in the background. (*Above, Marty Surdyk photo; below, Paul Woodring photo*)

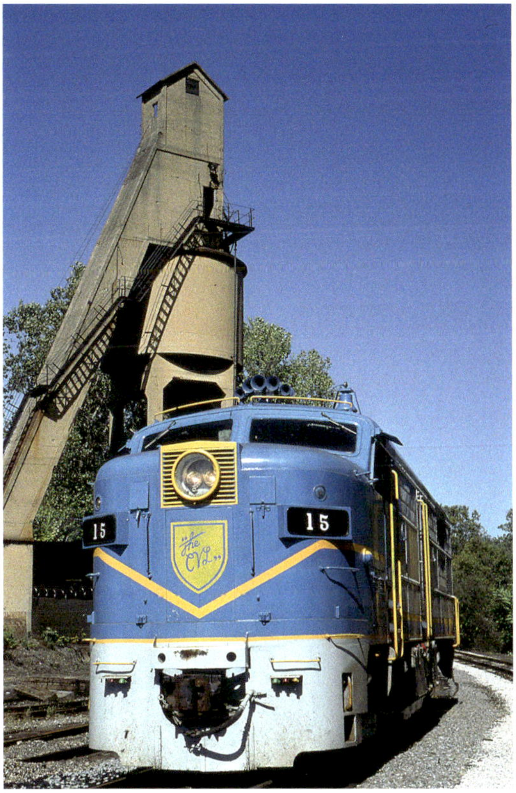

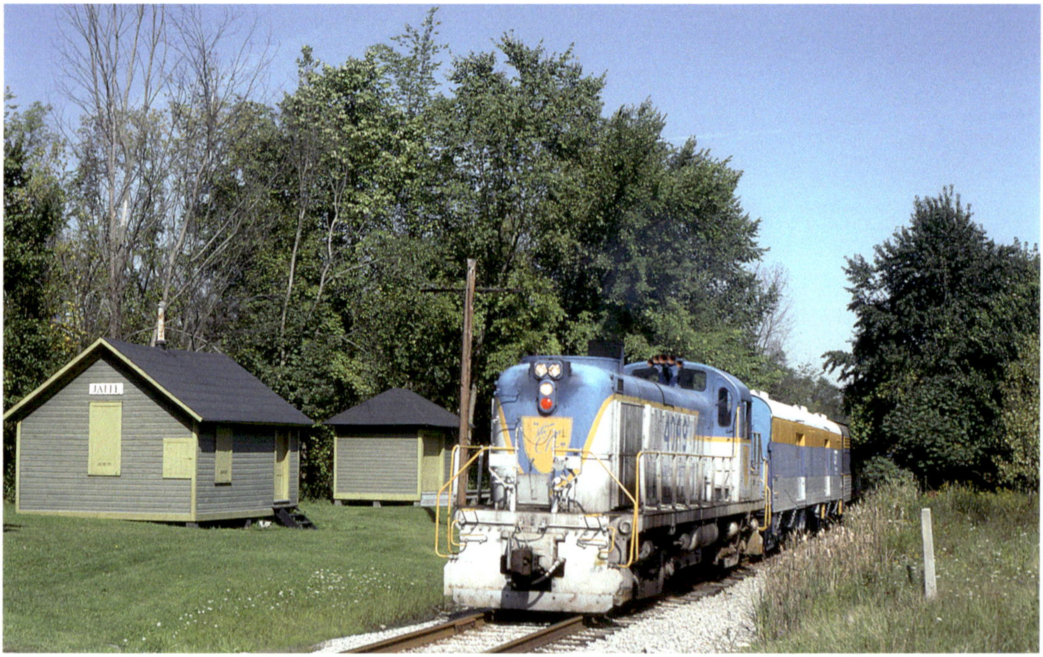

JAITE TRAIN ORDER STATION: The CVL nearly went out of business after losing $83,000 in 1990. It used $60,000 in private donations to start the 1991 season, operating on Saturdays, Sundays and Wednesdays. Ridership rose from 9,300 in 1990 to 15,700 in 1991 and revenue exceeded expenses by $73,000. Trains ran on Fridays in October and during holiday weekends. Above, a southbound train passes the former B&O Jaite train order station, which the Park Service has restored but moved back from its original location. Jaite was a flag stop for B&O's Cleveland-Wheeling, West Virginia, passenger trains until they made their last trips on September 29, 1951. Below, a northbound train passes Indigo Lake. (*Marty Surdyk photos*)

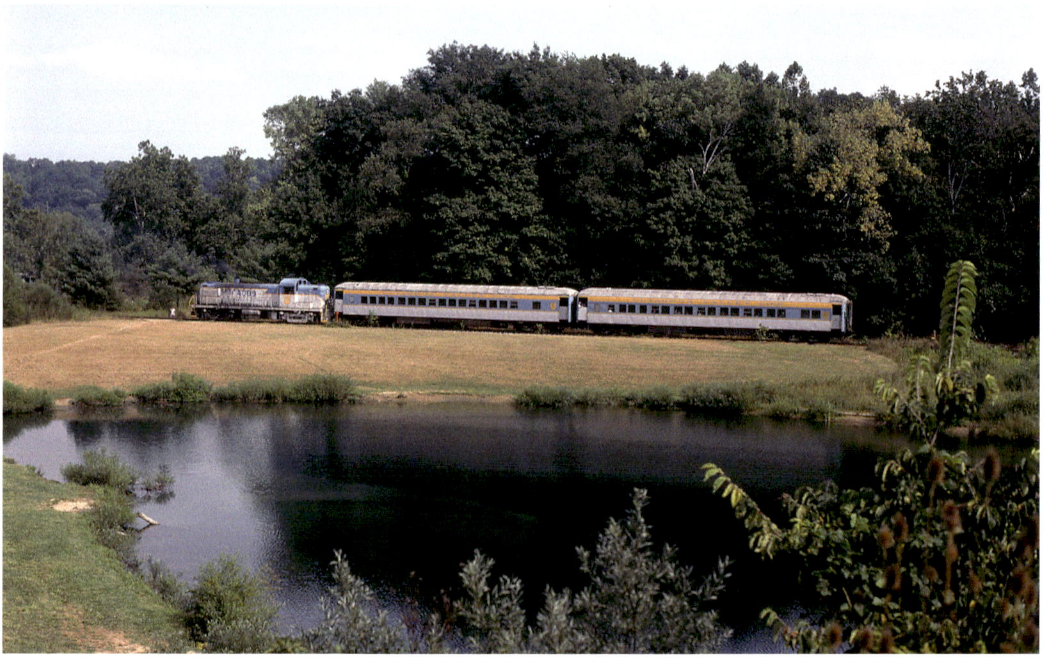

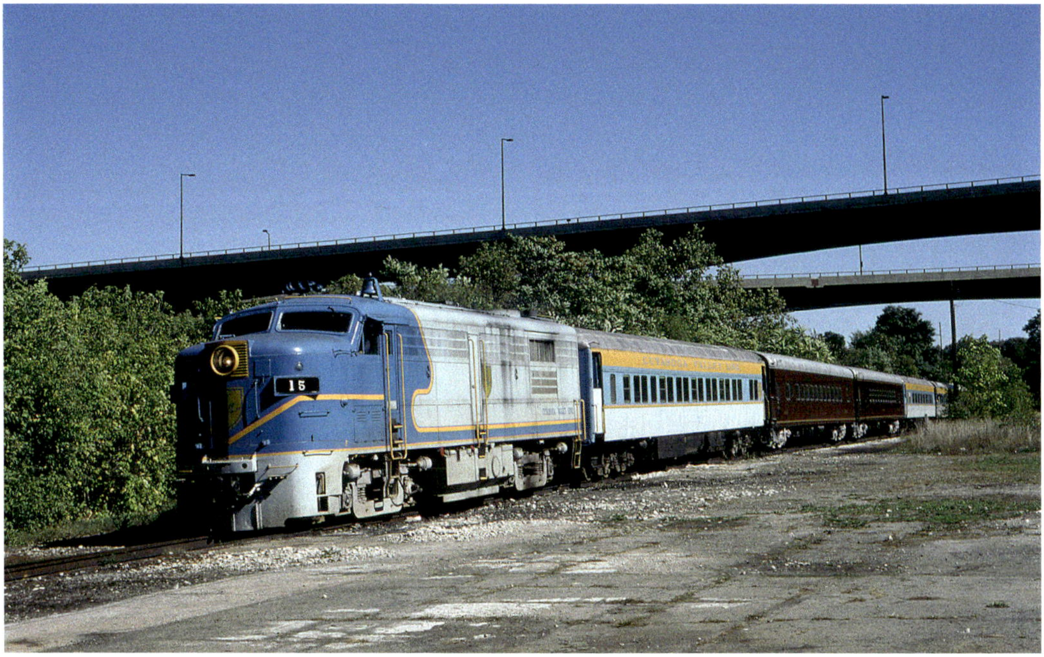

WHERE THE B&O ONCE BOARDED: Akron CVL passengers disembarked at the site of the former B&O Howard Street Station. Its last scheduled passenger trains were the *Cleveland Night Express* between Cleveland and Washington, D.C. Nos. 17 and 18 ran for the final time on January 3-4, 1962. In their final years, these trains carried a coach, a sleeping car and a lounge car that served a light breakfast northbound. There were no station stops between Cleveland and Akron. Howard Street Station was razed in 1965 and the CVL boarding site was a vacant lot until July 25, 2001, when the current CVSR station opened. Buses met trains and took passengers to Akron cultural and commercial attractions. *(Paul Woodring photos)*

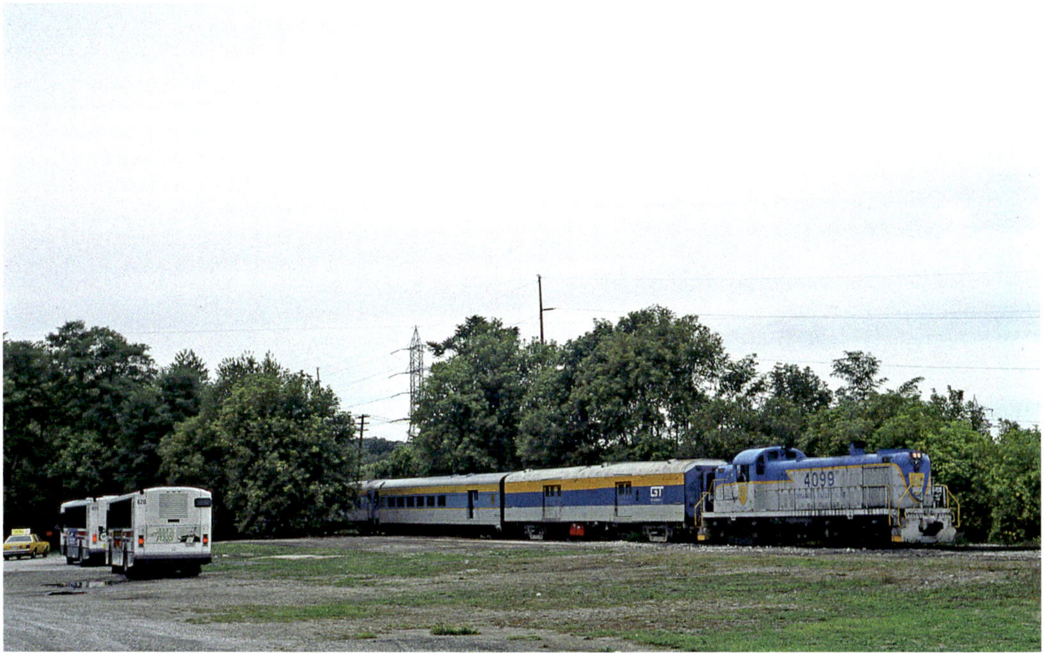

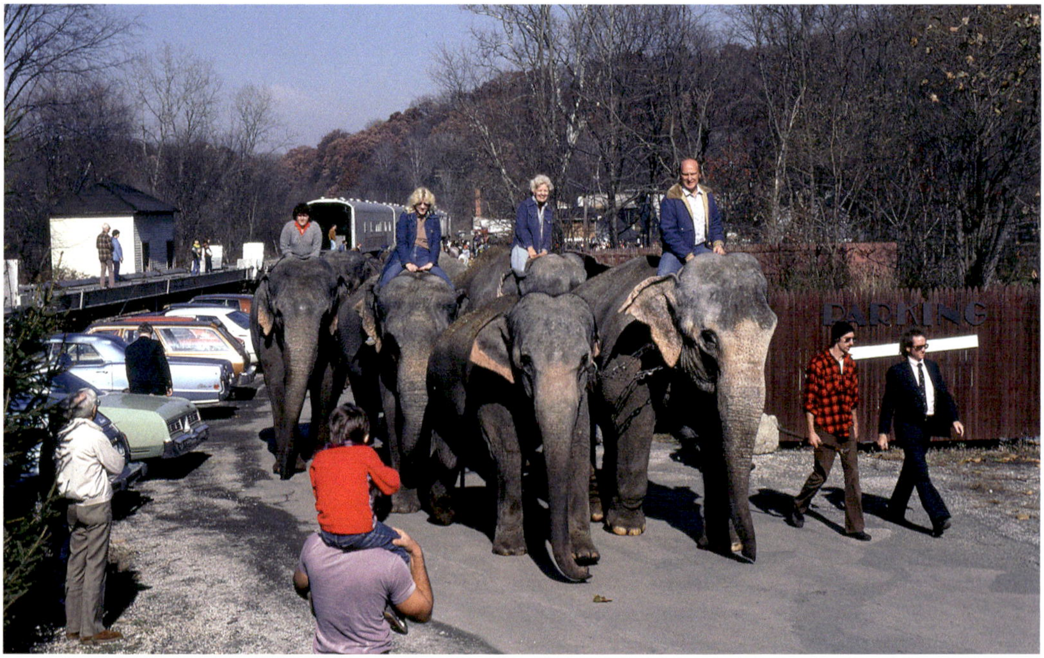

CIRCUS TRAIN: The Valley Line hosted a yearly visit of the Ringling Bros. and Barnum & Bailey circus train, which in November 1987 became the first train to use the Valley Line after its purchase by the National Park Service the previous September. Passenger cars carrying performers and staff members were parked and unloaded in Akron, but the animal cars were taken to Peninsula where the elephants disembarked and walked down Ohio Route 303 to the Richfield Coliseum. Above, the elephant parade has begun with local television celebrities catching a ride in November 1981. Below, the circus train is shown on the siding in Peninsula. (*Above, Paul Woodring photo; below, Tom Fritsch photo*)

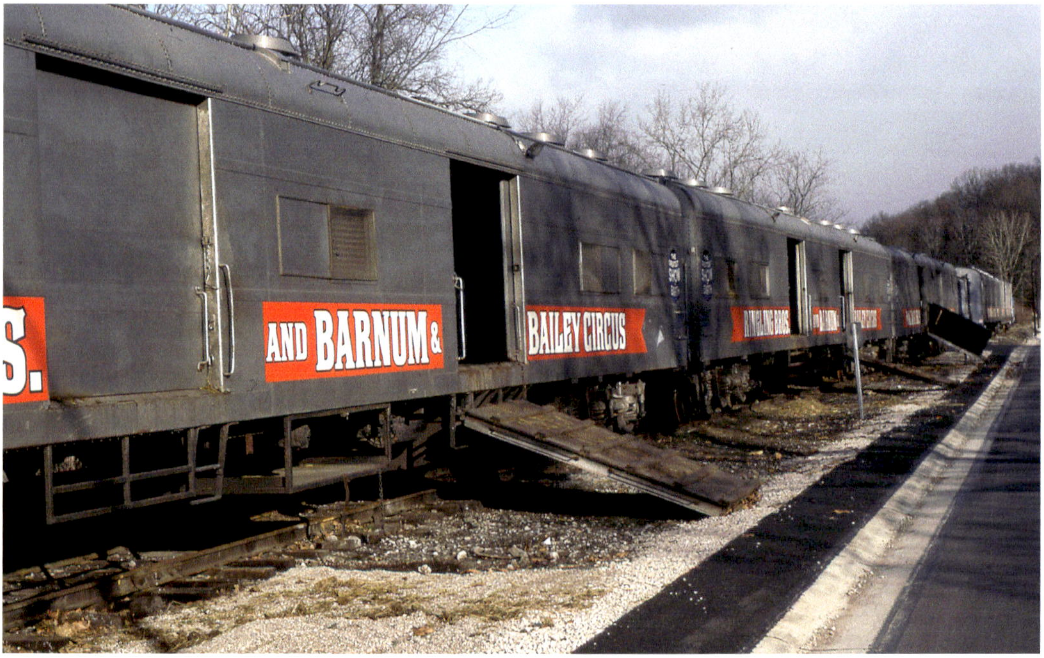

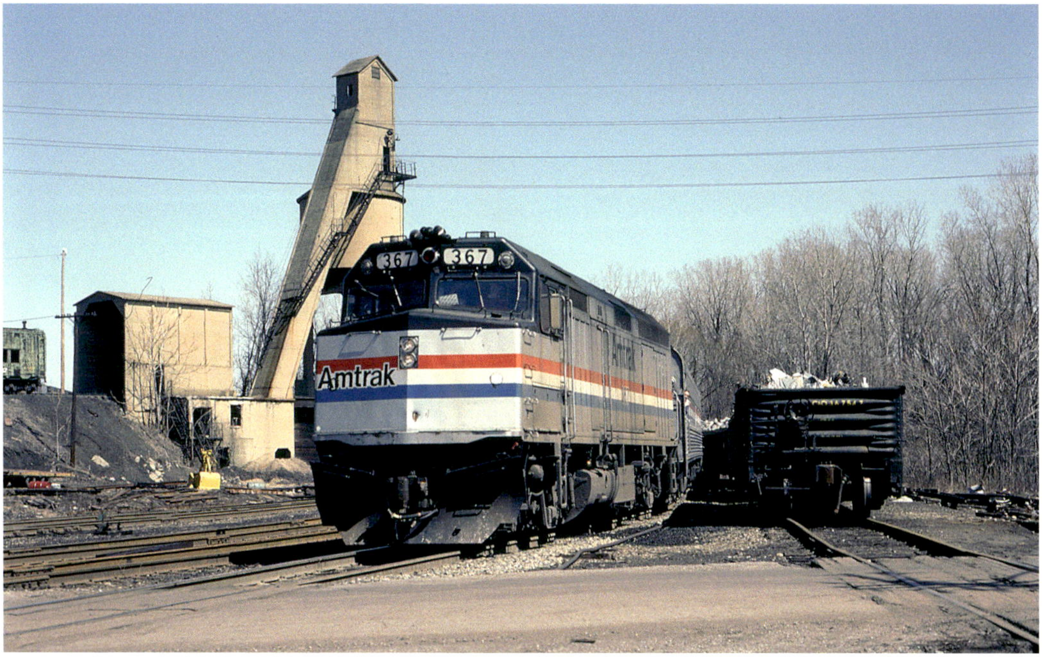

SPECIAL MOVES: On occasion, other passenger trains used the Valley Line. Above, an Amtrak inspection train passes Akron Junction en route to Cleveland on April 10, 1984. Some former Amtrak passenger cars have been used by the CVSR. Below, a chartered train for Pittsburgh Steelers fans ran from Pittsburgh to Cleveland via Akron on October 26, 1980, for a game against the Cleveland Browns at Cleveland Municipal Stadium, a game the Browns won 27-26. Below, the football special meets a southbound CVL train pulled by No. 4070 at Willow in Independence. The passenger cars were from the PATrain, a commuter service operated by the Port Authority of Allegheny County until 1989. (*Paul Woodring photos*)

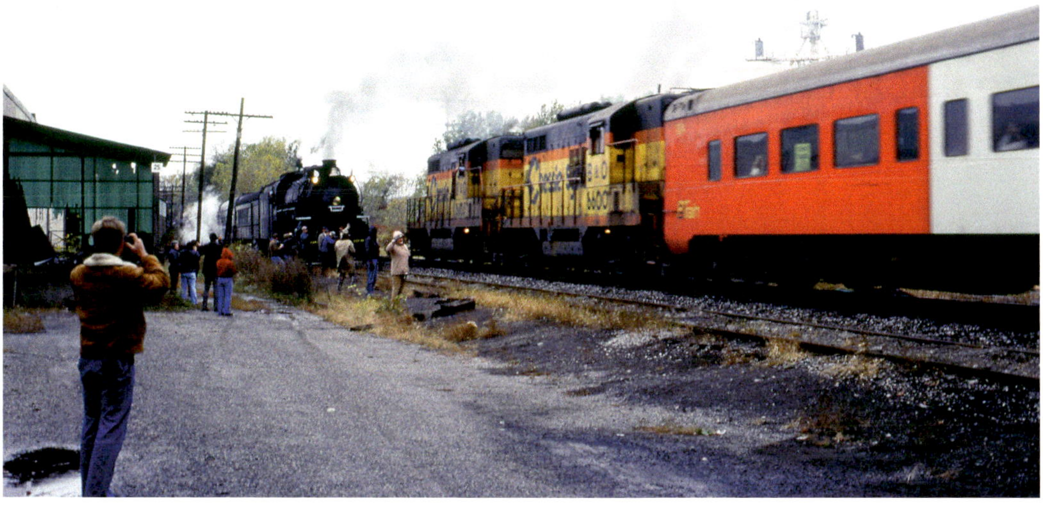

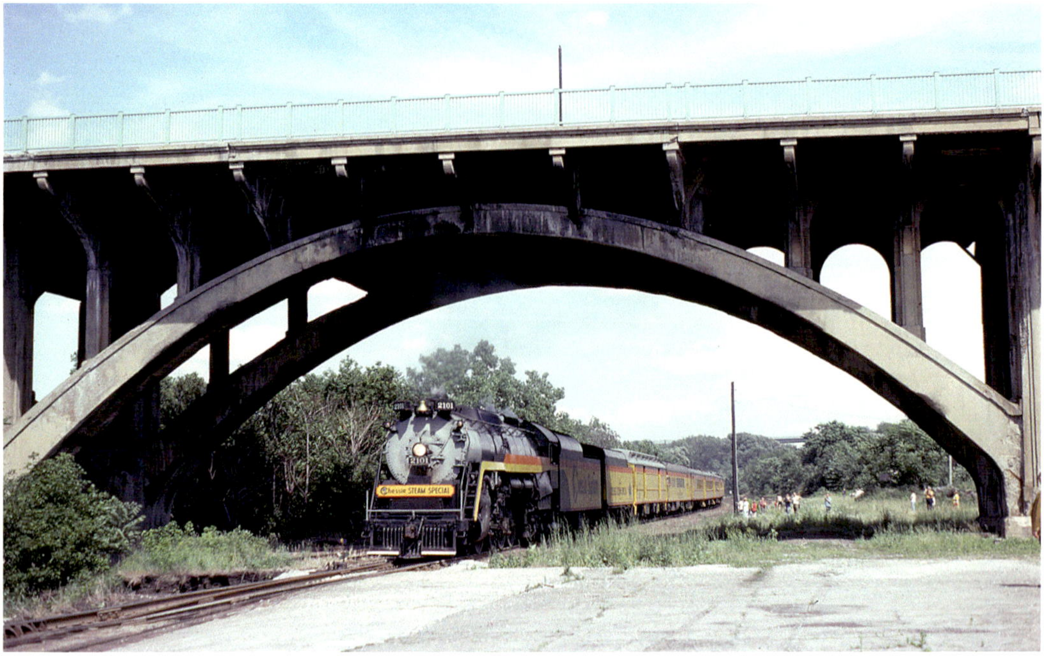

CHESSIE STEAM IN THE VALLEY: To celebrate the 150th anniversary of the founding of the B&O, Chessie ran a series of steam excursions. The eighteen-car Chessie Steam Special came to the Valley Line on June 19, 1977, on a deadhead move from Pittsburgh to Cleveland. Pulling the train was former Reading Company 4-8-4 T1 Class No. 2101. Above, the deadhead trip is shown passing beneath the North Hill Viaduct in Akron, and below, running between Boston Mill and Jaite. The Chessie Steam Special operated again in 1978, running from Cleveland to Pittsburgh via Akron on August 20 in a deadhead move that resulted in the cancellation of CVL service that weekend. (*Paul Woodring photos*)

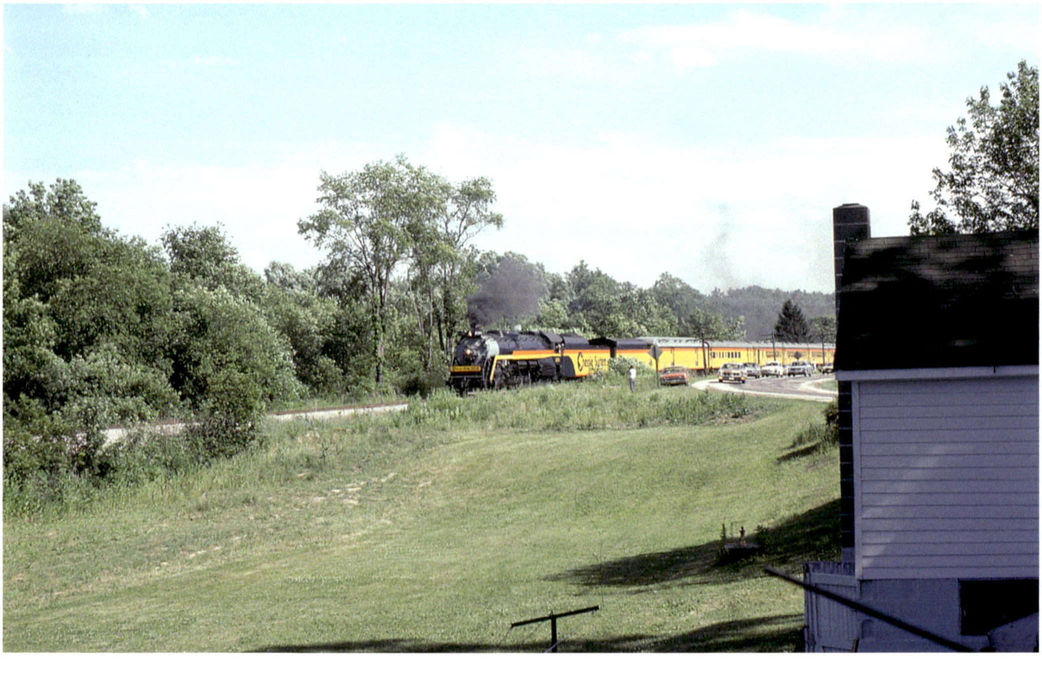

4 BROADENING THE APPEAL

Federal funding in the 1990s and 2000s enabled the CVSR to establish a new maintenance facility, rebuild its tracks and construct intermediate stations. Five miles of track were rebuilt in 1994 and seven miles were upgraded in 1995. Bridges were replaced over the Cuyahoga River near Peninsula and over Chippewa Creek in Brecksville.

In 2009, $2.4 million in federal stimulus funding paid for nine miles of new welded rail between Akron and Merriman Road, and Vaughn Road and Brecksville. Another $440,000 funded the replacement of 3,200 old ties.

Nine more miles of welded rail were installed in 2011 in a $3.35 million project that also included tie replacement, new ballast and rebuilding the Ohio 303 crossing in Peninsula. CVSR received $3.2 million in federal funding in 2012 for five projects, four of which involved rehabilitating passenger cars, locomotives and power cars.

Not every marketing idea to attract passengers succeeded. Patronage of 1994 ski trains to the Boston Mills and Brandywine ski resorts and an evening cocktail train was lackluster. But beer- and wine-tasting trains returned in the early 2000s and often sold out. The CVSR acquired dining cars to serve breakfast, brunch and dinner aboard select trains.

Conductors were directed to wear railroad-style uniforms and engineers to wear bib overalls to create the look of the 1940s to early 1950s. Engineers were instructed to wave at those on station platforms. "Our main function is to entertain and our mission is to serve the park, which is our landlord," CVSR Executive Director President Peter Birgeles told the *Akron Beacon Journal* in May 1994.

By 1996 the CVSR's annual budget was $1.4 million with corporate sponsorships accounting for $600,000 of it. The black tie All Board Ball began in 2005 to raise money. It has been held in a variety of venues including the Fitzwater maintenance shop. The railroad's fundraising activities were focused more on funding specific projects than on underwriting daily operating expenses.

On June 1, 2007, service to Akron expanded to three times a day on Wednesdays through Sundays to match the level of service operating between Independence and Peninsula. One train set operated between Akron and Independence, replacing the change of trains that had been required in Peninsula. CVSR service to Akron had been twice a day on Saturdays and Sundays.

A 2006 survey found 12 percent of Cuyahoga Valley National Park visitors rode the CVSR. A survey conducted a decade later found 15 percent of park visitors rode the train and 44 percent of them had ridden the train previously.

The CVSR website went live in mid-2009, giving potential passengers another option for buying tickets and obtaining train and seat availability information.

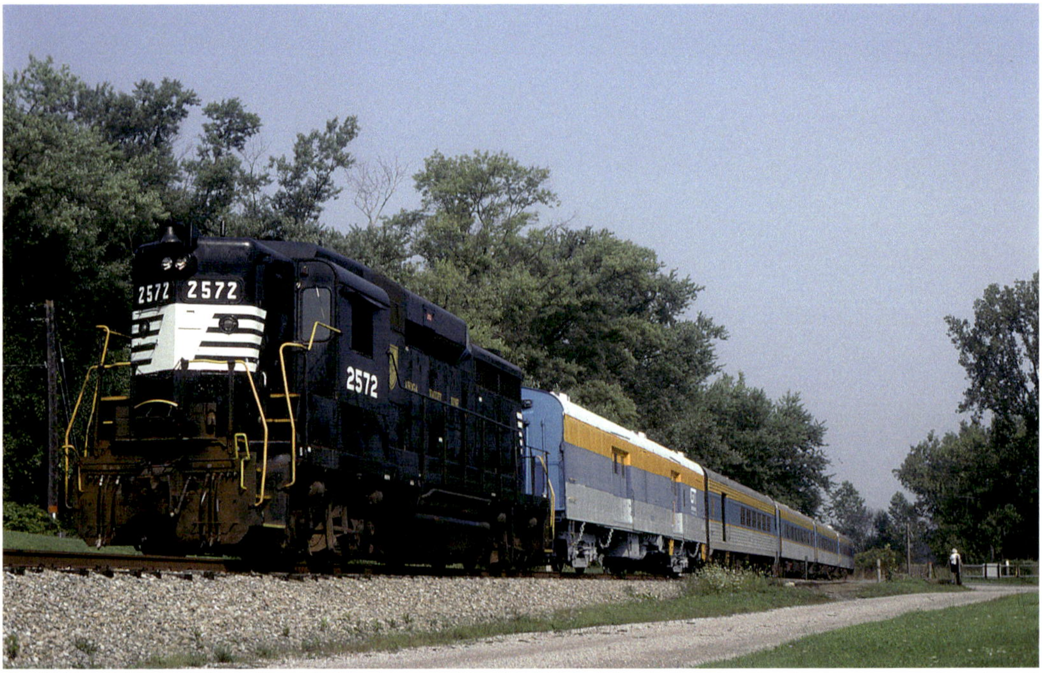

ONE-SEASON WONDER: CVL and CVSR trains have been pulled by an assortment of motive power that worked on the railroad for a short time and were not repainted. For the 1992 season, the CVL acquired former Norfolk Southern EMD GP30 No. 2572, which had been built in October 1962 for the Southern Railway. Although some of its NS markings were painted over, No. 2572 never wore CVL colors, sporting only a small CVL logo and the CVL name on its flanks. Above, it is shown in September along Riverview Road, and below, a month later at Boston Mill with a former Amtrak car in the passenger car consist. (*Marty Surdyk photos*)

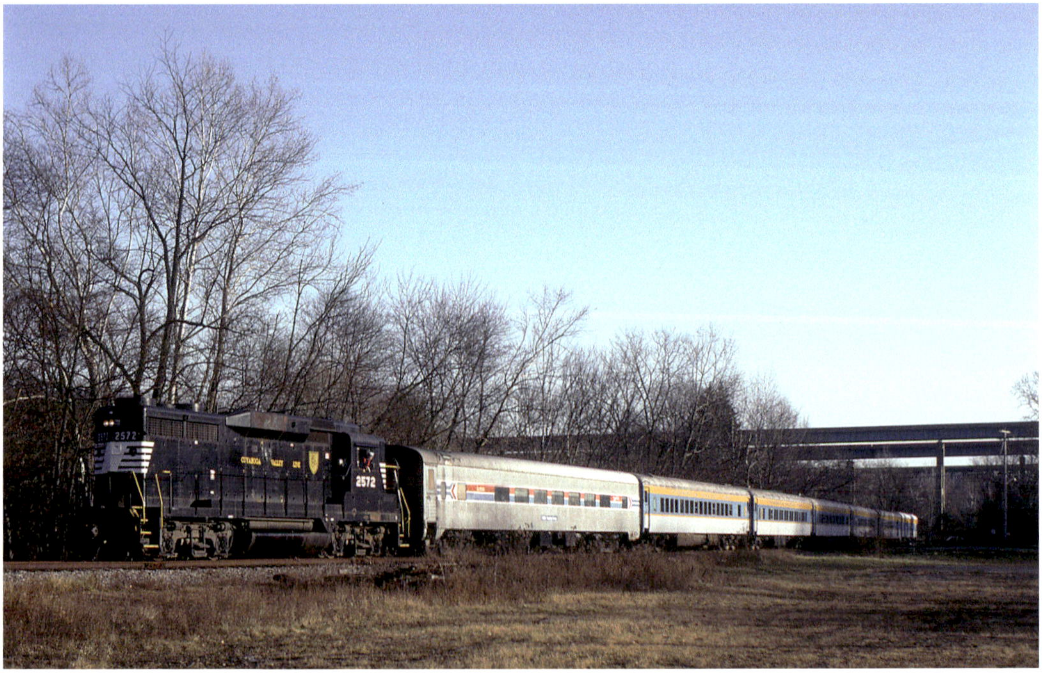

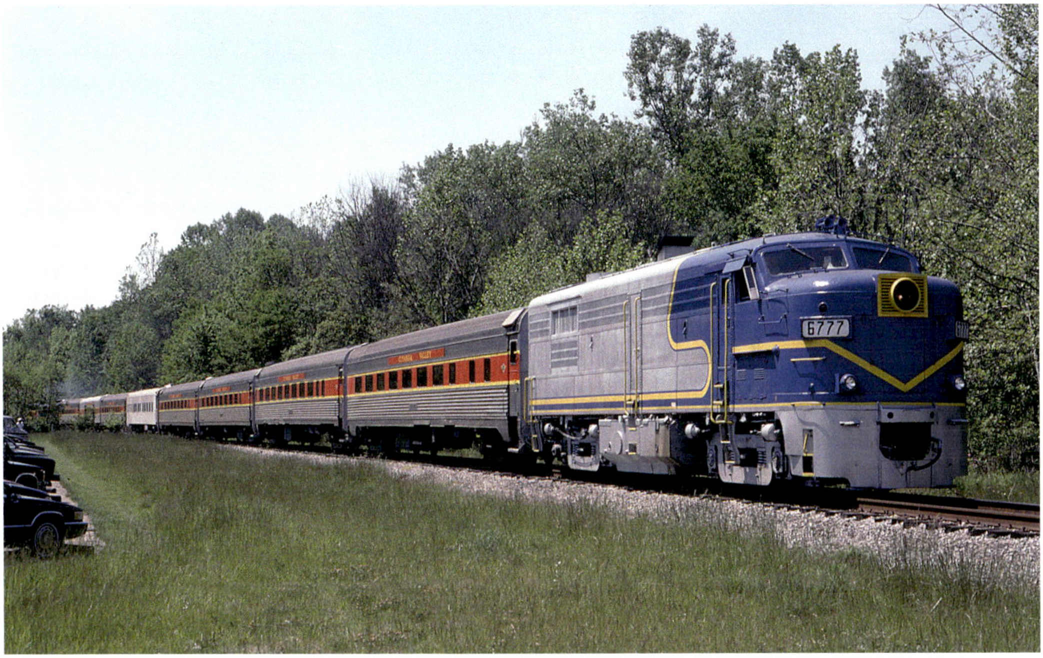

MIXED APPEARANCE: Upon renaming itself the Cuyahoga Valley Scenic Railroad in April 1994, the railroad adopted a livery of red, gold and black. For a while, the new colors appeared on passenger cars, but not on all locomotives. FPA-4 No. 6777 is shown at Brecksville in June 1994 wearing a darker shade of blue and a V stripe on its nose, but without the shield that had been part of the early CVL diesel livery. No. 6777 would be given roster No. 14 when it was repainted. Below, No. 15 pulls a train along Riverview Road south of Peninsula in April 1994, still in its old livery, but with the passenger cars wearing the new colors. (*Marty Surdyk photos*)

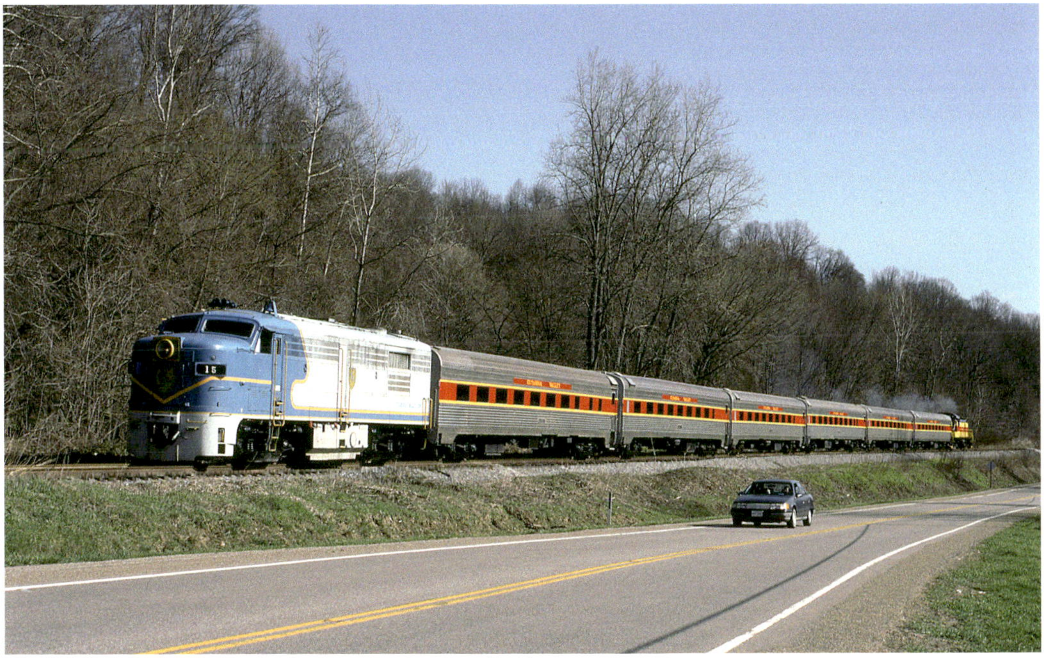

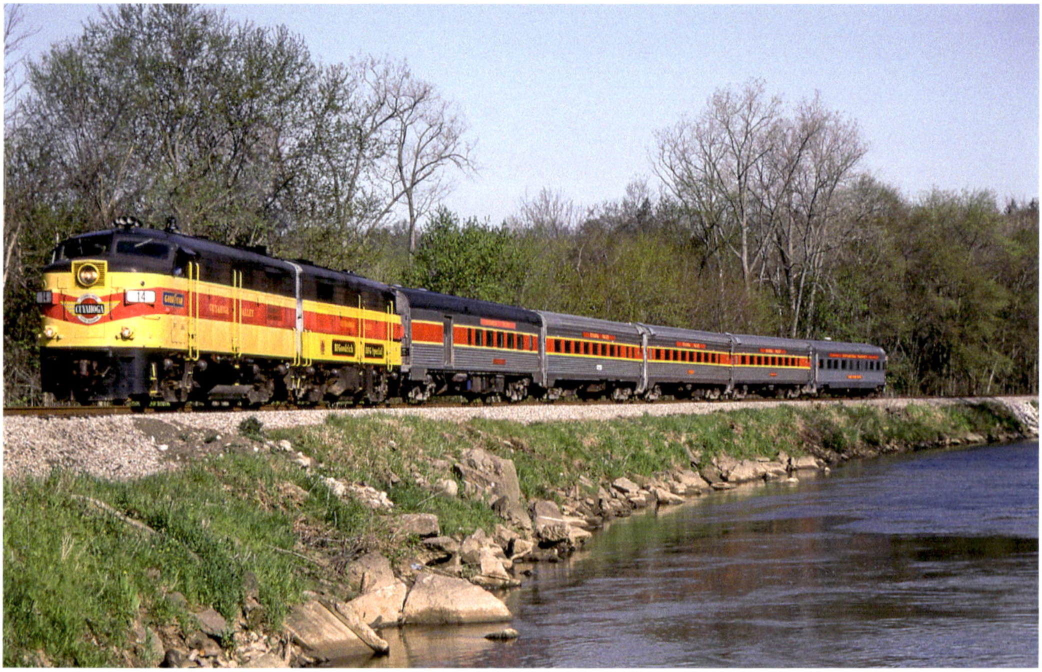

RAILFAN EXCURSION: The first CVSR locomotive livery emphasized gold with broad red stripes. The tops of the locomotives were black. On May 17, 1997, Nos. 14 and 15 led an all-day railfan excursion that covered the length of the line between Independence and Akron. Above, photo runbys were conducted at numerous scenic locations, including along the Cuyahoga River near Brecksville. Below, crew members re-created timeless railroad scenes, including this one of crew members comparing their watches that was staged at Rockside Road Station in Independence. *(Above, Robert Farkas photo; below, Marty Surdyk photo)*

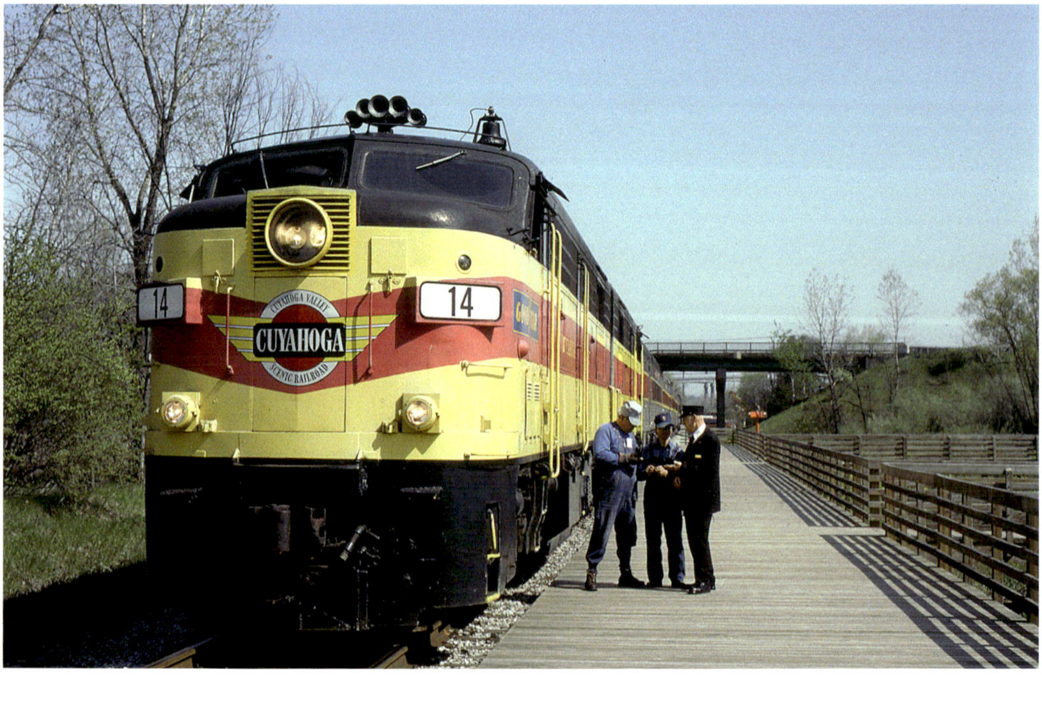

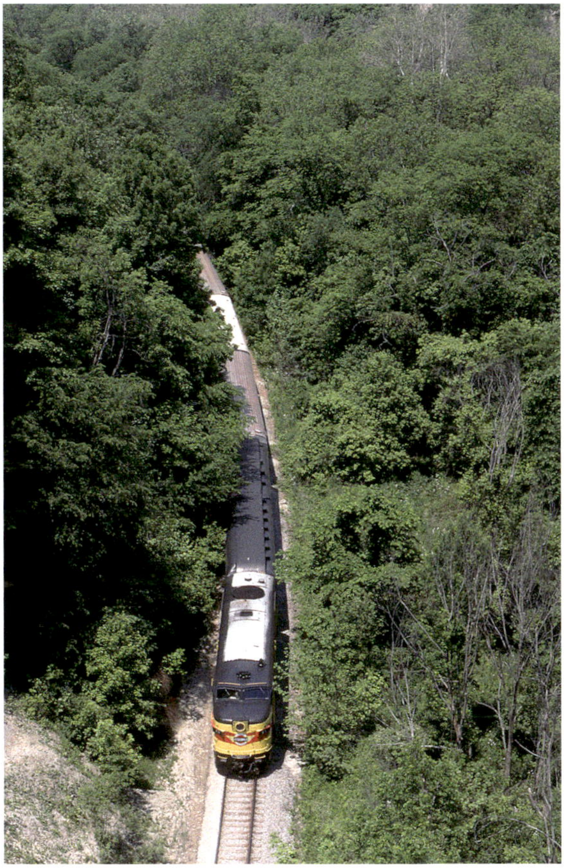

EXPANSION IDEAS: The CVSR awarded a $10,000 consultant's contract in 1993 to study extending service to three destinations: downtown Cleveland, Canton and Akron's Quaker Square. It was part of a planned $12 million expansion project that included the acquisition of additional locomotives and passenger cars, and new station facilities. Funding was expected to come from the federal and state government and grants from private foundations. One estimate was that buying the CSX-owned track from Independence to Cleveland would cost $3.5 million. The Cleveland extension has yet to occur because CSX still uses the route in Cleveland and the tracks are not suitable for passenger operation. Shown are CVSR trains in Brecksville in June 1994. (*Marty Surdyk photos*)

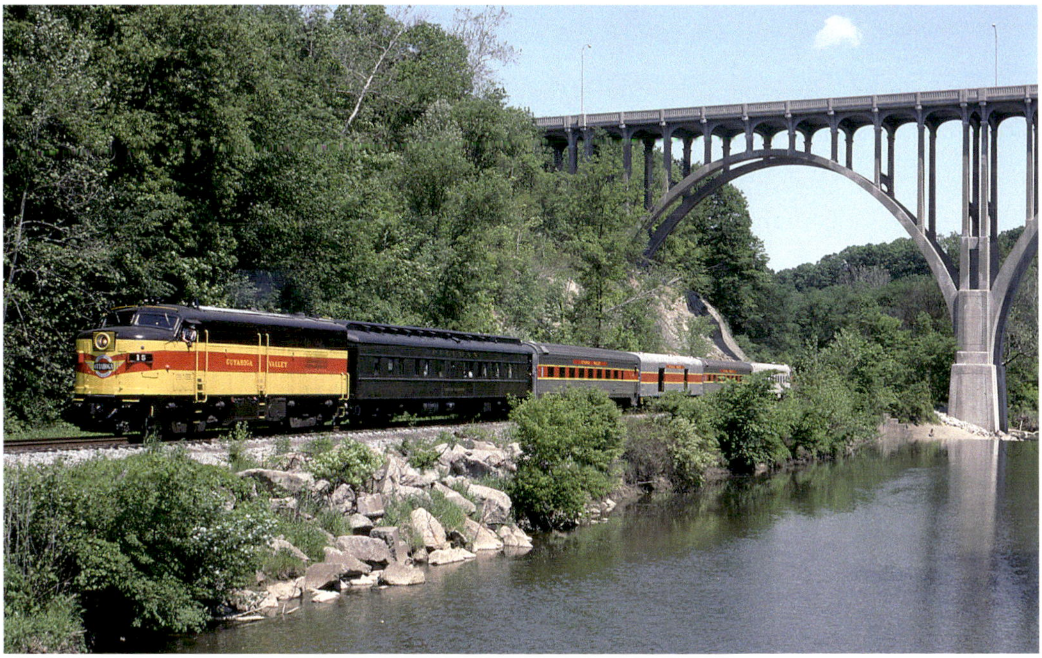

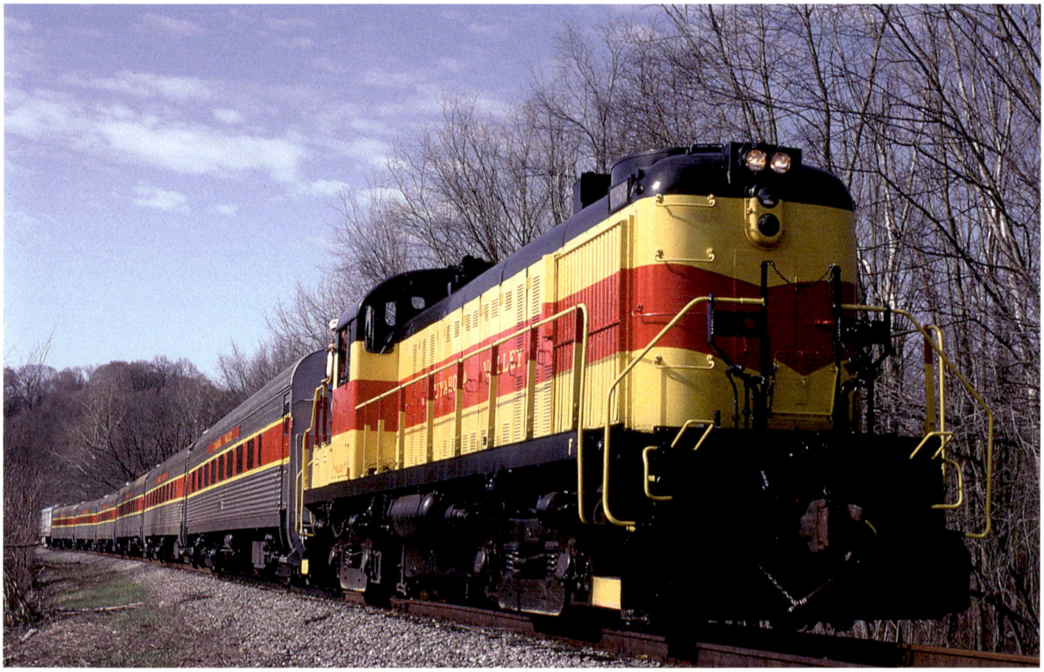

RELIABLE NO. 4099: RS-3 No. 4099 was built by Alco in September 1952 for the Delaware & Hudson Railway, which used it in freight and passenger service. The second diesel locomotive to join the CVL fleet, No. 4099, was the primary CVL motive power in the 1990s and continued to pull trains through 2004. It left the CVSR in November 2011 and is now part of the collection of the Age of Steam Roundhouse in Sugarcreek, Ohio, where it continues to wear its CVSR livery. Above, No. 4099 leads a train in April 1994. Below, No. 4099 crosses Furnace Run at Everett. (*Marty Surdyk photos*)

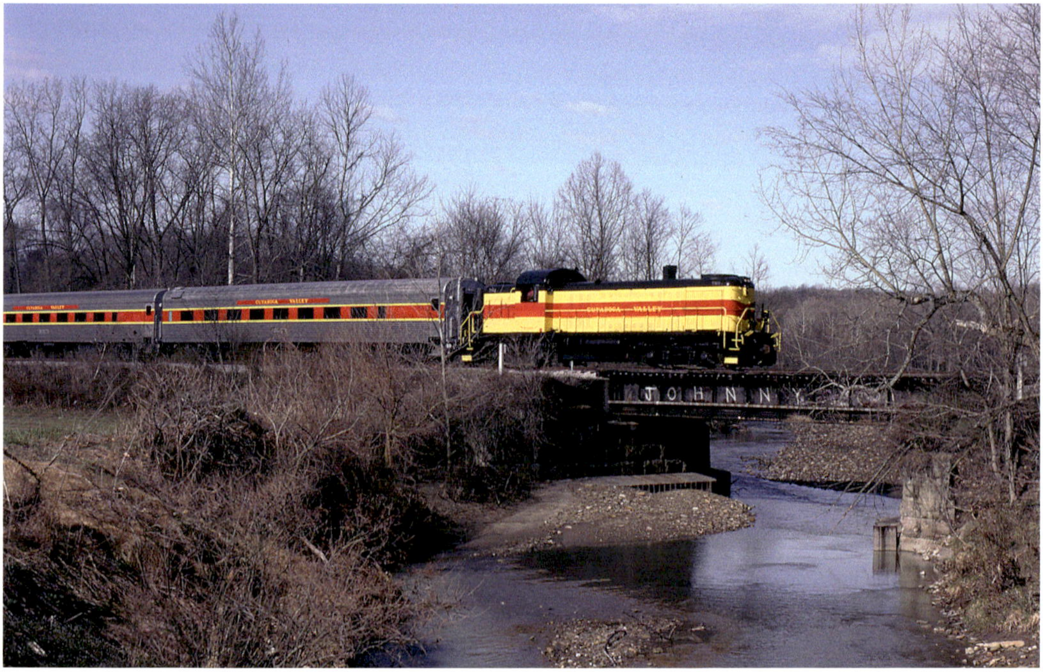

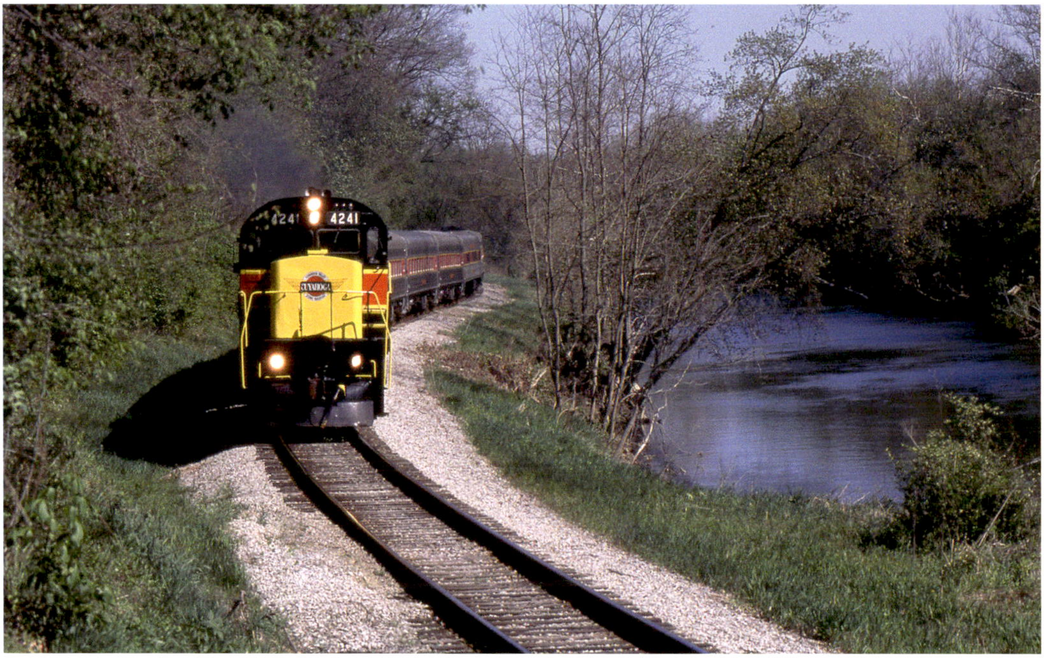

FOLLOW THE RIVER: CVSR began repainting its locomotives in late 2002 into a livery that emphasized black and limited gold paint to the engine nose and flank stripes. Above, a southbound train hugs its namesake river on May 6, 2007, between East Pleasant Valley and Hillside roads. The tracks also skirt the river in Brecksville, along Riverview Road near Boston Mill, and in Peninsula. Not all of the CVSR runs through the Cuyahoga Valley National Park. Below, a portion of the CVSR passes behind the backyards of private homes in the Merriman Woods housing development in northwest Akron, where the track begins a two percent grade southbound. *(Above, Mark Demaline photo; below, Craig Sanders photo)*

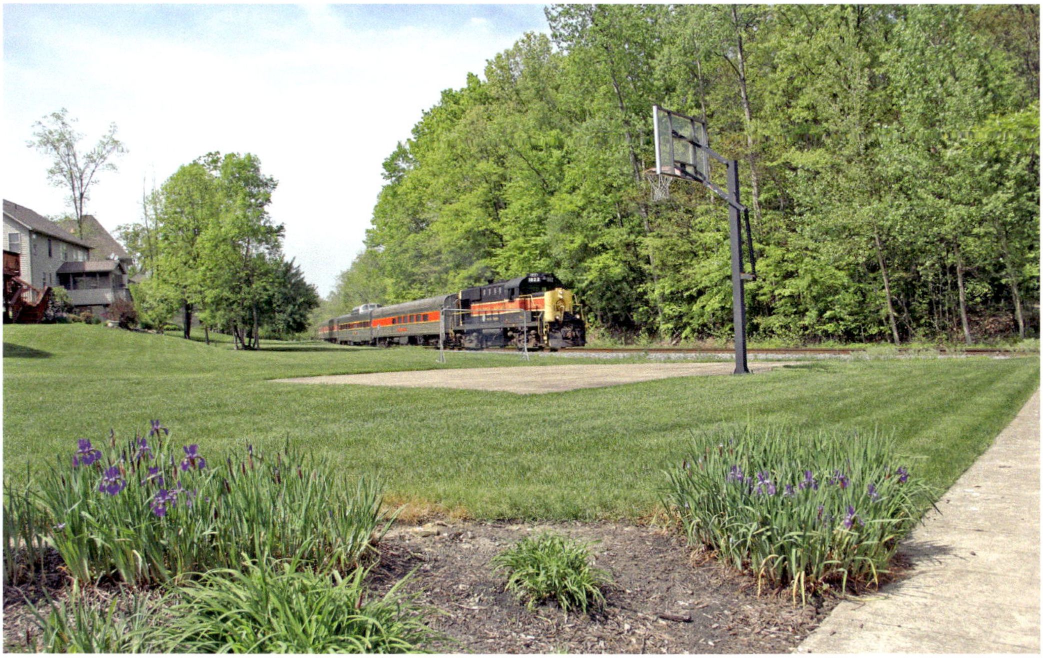

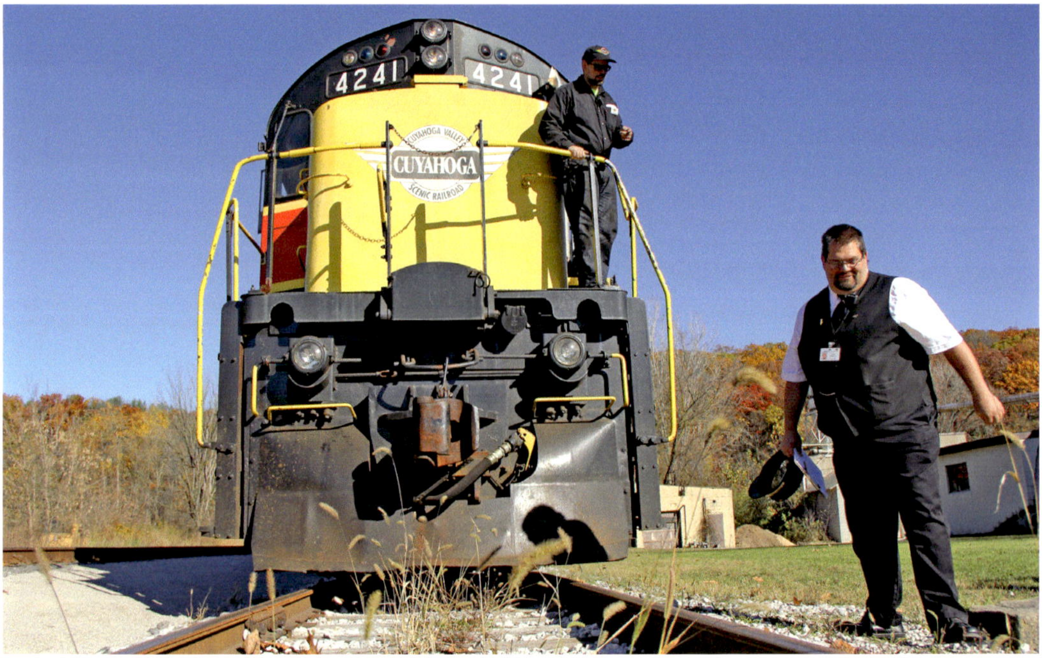

CVSR'S BACKBONE: More than half of CVSR's patronage rides the *National Park Scenic* between Independence and Akron. Between June and late October, trains run three roundtrips a day Friday through Sunday and two roundtrips a day Tuesday through Thursday. The *Scenic* operates twice a day on weekends during the late fall, winter and spring. Five-day-a-week operation began on May 24, 1995, between Independence and Peninsula. Above, on October 26, 2014, two crew members pose by CVSR 4241, a C424 built by Montreal Locomotive Works in January 1966 for Canadian Pacific Railway. Below, the *Scenic* passes a colorful autumn scene at Indigo Lake on October 25, 2015. The lake is a former sand and gravel pit. (*Craig Sanders photographs*)

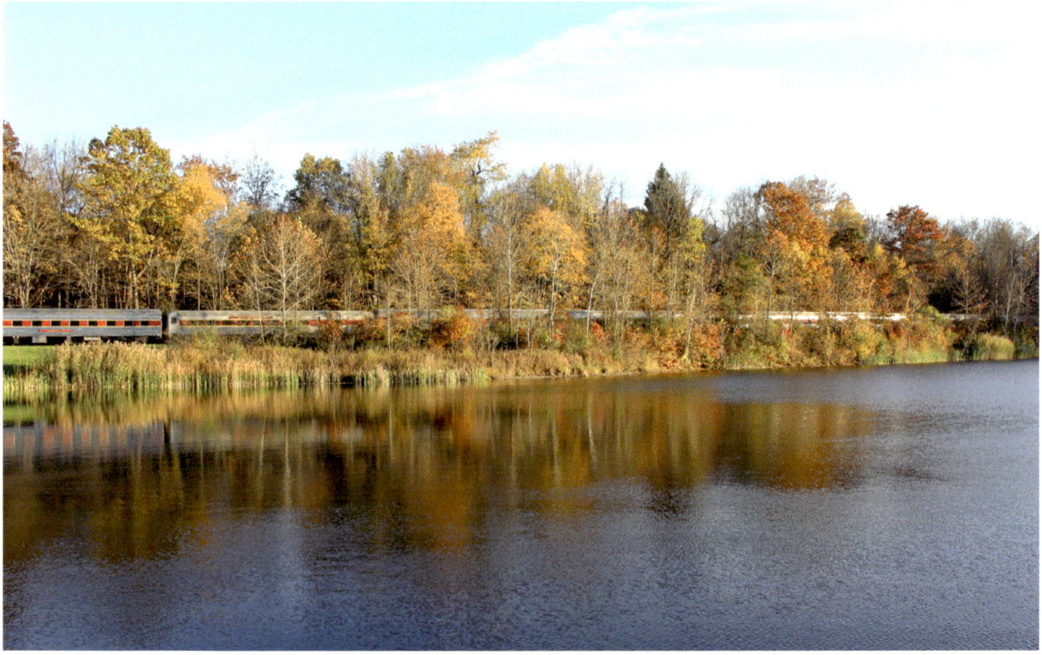

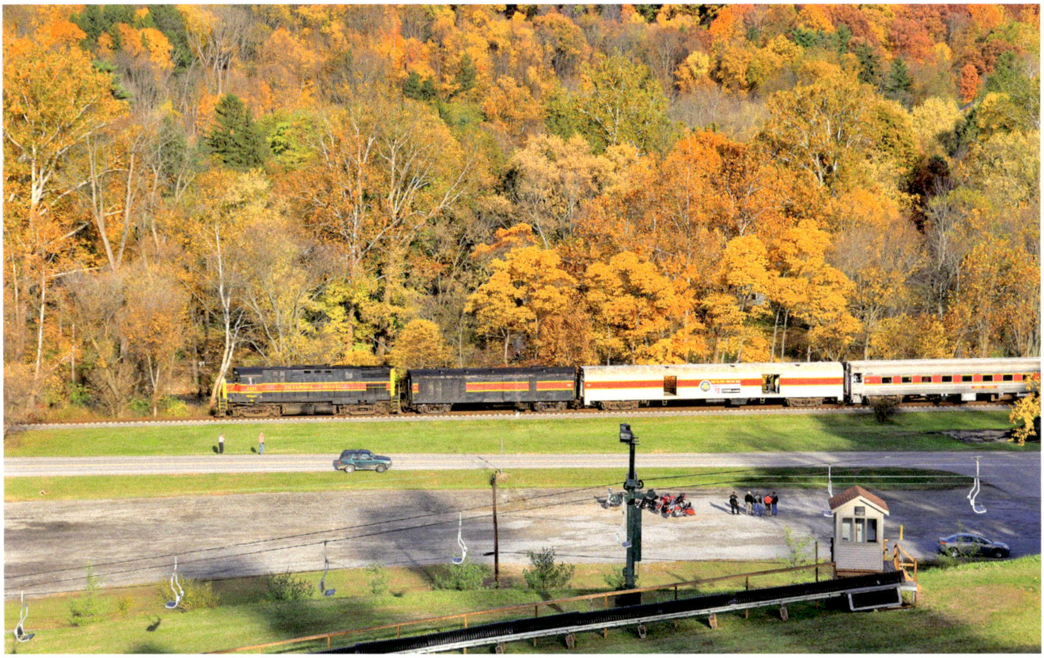

AKRON EXPANSION: In a bid to boost Akron ridership by as much as 10,000 a year, CVSR expanded service on June 9, 2007, to three roundtrips between Akron and Peninsula on Wednesday through Sunday during June, July and August. Previous Akron service had run only on Saturday and Sunday and connected in Peninsula with Independence-Peninsula trains. Above, the photographer is standing atop a slope of the Boston Mills ski resort west of the tracks on October 25, 2009, to capture a *Scenic* train amid autumn splendor. Below, a southbound train passes a wall of fall color along Riverview Road south of Peninsula on October 21, 2012. *(Above, Peter Bowler photo; below, Craig Sanders photo)*

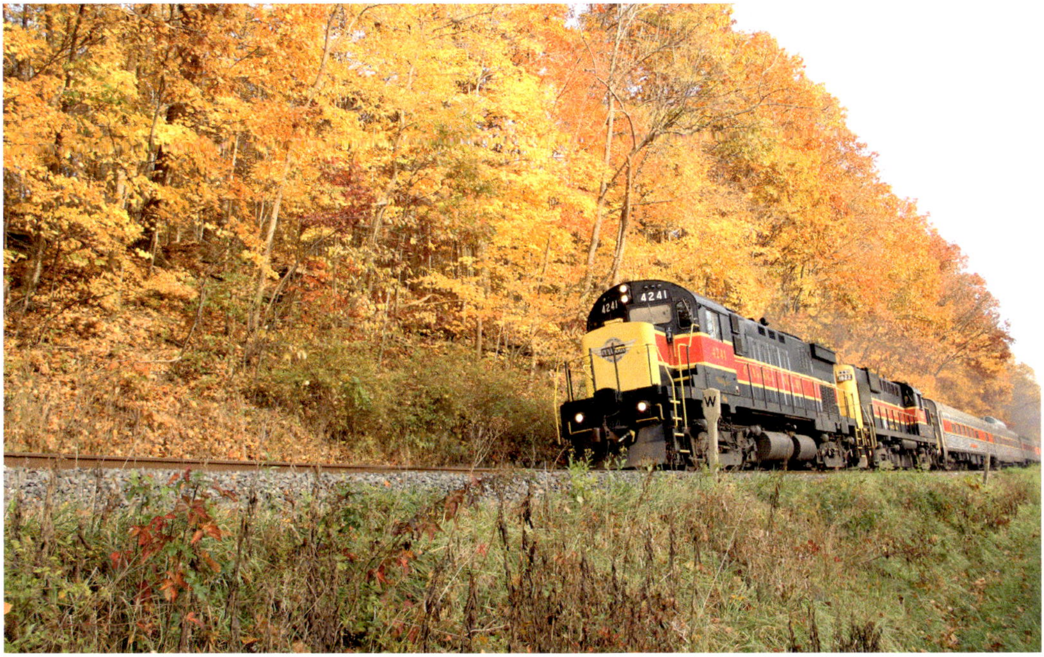

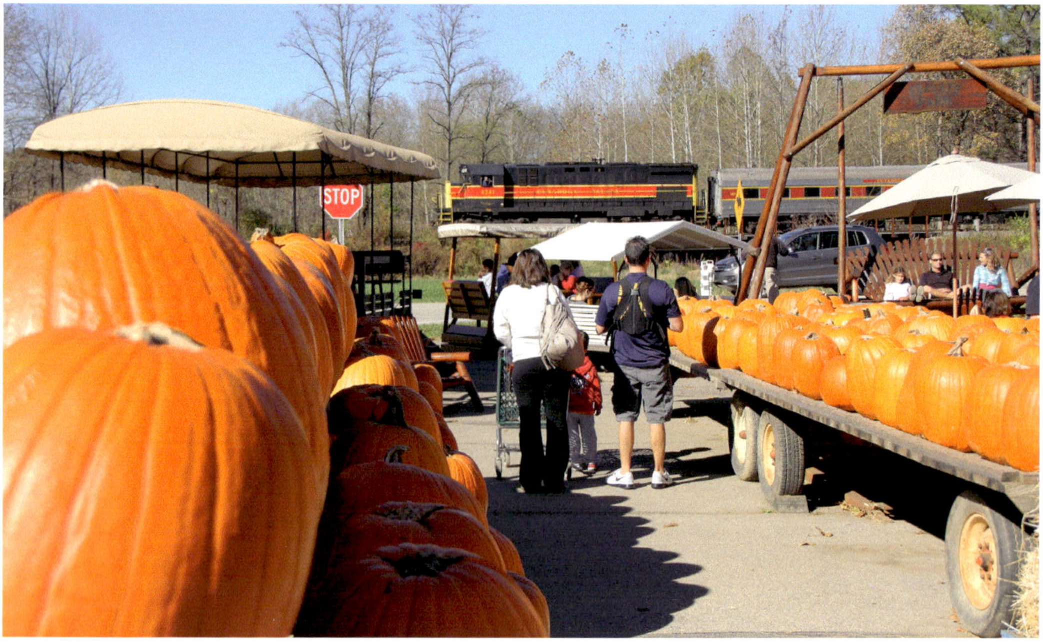

ALL THE WAY THROUGH: For the 2008 season, the CVSR ceased operating separate Akron-Peninsula and Peninsula-Independence trains in favor of one train that shuttled between Independence and Akron. Trains operated Wednesday through Sunday between June and August and in October for the fall foliage season. Weekend-only service operated in September and between November and May. This remained the general service pattern until June 2017 when Tuesday service began. Above, a CVSR train passes Szalay's Farm and Market on October 26, 2014. Below, a train sits at the Indigo Lake Station, which is out of sight around a curve. During the foliage season, trains often operate with two locomotives on the south end, particularly on weekends. (*Craig Sanders photos*)

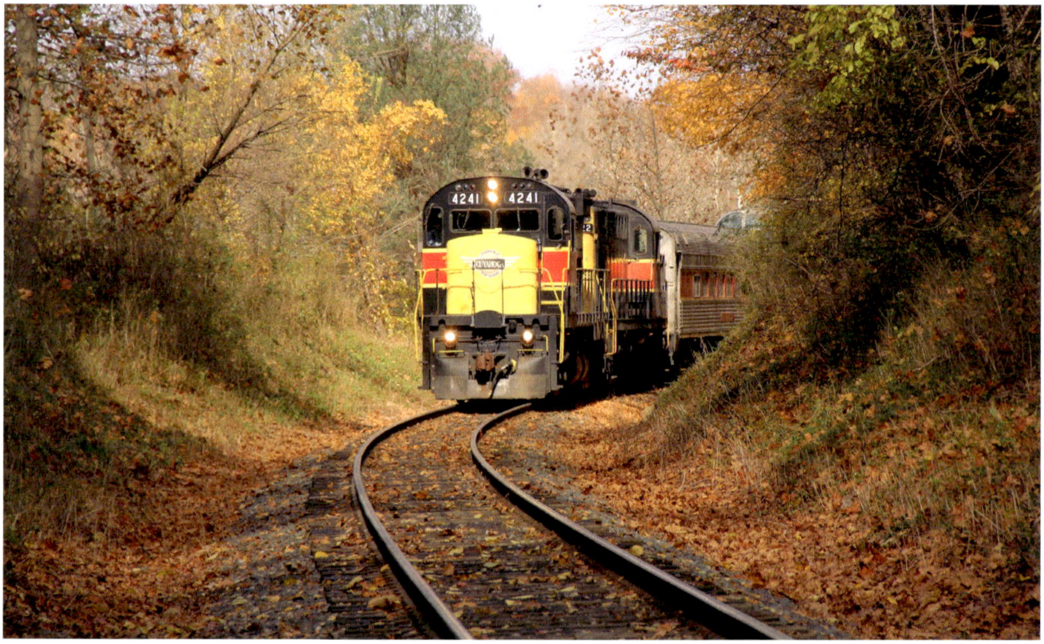

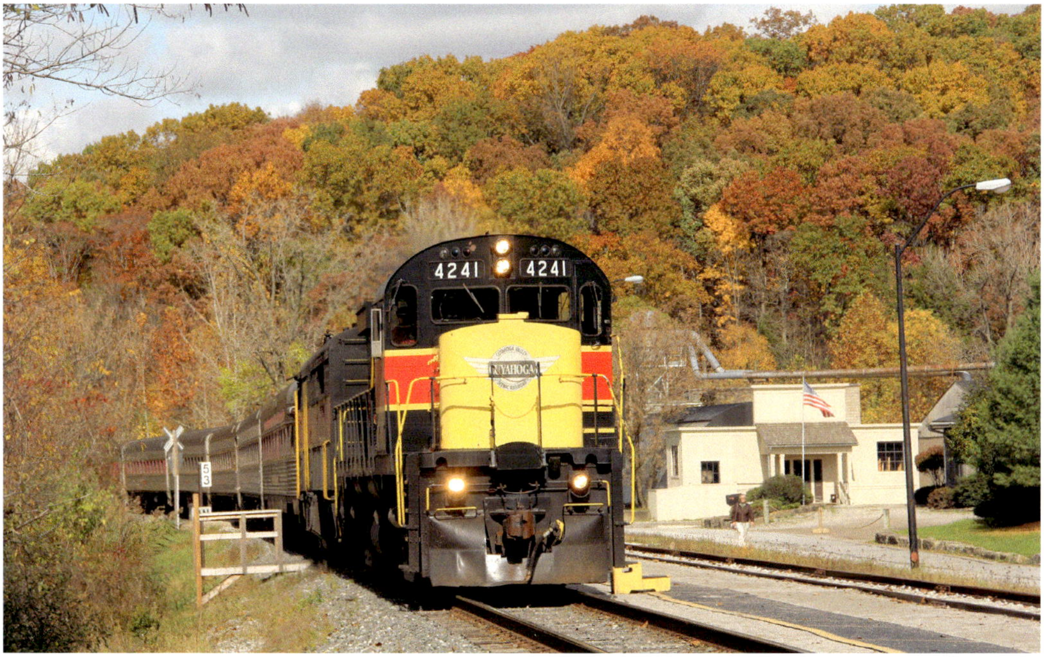

THEME TRAINS: In the ongoing effort to win a share of the discretionary spending of Northeast Ohio residents, the CVSR operates numerous theme trains throughout the year. Among its most popular are the *Grape Express*, a wine-tasting train, and *Ales on Rails*, a beer-tasting train. These trains serve samples based on the type and/or geographic location of the winery or brewery. Passengers also receive hors d'oeuvres. The alcohol-tasting trains do not permit minors and thus operate separately from the *National Park Scenic*, usually in late afternoon or evening. Above, a *Scenic* train arrives in Peninsula on October 19, 2014, while an *Ales on Rails* train passes Brecksville station on November 5, 2016. (*Craig Sanders photos*)

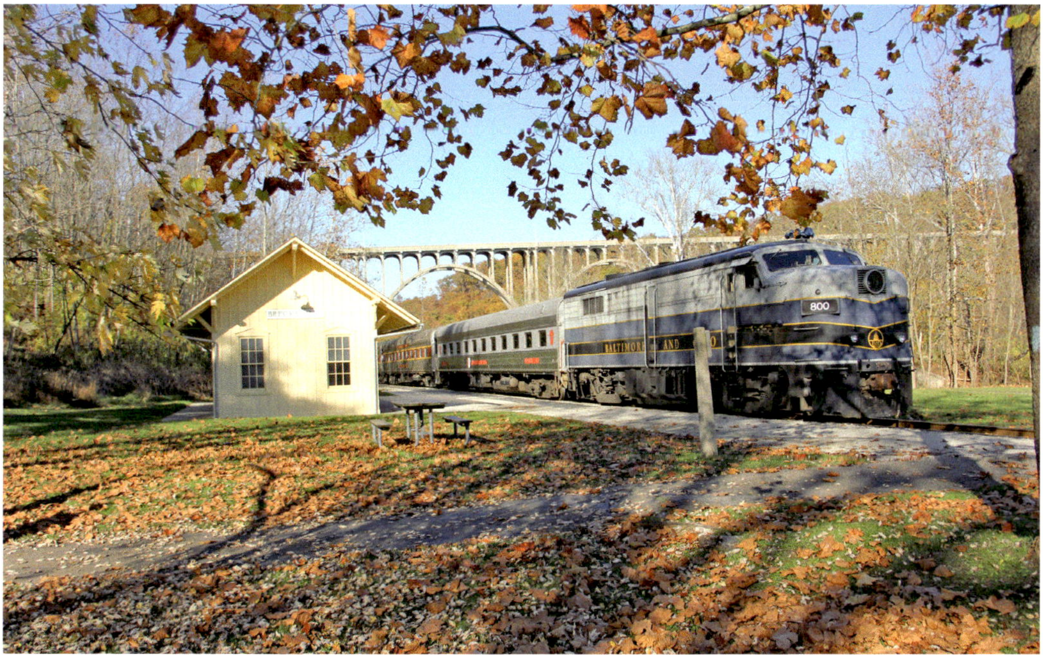

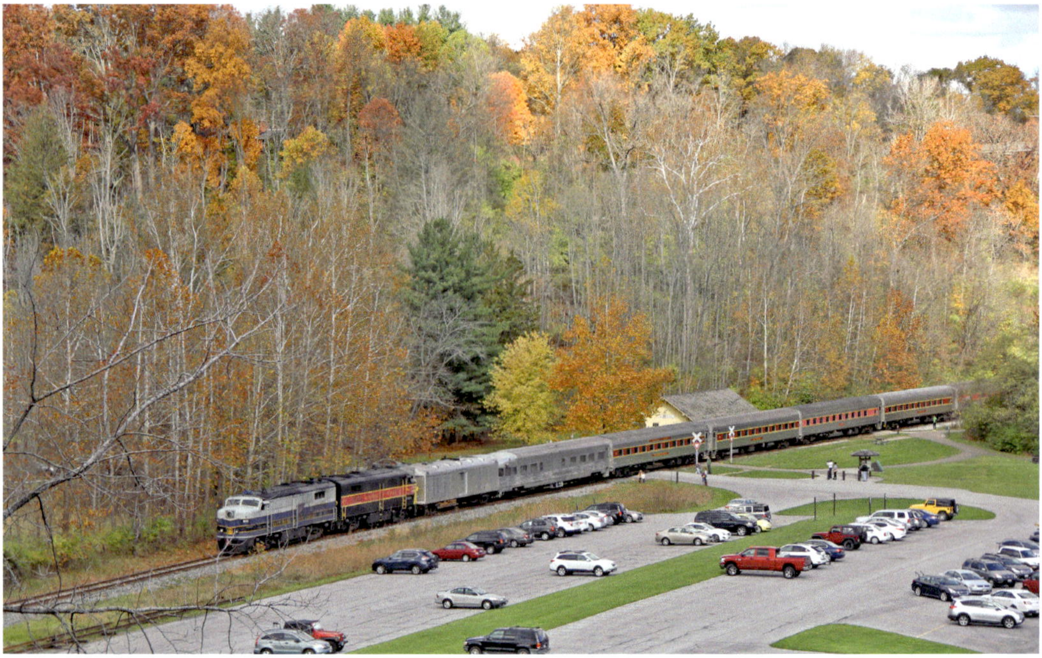

AUTUMN IN THE VALLEY: October is a busy month with many riding to view the fall foliage. Trains may run late due to the high number of passengers and bicyclists. Above, a *Scenic* passes Brecksville station on October 25, 2015, as seen from a nearby hillside. Below, the theme train *Pumpkin Express* nears Deep Lock Quarry on its October 27, 2013, journey from Szalay's Farm and Market to Brecksville. Funded by a $35,000 federal grant, the CVSR, in June 2009, launched "Voices in the Valley," a GPS-activated series of recordings that provide narration via individual headsets about what passengers are seeing. Volunteers portray historic figures telling stories, talking about nature and history, and even provide music. (*Craig Sanders photos*)

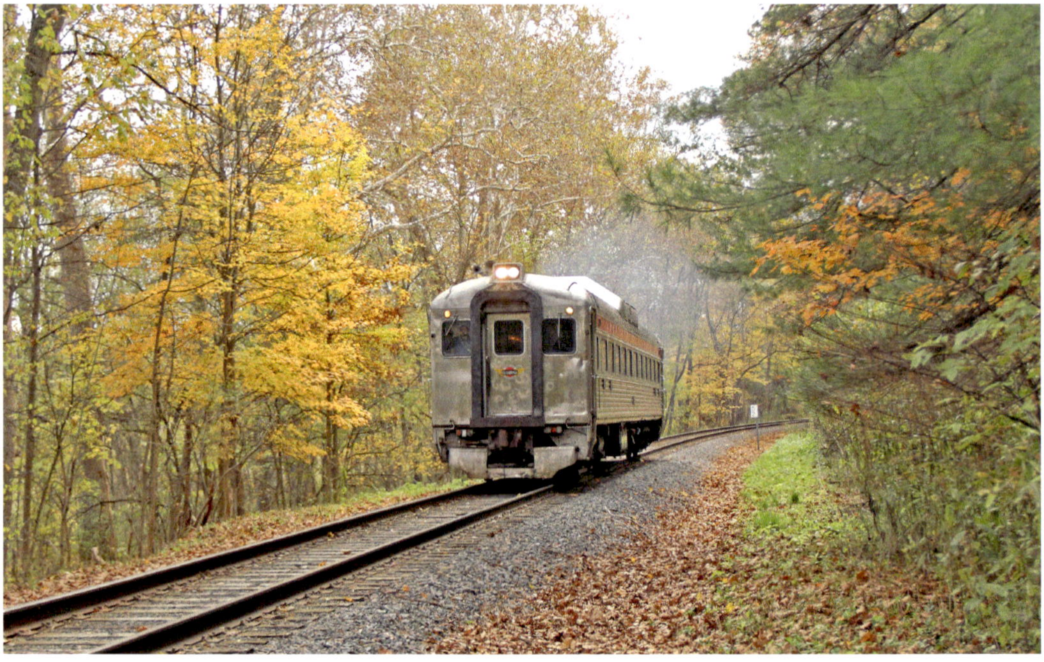

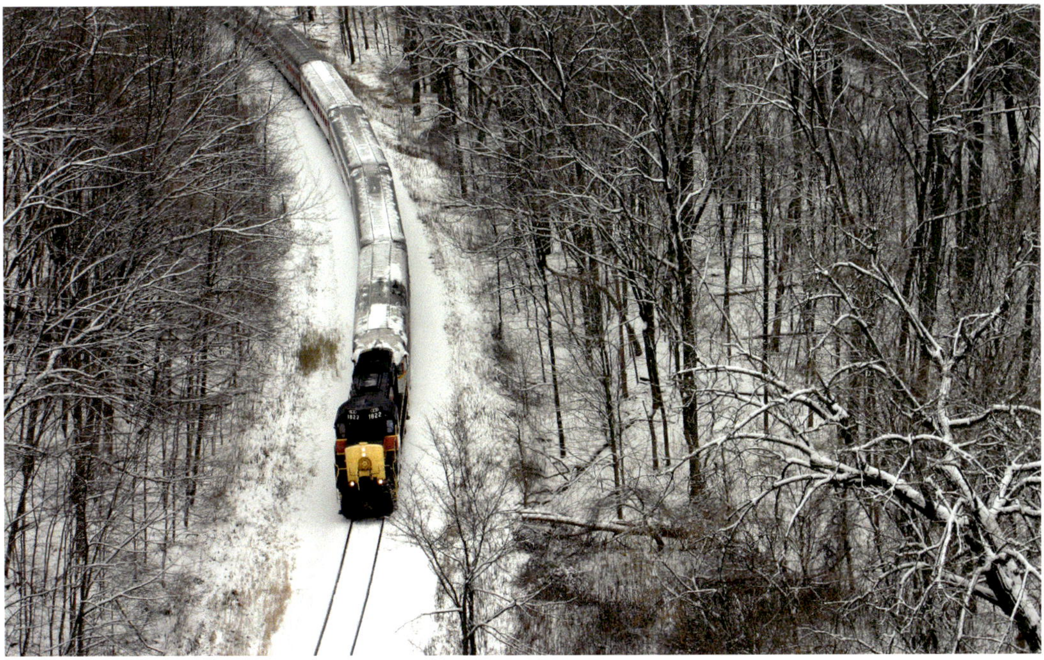

WINTER OPERATION: For more than a decade, CVL trains operated between June and late October or early November. The first winter trains were *Polar Express* trips. The season lengthened in the 1990s, starting in May, then April, then February. The CVSR now operates twelve months a year but takes a break from latter December to latter January. Above, a *Scenic* passes beneath the Ohio Route 82 Bridge in a wintery scene on December 4, 2005. Below, acquired in 2001, FPA-4 No. 800 wears a B&O tribute livery. It is coated in snow as it passes Jaite on February 14, 2005. It is the only CVSR FPA-4 that doesn't wear its original CN roster number. (*Peter Bowler photos*)

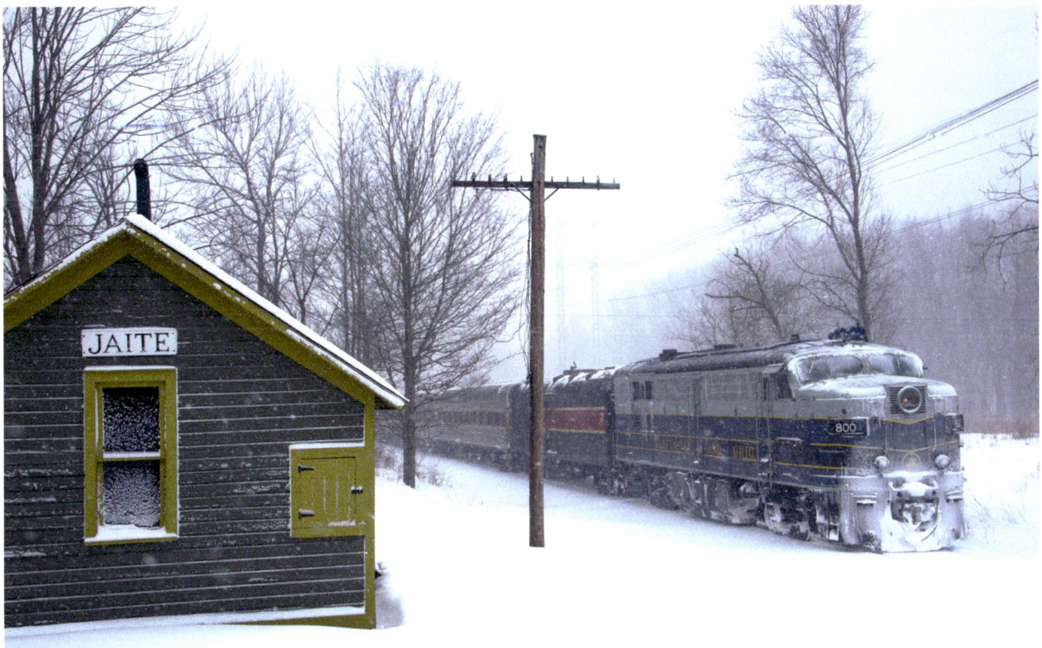

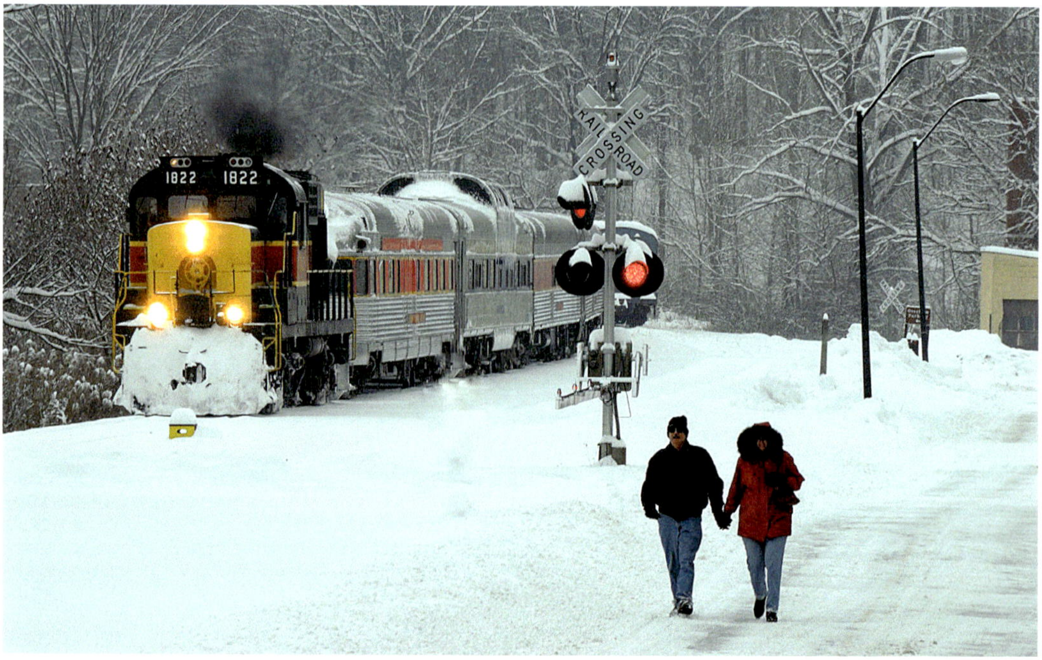

DEEP SNOW: Snow caked on the pilot of RS18u No. 1822 is testimony to the deep snow along the tracks on January 10, 2009, and how the train had to break a few snowdrifts. A couple walks along West Mill Street in Peninsula as a southbound train arrives in town. During the winter, CVSR trains usually run only on Saturdays in January and February with Peninsula the only scheduled stop between Independence and Akron. Below, the ruts in the snow show how deep the snow was on February 28, 2015, as a northbound *Scenic* is about to cross Chippewa Creek near Brecksville station. (*Above, Peter Bowler photo; below, Craig Sanders photo*)

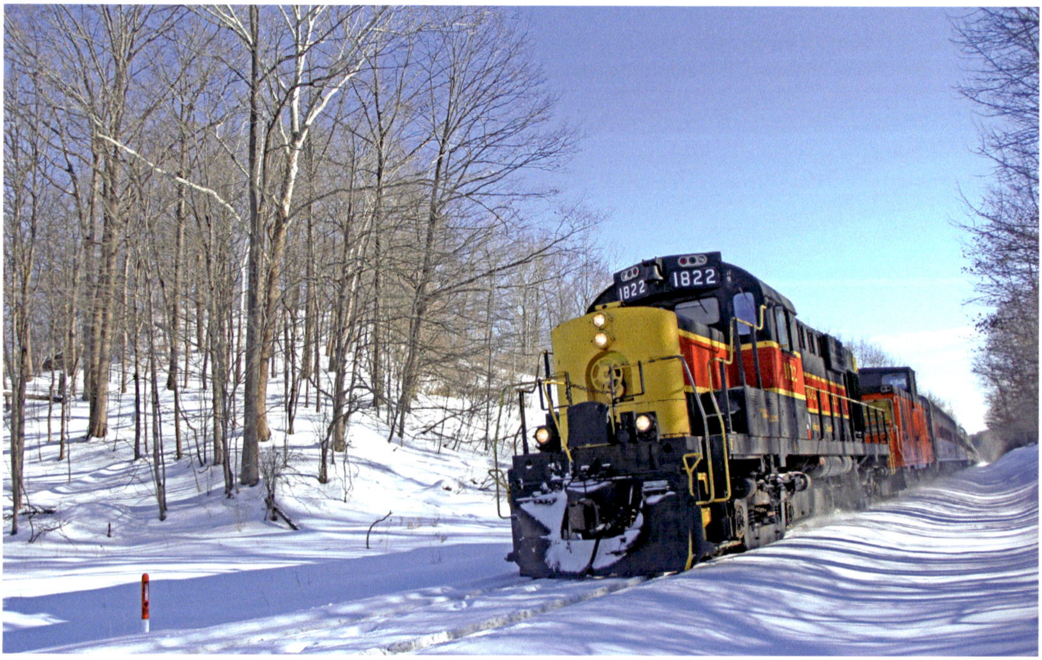

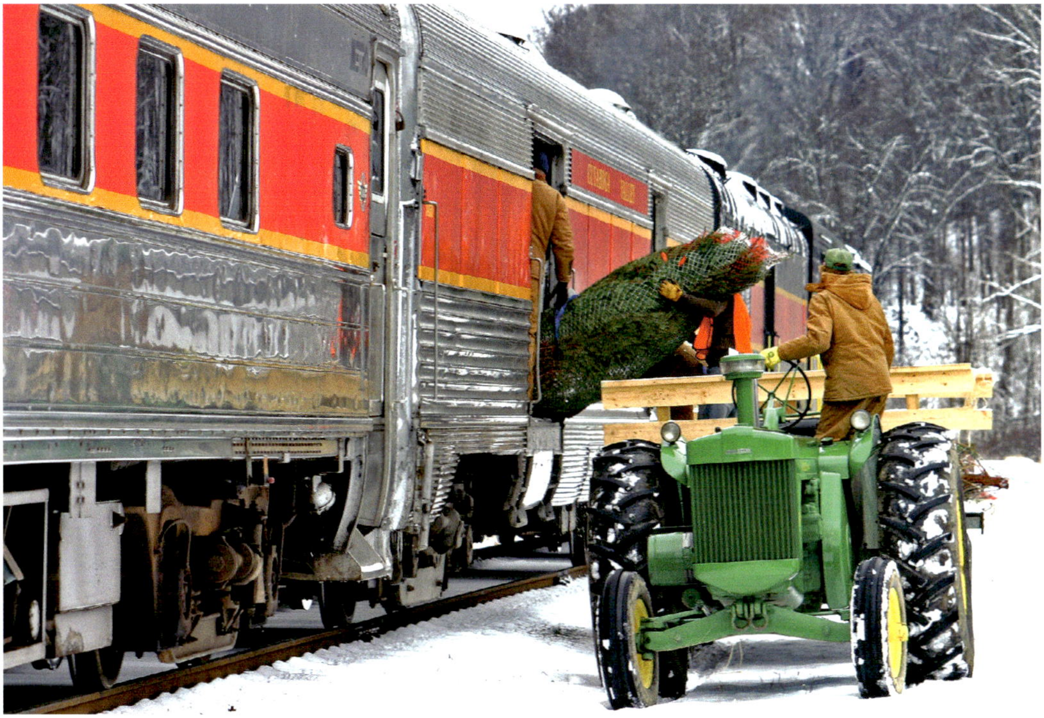

CHRISTMAS TREE ABOARD: In December, the CVSR offers passengers the opportunity to visit a Christmas tree farm and select a tree to take home. Above, a tree is loaded into the baggage car in Peninsula. Below, Akron Northside station was dedicated on July 25, 2001. Owned by the City of Akron, which received a $50,000 federal grant to build the parking lot, it was the third station built by the Park Service for the CVSR following the opening of stations at Indigo Lake and Brecksville. In 2002, the Park Service began building stations at Botzum, Hillside Road (Canal Education Center), Boston Mill, and Independence (Rockside Road). (*Peter Bowler photos*)

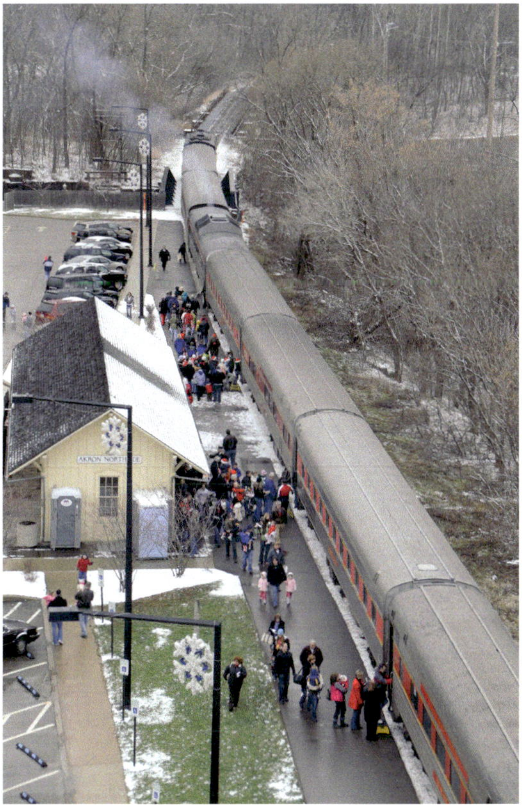

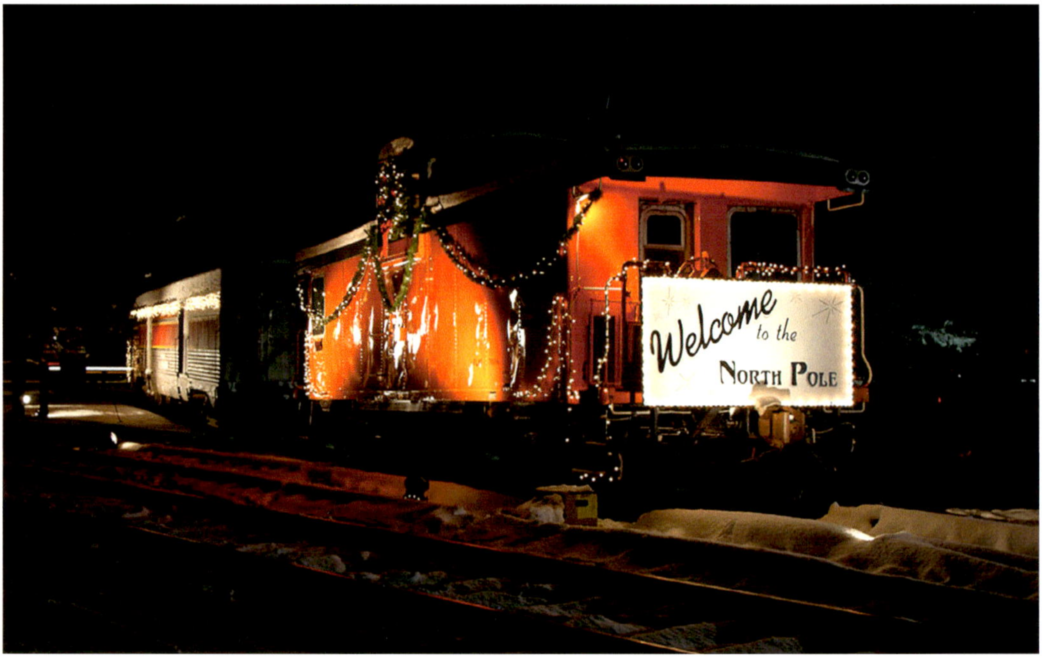

THE NORTH POLE: The CVSR's first Christmas-themed train was the *Polar Bear Limited*, on November 27, 1992. The Saturday and Sunday trips ran through December 20 to the "North Pole" at Peninsula and were repeated in 1993. The first *Polar Express* ran in 1994 with three trips carrying 1,000 passengers. Based on the 1985 story of the same name by Chris Van Allsburg, passengers heard a tape-recorded narration. Ridership grew and volunteers reading the story replaced the recording. In 1995, the 400 tickets sold out in September. A year later, the 6,000 tickets sold in less than four hours and a ticket lottery was established. In 1999, 12,480 rode the two-hour trip to the "North Pole." (*Jerry Jordak photos*)

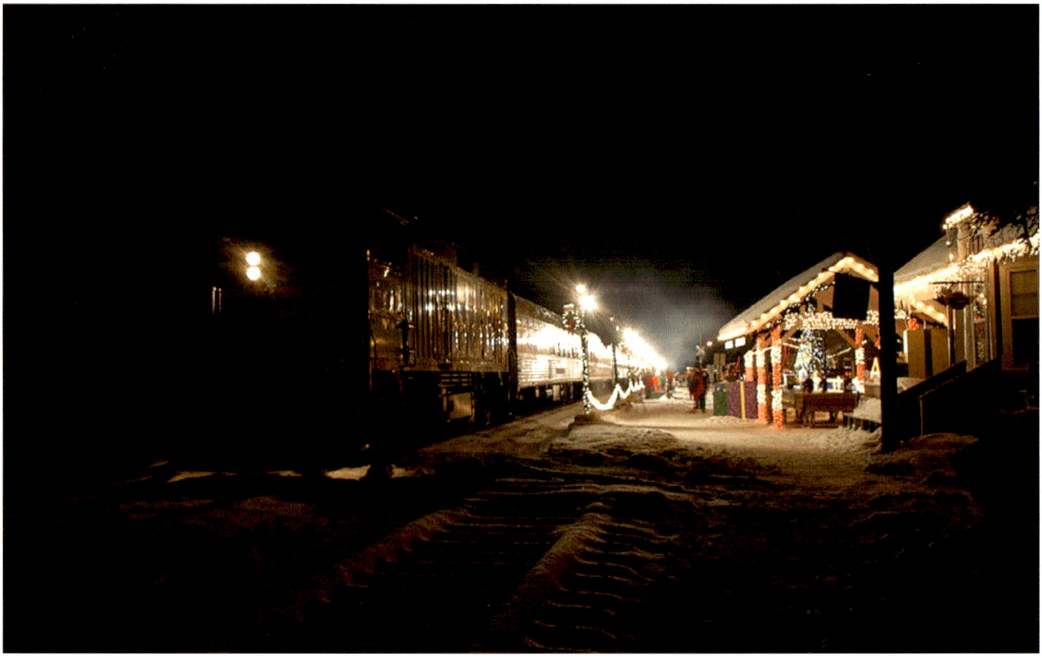

POPULAR TRAIN: The family-oriented *Polar Express* departs in November and December from Akron and Independence for the "North Pole" in Peninsula, where Santa Claus boards the train. Children, many wearing pajamas, receive cookies, hot chocolate and a bell. *Polar Express* ridership in 2016 was more than 42,000, which was 20 percent of CVSR's yearly ridership. CVSR renamed the train *North Pole Express* in 2005 after Warner Bros. Entertainment bought the proprietary rights to the Van Allsburg story from Houghton Mifflin. The latter had not charged CVSR a royalty. The railroad and Warner Bros. in June 2006 reached an agreement on continued use of the *Polar Express* name, but the parties declined to provide details about it. (*Peter Bowler photos*)

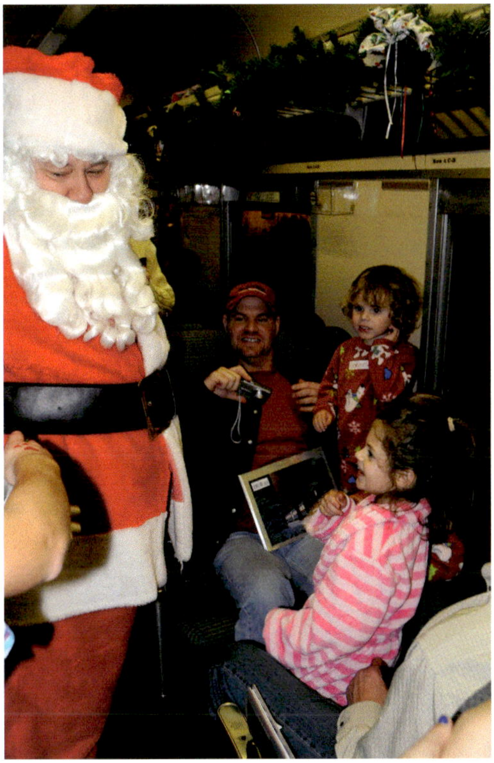

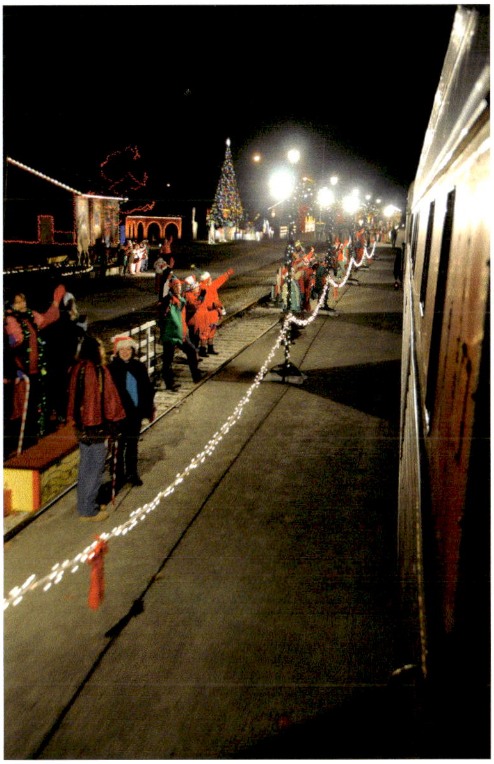

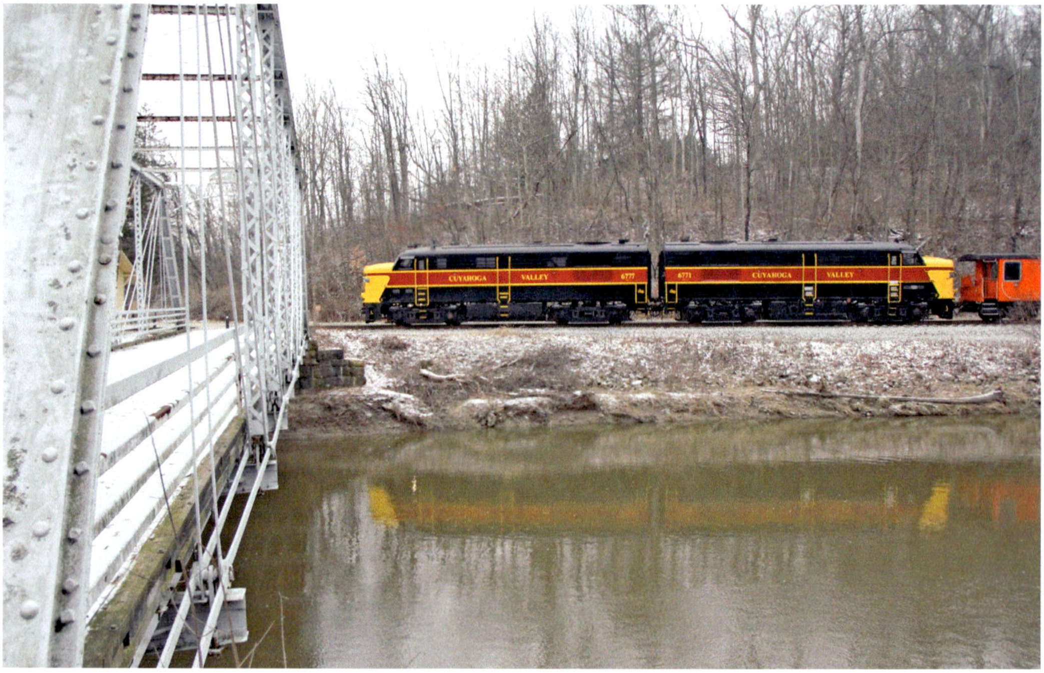

NEW LIVERY: FPA-4 No. 6771 rolled out of the paint booth in 2016 sporting a new look. Although the basic scheme was retained, the CVSR herald was removed from the nose in favor of a narrow V-shaped stripe that was an extension of the broader red stripe on the flanks. No. 6777 received that same livery in early 2017 and for a few weeks the two "new look" locomotives were paired on the south end of the *Scenic*. Above, Old Station Road Bridge frames Nos. 6771 and 6777 along the Cuyahoga River at Brecksville on January 28, 2017. Below, a northbound train runs along the river in Brecksville on February 4, 2017. (*Craig Sanders photos*)

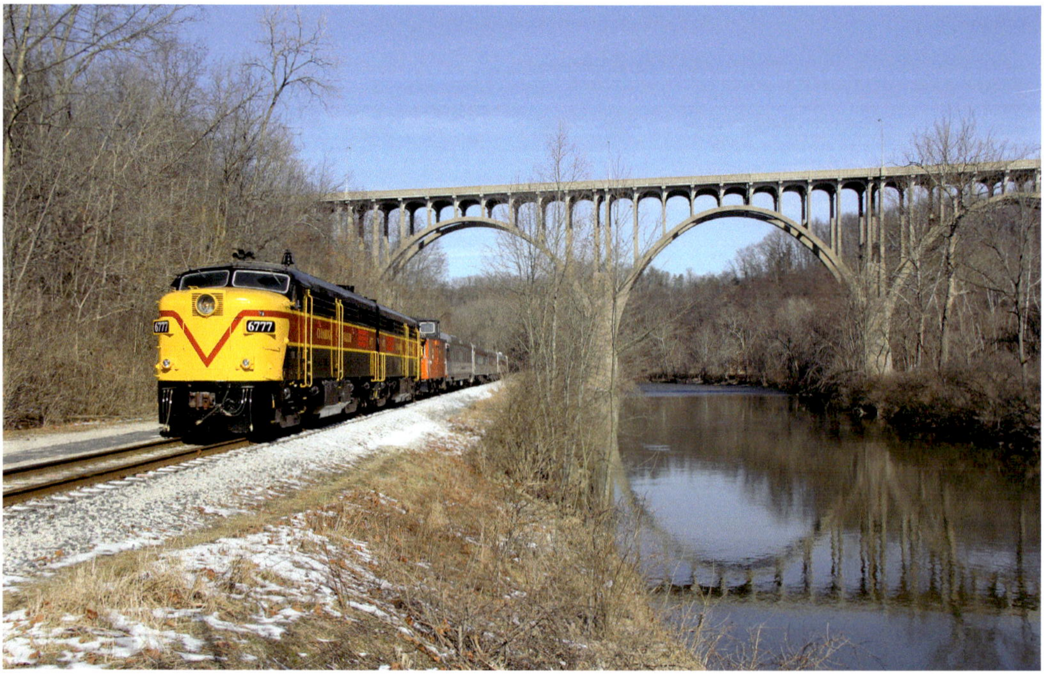

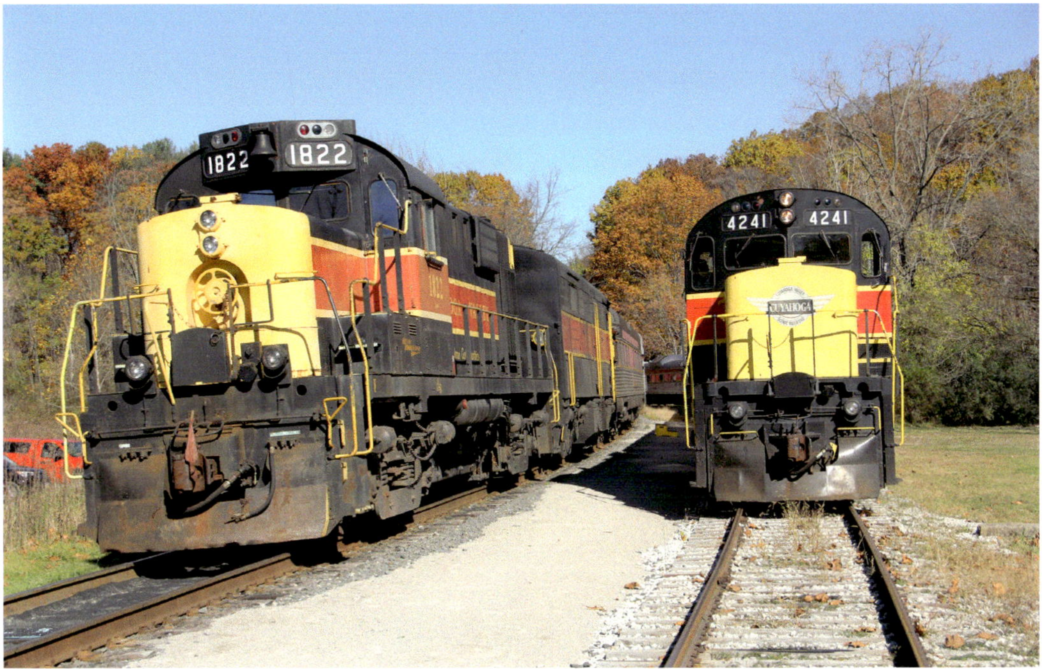

PASSING TRAINS: On most days, just one CVSR train is out on the road. On the infrequent occasions when two trains must pass each other, they usually meet in Peninsula, although it could be done at Fitzwater Yard. Above, a northbound *Scenic* (left) passes a *Pumpkin Express* train in the Peninsula siding on October 26, 2014. No. 1822 is an RS18u built by Montreal Locomotive Works in May 1958 for Canadian Pacific. CVSR acquired it in late 1998. Below, a *Scenic* passes a rail diesel car waiting in Peninsula on October 27, 2013. Meets are most likely to occur between the *Scenic* and a theme or steam train. (*Craig Sanders photos*)

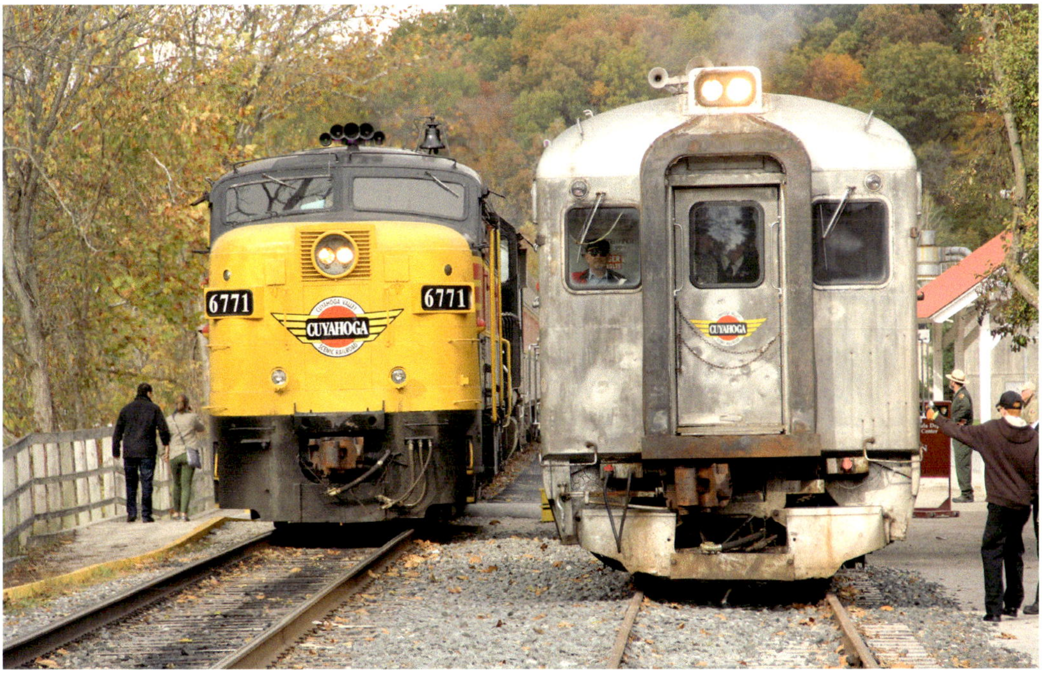

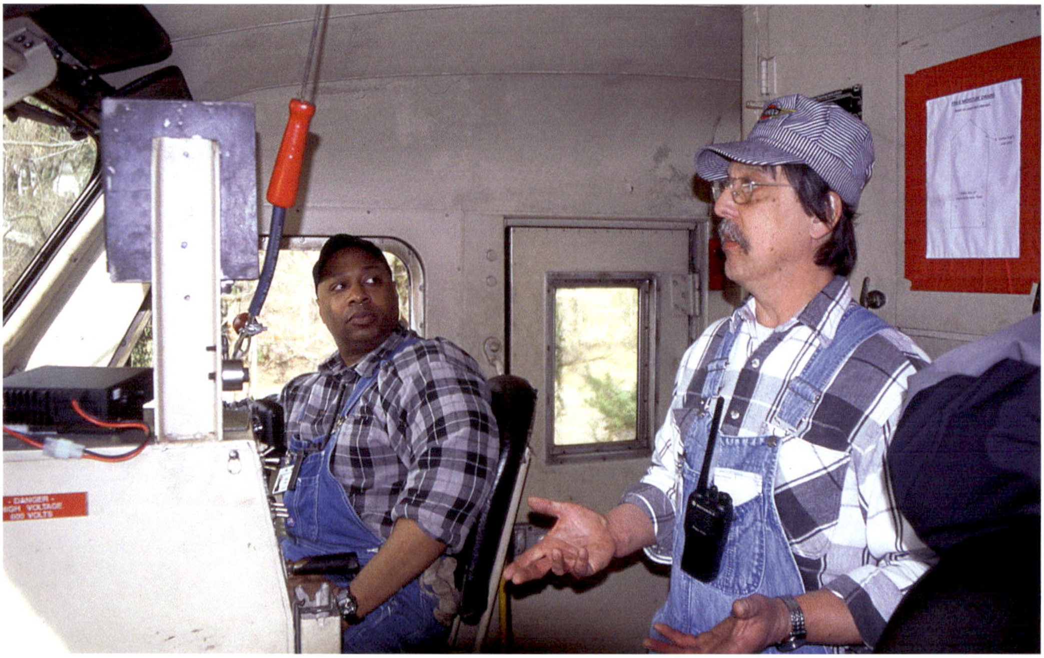

IN THE CAB: The author rode in the cab of FPA-4 No. 800 on April 23, 2011, from Independence to Akron. Above, then-engineer trainee Sean Veney sits in the engineer's seat as instructor Tim Osyk provides tips about operating a train during the station stop in Peninsula. Veney is a biology professor at Kent State University who started on the CVSR as a trainman in 2008. Osyk was named the CVSR volunteer of the year in 2015. At the time, he had been with the CVSR for fourteen years and had volunteered 6,000 hours as an engineer and brakeman. Below, the train is crossing the Cuyahoga River south of Peninsula. (*Craig Sanders photos*)

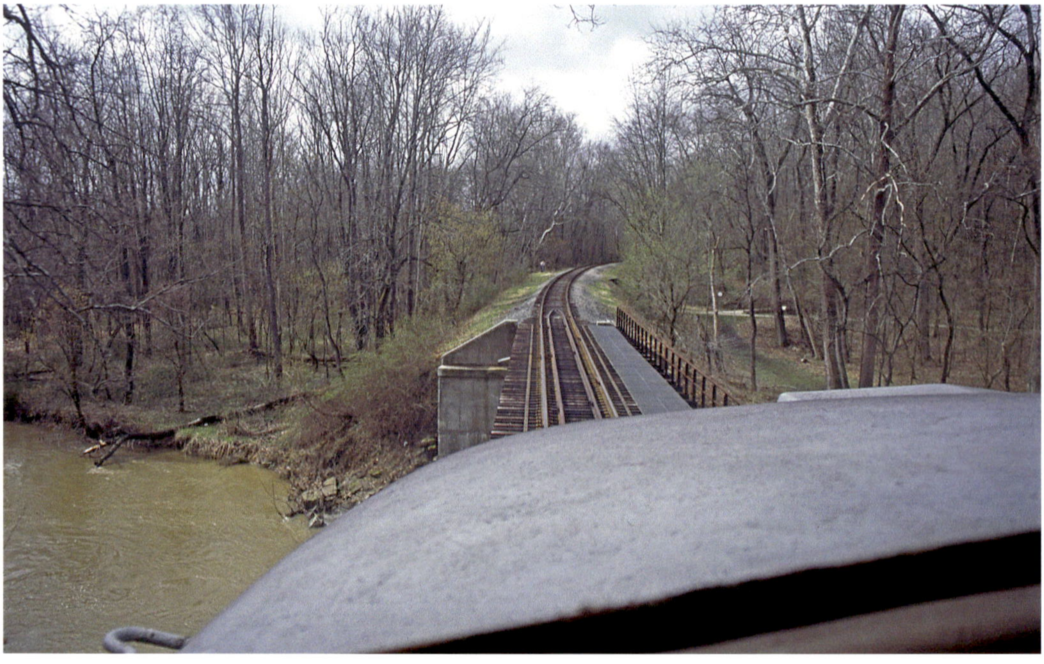

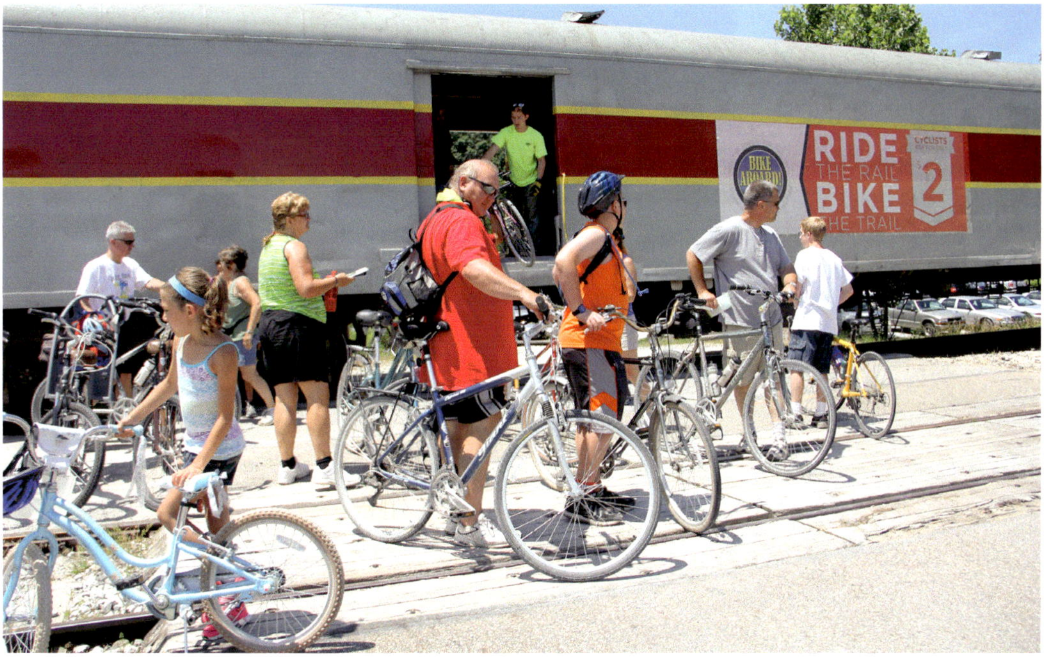

BIKES ABOARD: The CVL began carrying bicycles in a baggage car in October 1992. Bicyclists could bike one way on the Cuyahoga Valley National Recreation Area's new Towpath Trail and return by train. The program was renamed Bike Aboard! in June 2007 when the fare fell to $2. Previously, bikers paid the regular fare. Bike Aboard! drew 6,500 in 2007 and 18,691 in 2008 when the CVSR dedicated a coach next to the baggage car for Bike Aboard! passengers. Participation zoomed to 21,500 in 2009, which was sixteen percent of the annual ridership. The summer and fall program drew a record 23,911 participants in 2016. The fare increased to $3 in 2011. (*Craig Sanders photos*)

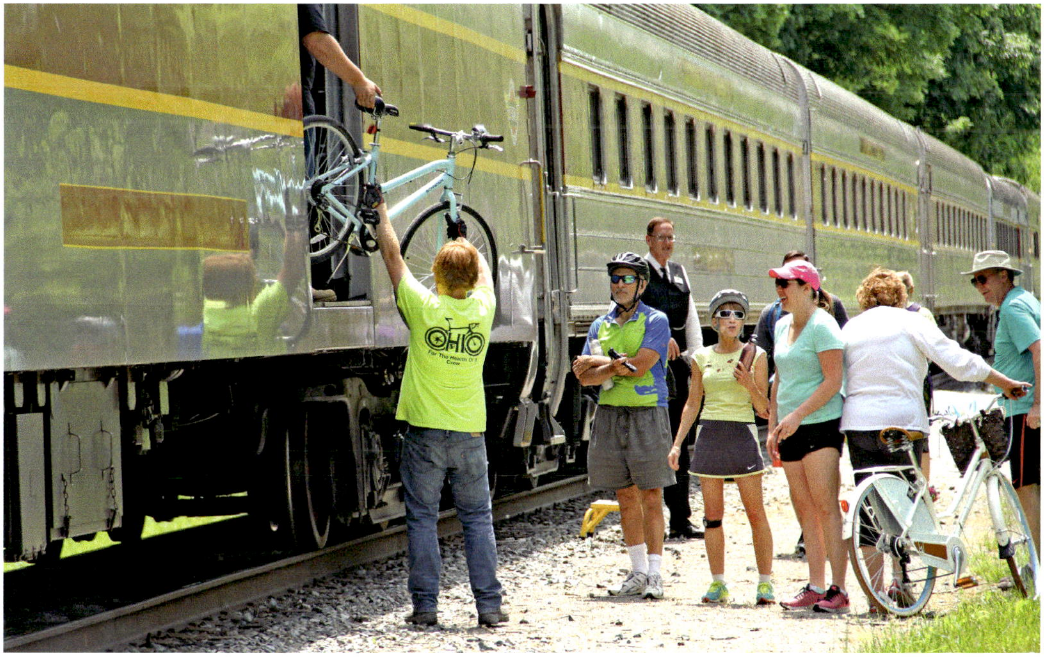

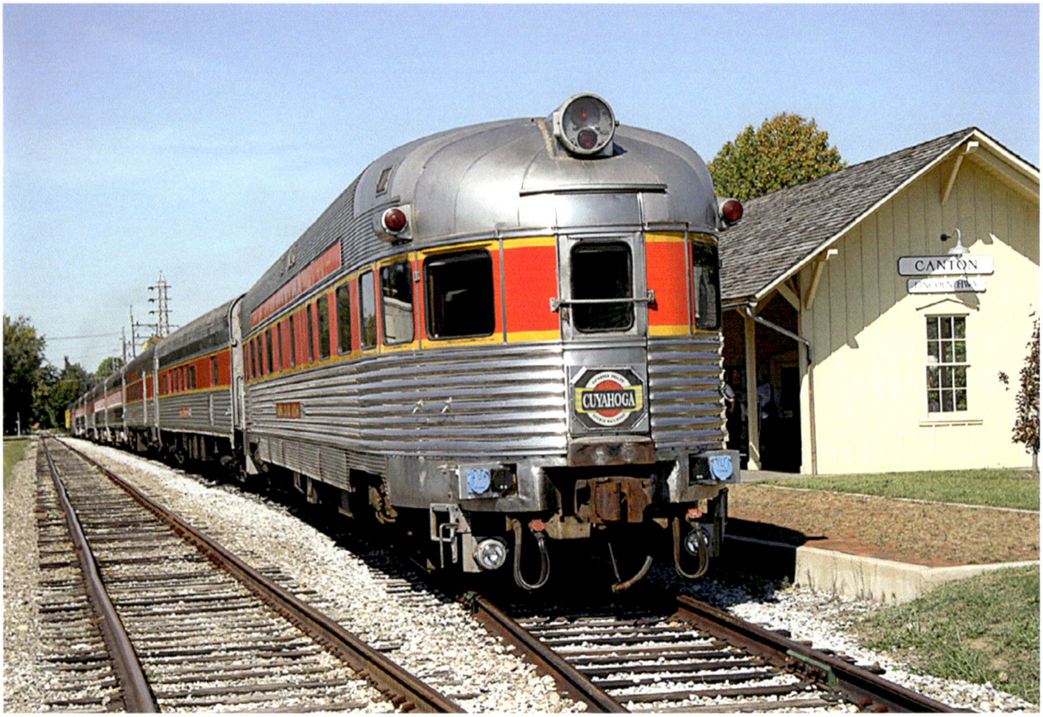

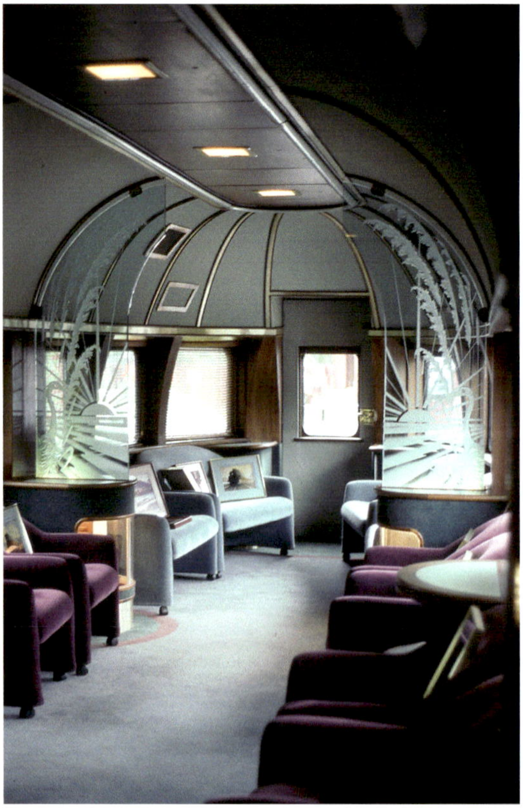

SAINT LUCIE SOUND: Dennis B. Haslinger, a former president of the CVSR board of trustees, bought the *Saint Lucie Sound* in 1994 for about $175,000 and willed it to the railroad after his 1995 death. Built by the Budd Company in 1946 for the Florida East Coast Railway, the observation-lounge car has a bar, three sleeping rooms, pantry, kitchen and etched glass dividers. It is used for extra fare executive class service. The *Saint Lucie Sound* is seldom uncovered because CVSR trains operate with locomotives at each end. Above, the car is in Canton during a September 29, 2007, total track tour. Below, the observation end interior is shown in October 1994. (*Above, Jerry Jordak photo; below, Paul Woodring photo*)

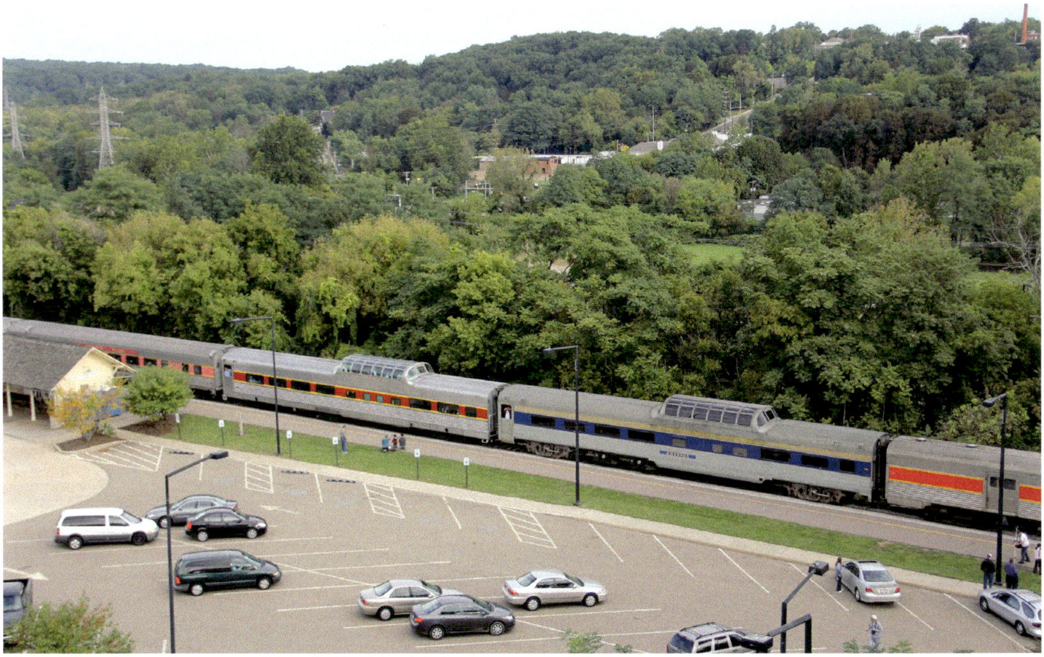

DOME CARS: CVSR has had two dome cars. Former Great Northern Railway 1331 was built by Budd in 1955 and leased from Mid America Rail Car Leasing. The blue, gold and gray car ran on the CVSR between 2009 and 2011 and never wore its colors. The former Denver & Rio Grande Western Railroad's *Silver Bronco* arrived in 2011. Built by Budd in 1948, No. 1105 ran on the original *California Zephyr*. Both domes were named *Emerson* after a corporate donor, but No. 1105 reverted to the *Silver Bronco* name in 2015. Above, both domes pass through Akron on September 17, 2011. Below, passengers enjoy the dome section of No. 1105 on February 9, 2014. (*Craig Sanders photos*)

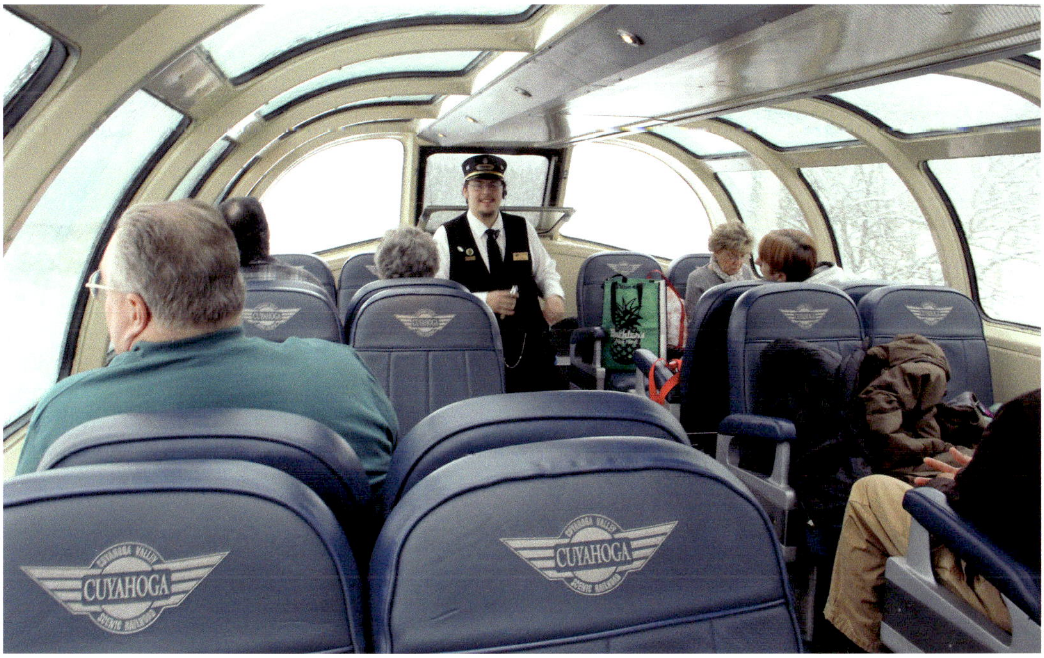

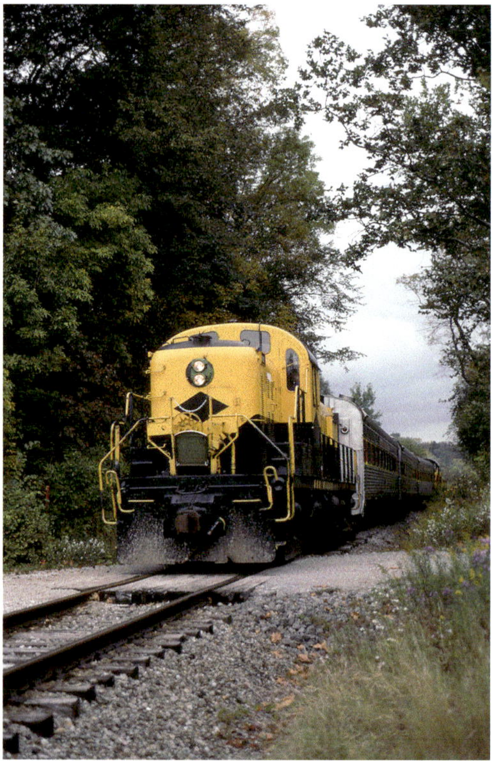

NEVER WORE CVSR COLORS: Alco RS-3 No. 4088 was built for the Delaware & Hudson Railway in August 1953 and arrived on the CVSR in New York, Susquehanna & Western Railway colors in April 1994. Above, No. 4088 pulled only a few CVSR trips and is shown in October 1994 at Everett. General Electric 44 tonner No. 21 was built in February 1953 for the U.S. Air Force and used at Whitman AFB. It was restored in Peninsula and repainted as Baltimore & Ohio Railroad No. 21. Shown on December 9, 2006, it was sold to the Kentucky Railway Museum in 2009 and moved there by flatcar. (*Above, Paul Woodring photo; below, Mark Demaline photo*)

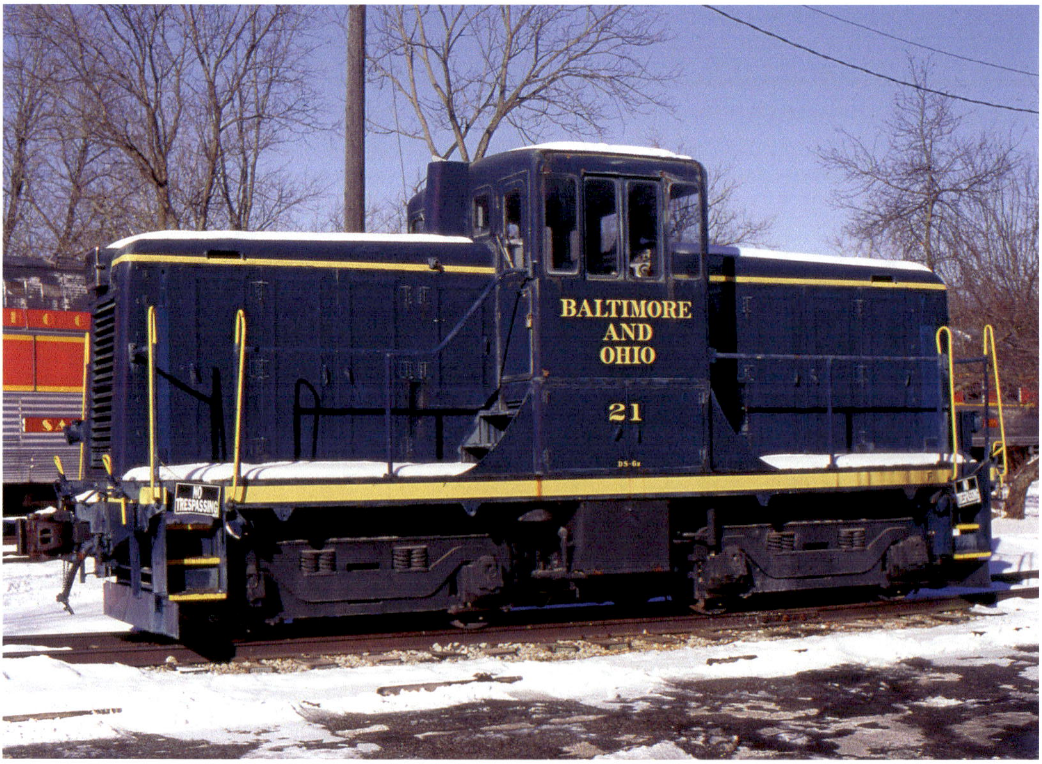

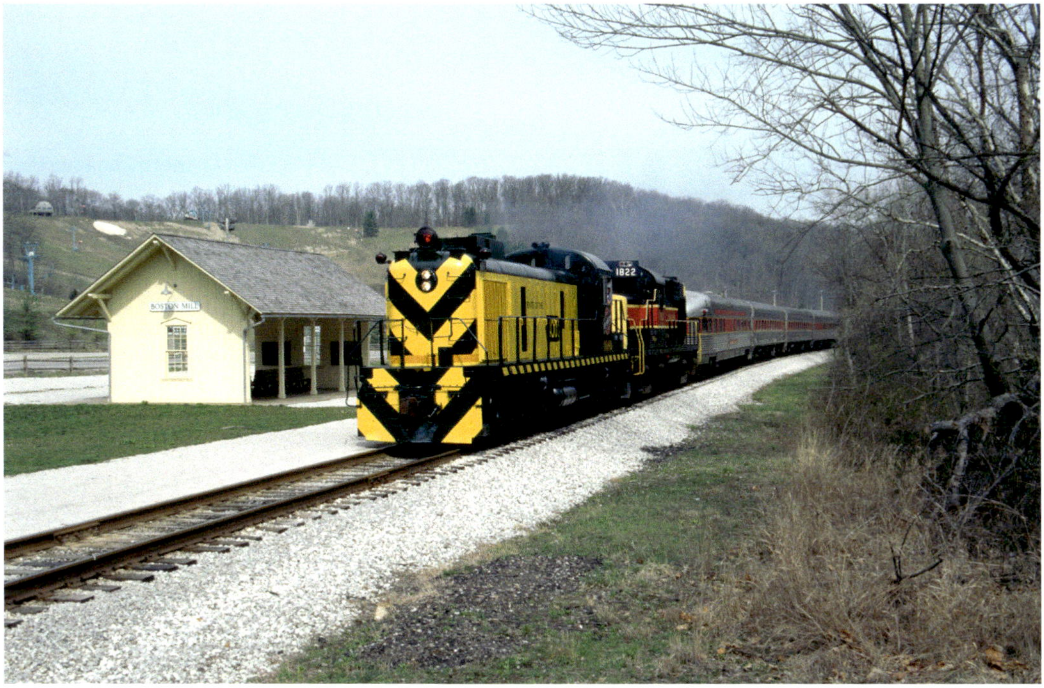

FOREIGN POWER: Alco RSD-5 No. 1689 operated on the CVSR, but the railroad never owned it. It came to the CVSR from the Western Maryland Scenic Railroad and was repainted into the colors and markings of the Chicago & North Western Transportation Company, for which it was built in April 1954 for use in Chicago suburban passenger service. It is shown above on April 17, 2004, at Boston Mill station, and on October 15, 2005, at Everett. No. 1689 is now in the collection of the Illinois Railway Museum. *(Jerry Jordak photos)*

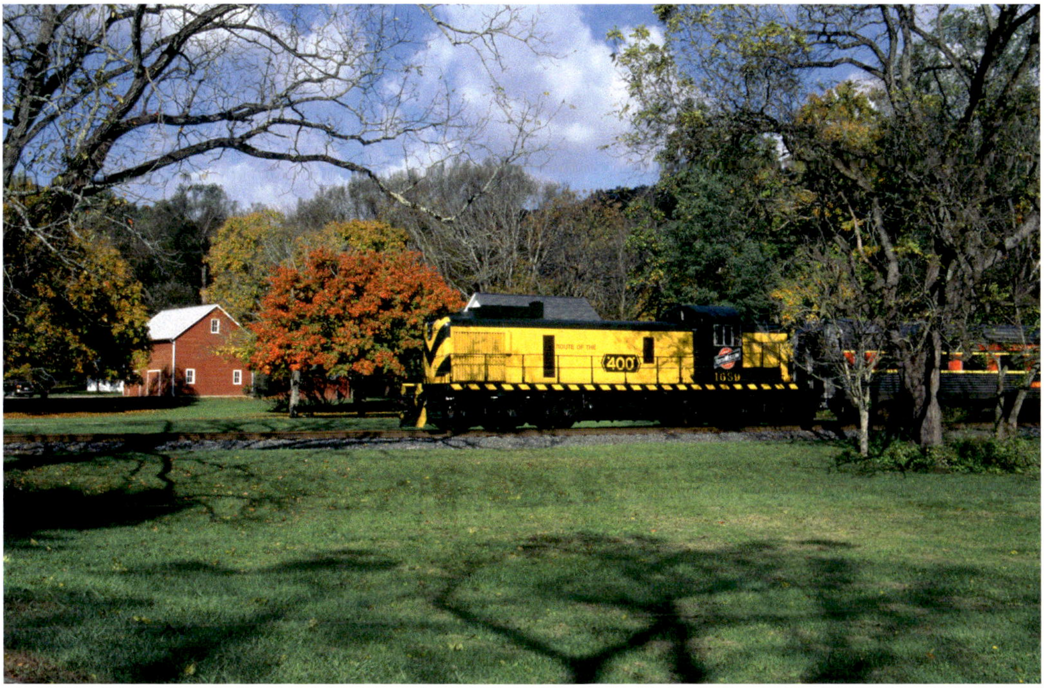

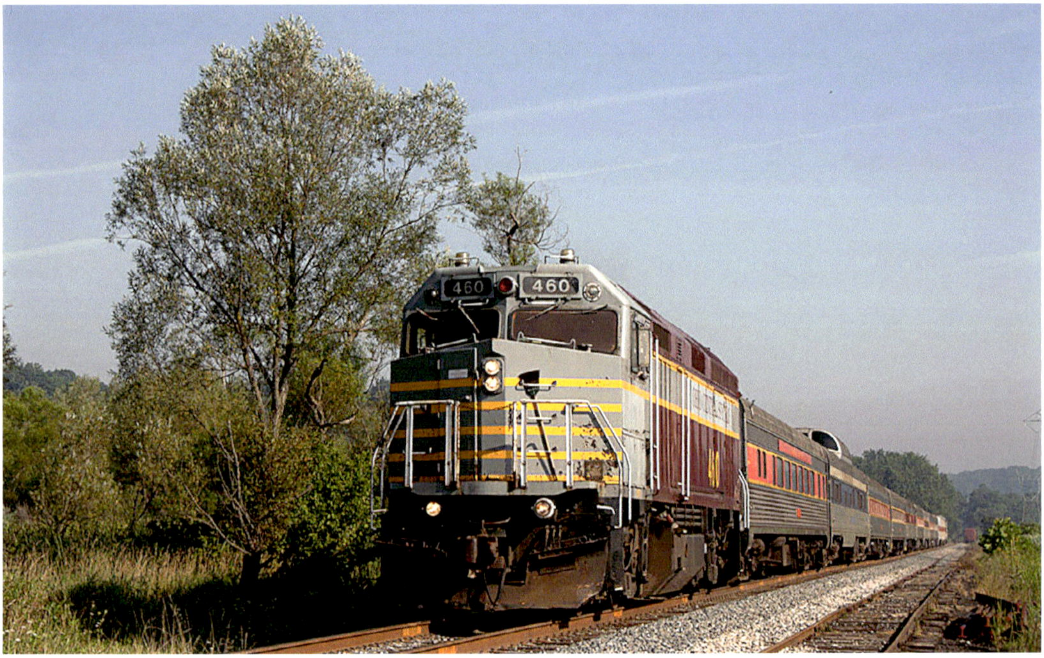

FORMER AMTRAK LOCOMOTIVES: Former Amtrak locomotives have pulled trains on the CVSR, although not while wearing Amtrak colors or markings. Above, Ohio Central System F40M-2C No. 460, formerly Amtrak F40PHR No. 269, pulled *Polar Express* and other trains in winter 2010-2011. No. 460 and OC No. 452 were on the CVSR for most of 2011. Below, FL9 No. 484 pulled Amtrak trains through the mid-1990s. Built in November 1957 for the New York, New Haven & Hartford Railroad, it arrived on the CVSR in late 2009, owned by F. P. Flynn. It remained through late February 2012. It pulls a train over Cascade Lock in Akron on September 17, 2011. *(Above, Jerry Jordak photo; below, Craig Sanders photo)*

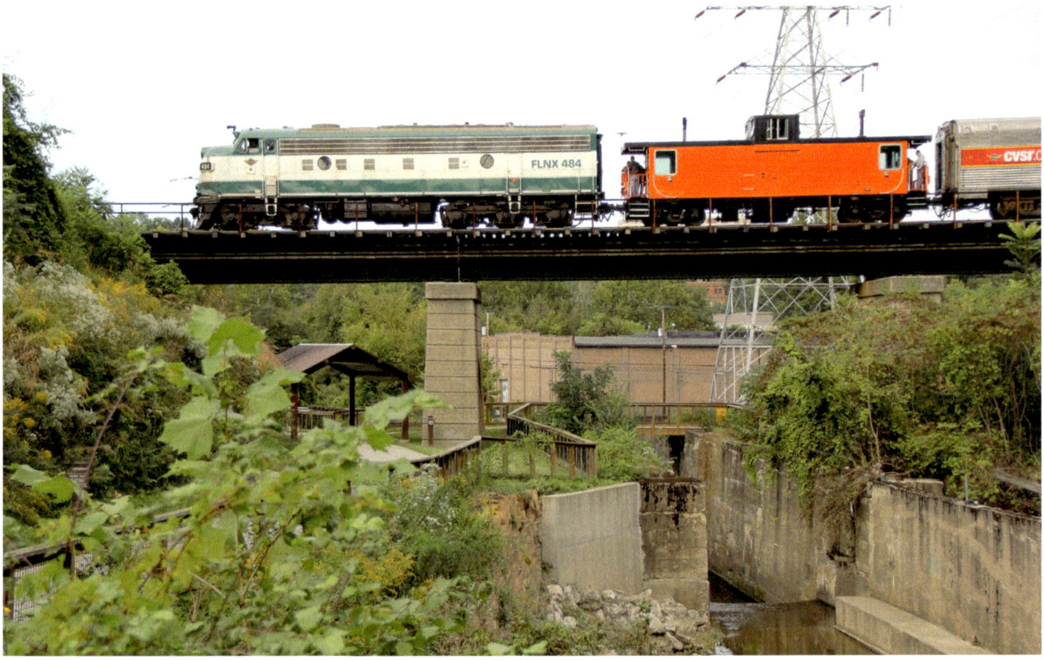

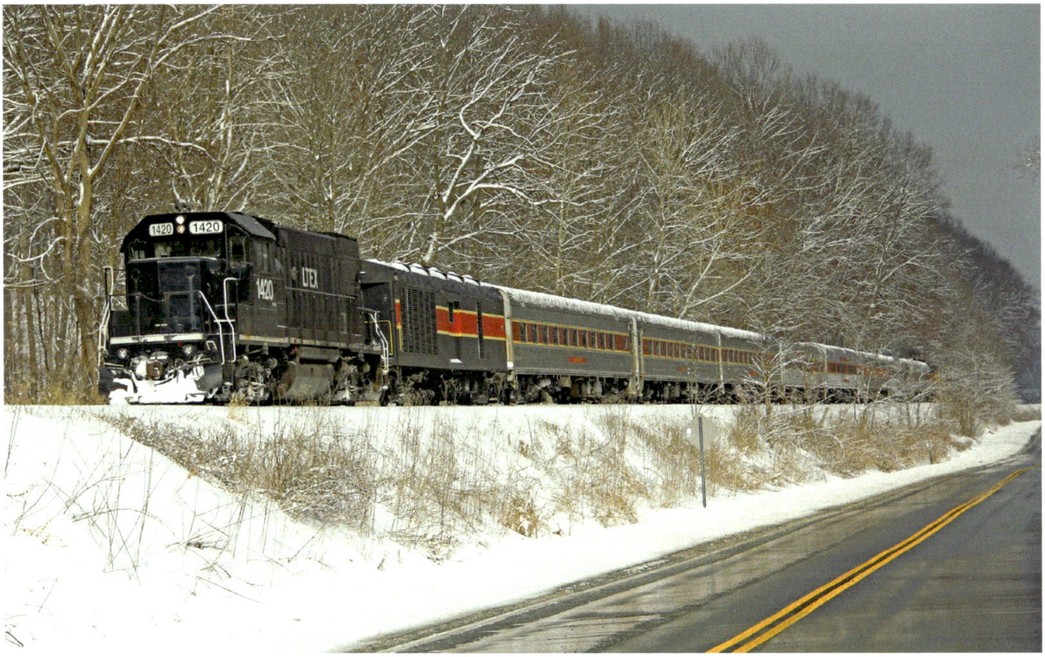

LTEX LOCOMOTIVES: CVSR has leased three locomotives from Larry's Truck Electric, a McDonald, Ohio, locomotive leasing company. GP15-1 No. 1420 operated on the Cleveland Commercial Railroad before coming to the CVSR in late 2011, where it was a mainstay through summer 2015. LTEX No. 2436, a GP30u, arrived in October 2012 and operated into 2013, still wearing its former Atchison, Topeka & Santa Fe Railway colors, but with the markings painted over. Above, No. 1420 trails in a wintery scene along Riverview Road on February 9, 2014. Below, No. 2436 leads a northbound in a snow shower through Boston Mill on March 3, 2013. LTEX GP35 No. 355 ran on the CVSR in November 2012. (*Craig Sanders photos*)

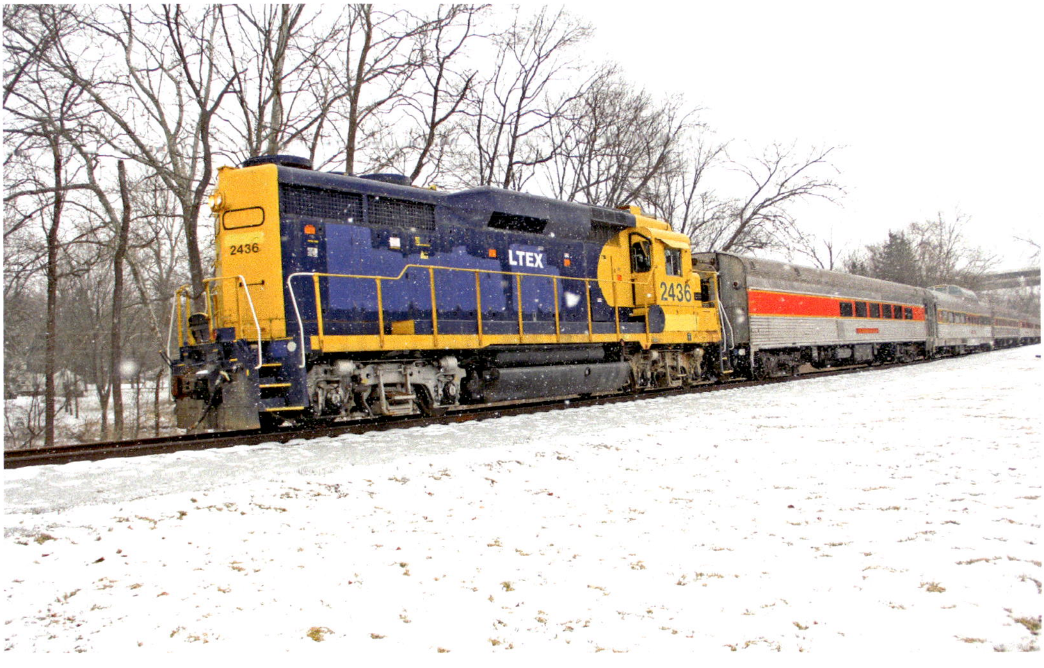

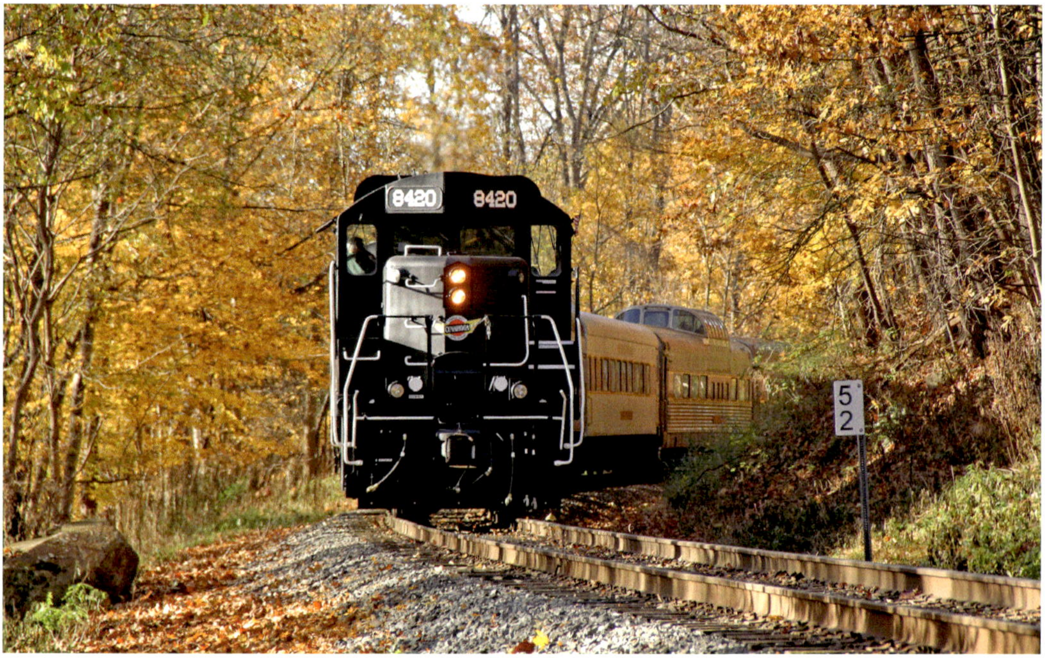

ON THE HORIZON: GP10-1 No. 8420 arrived in summer 2015, after being leased from Horizon Rail of Euclid, Ohio. Built in February 1952 for the St. Louis-San Francisco Railway as a GP7, it was rebuilt by the Illinois Central Gulf Railroad. Like other leased locomotives, No. 8420 never wore CVSR colors, but did have a CVSR herald. It is shown amid autumn beauty at Milepost 52, measured from Valley Junction, near Deep Lock Quarry, on October 23, 2015. When No. 8420 had to be repaired in summer 2016 after being involved in a grade crossing accident, Horizon sent GP40 No. 3134 as a short-term replacement. It is shown in Peninsula on July 23, 2016. (*Craig Sanders photos*)

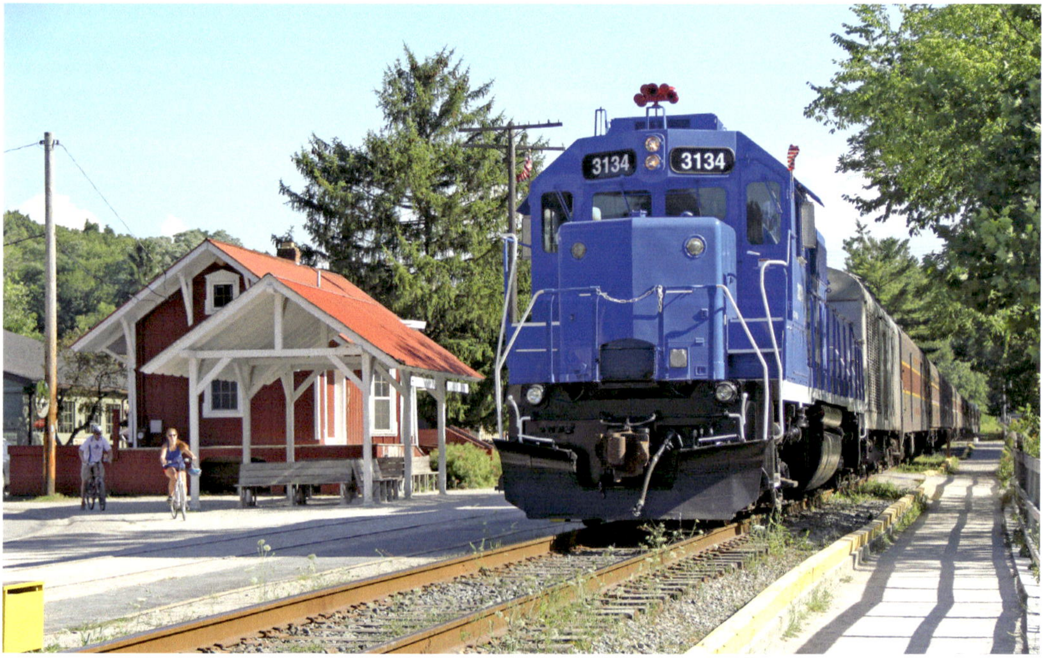

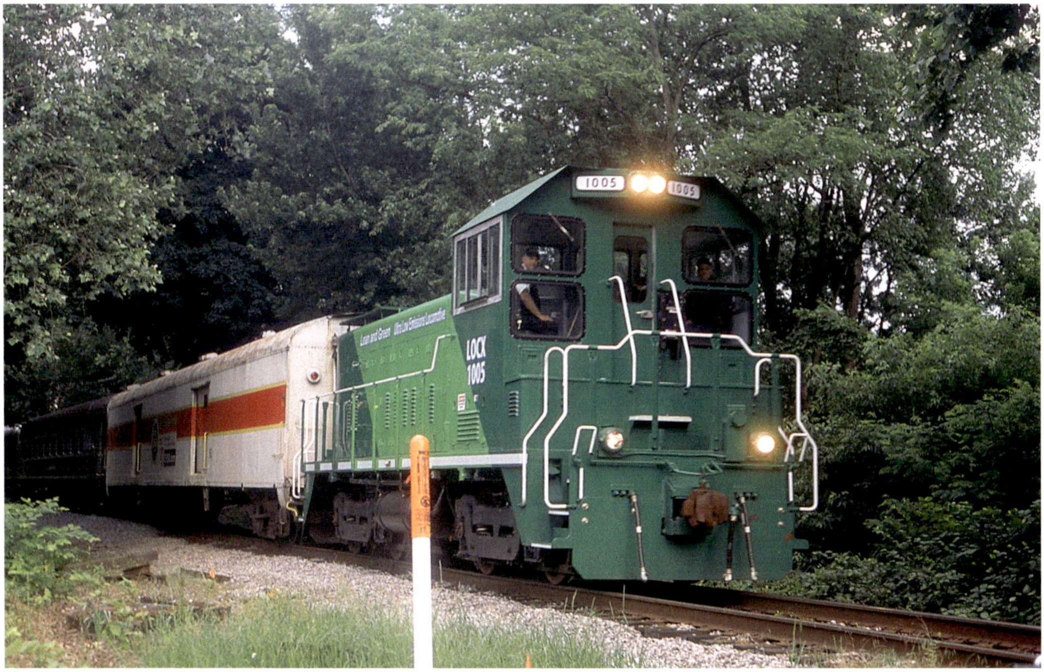

GREEN MACHINES: As part of a National Park Service focus on environmental sustainability, the CVSR tested two "green" locomotives. Above, LOCX 1005 was a former SW8 rebuilt by Industrial Railway Switching and Services of Lorain, Ohio, and leased from Mobile Locomotive Services for operation on the CVSR in 2011. Below, NREX 1400 was a model 2GS14B leased from National Railway Equipment, which rebuilt it from former AT&SF GP7 No. 2785. It operated on the CVSR in 2012. No. 1400 is shown along Merriman Road in Akron near the intersection of Portage Path. (*Above, Jim Mastromatteo photo; below, Marty Surdyk photo*)

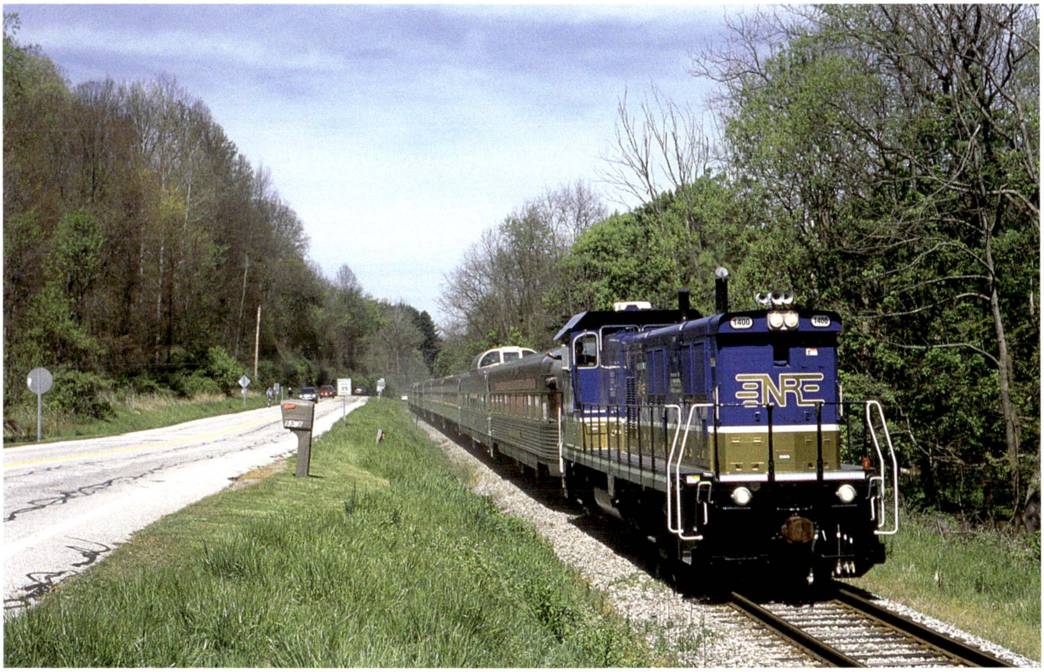

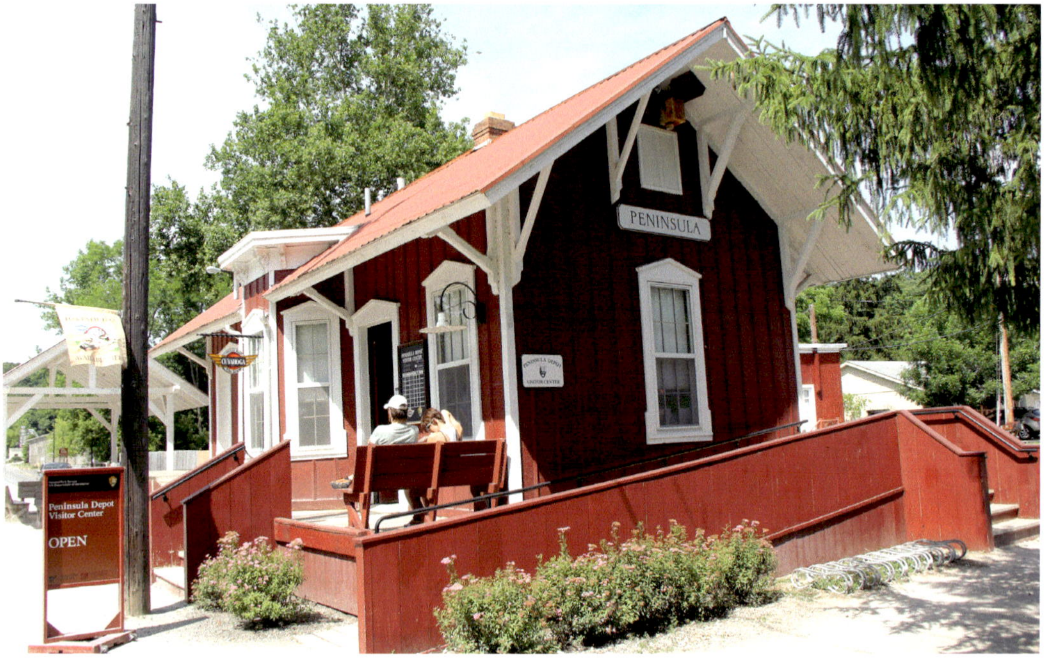

CVSR STATIONS: Peninsula has the only former B&O depot that remains on the CVSR. It was the Boston Mill station until being moved to Peninsula in December 1967. The Park Service funded construction of shelters for Independence (Rockside Road), Canal Exploration Center, Brecksville, Boston Mill, Indigo Lake, Botzum (formerly known as Indian Mound), Akron Northside and Canton. Designed to resemble a traditional railroad depot with Victorian styling, the first of these shelters was built in May 1998 at Indigo Lake. Major CVSR stations have restrooms but only Peninsula features an indoor space. All stations have benches, but the Big Bend station in Akron does not have a shelter, just a boarding area. (*Craig Sanders photos*)

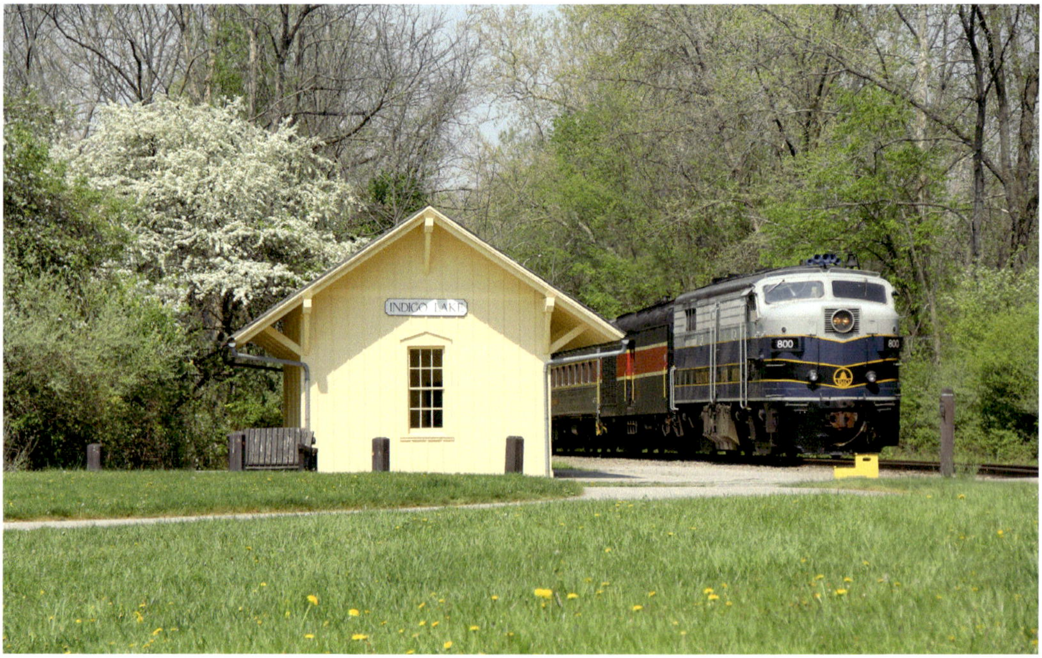

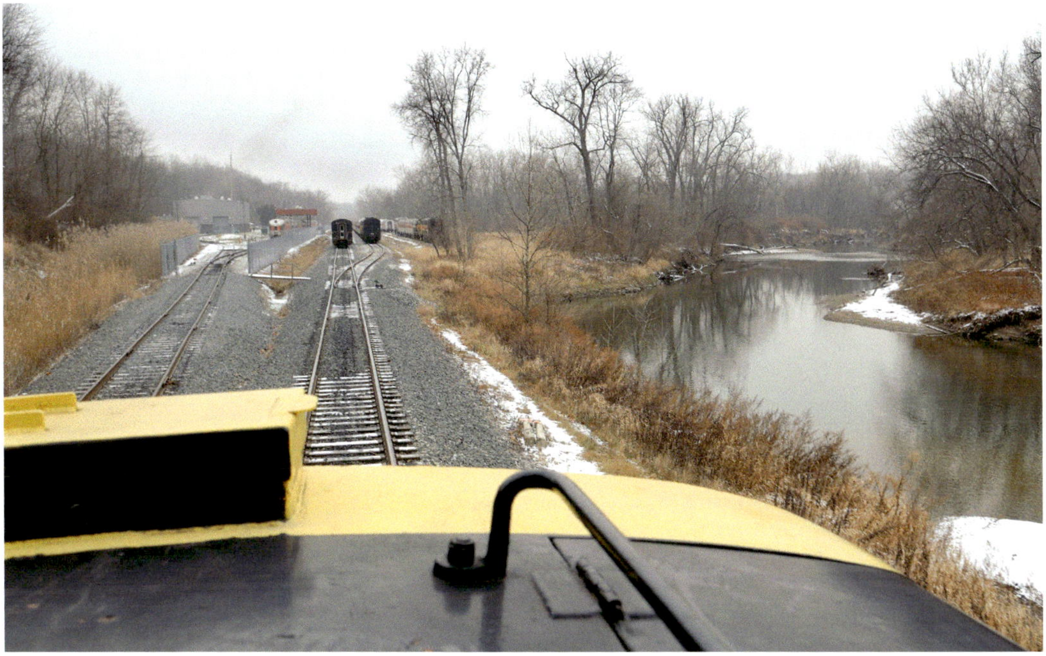

FITZWATER SHOPS AND YARD: The CVSR took possession of Fitzwater Yard on November 4, 1994. The 22-acre site had been a Cuyahoga County highway garage since 1934. It gave the CVSR more room to store equipment, establish a maintenance headquarters and build a shop. The Park Service provided $4.6 million to buy the property and build the shop, which opened in June 1999. Above, the complex is shown on December 22, 2009, looking north from the cab of No. 1822 during a maneuver to shake coolant out of the locomotive for the winter. Below, No. 365 sits inside the shop. It is an Alco C420 built in June 1965 for the Seaboard Air Line Railroad. (*Peter Bowler photos*)

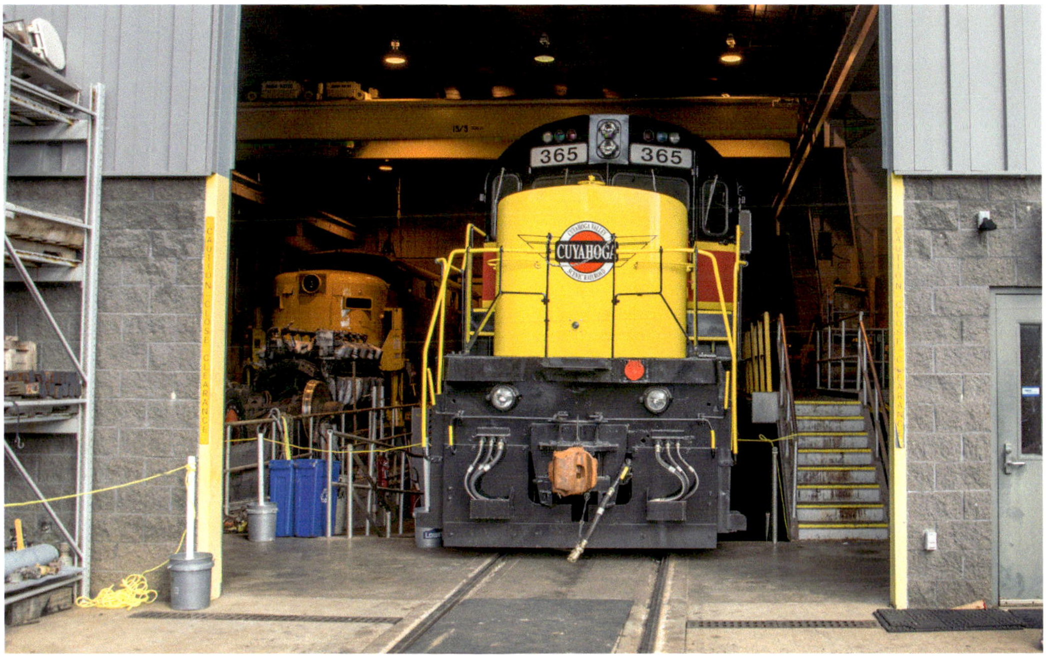

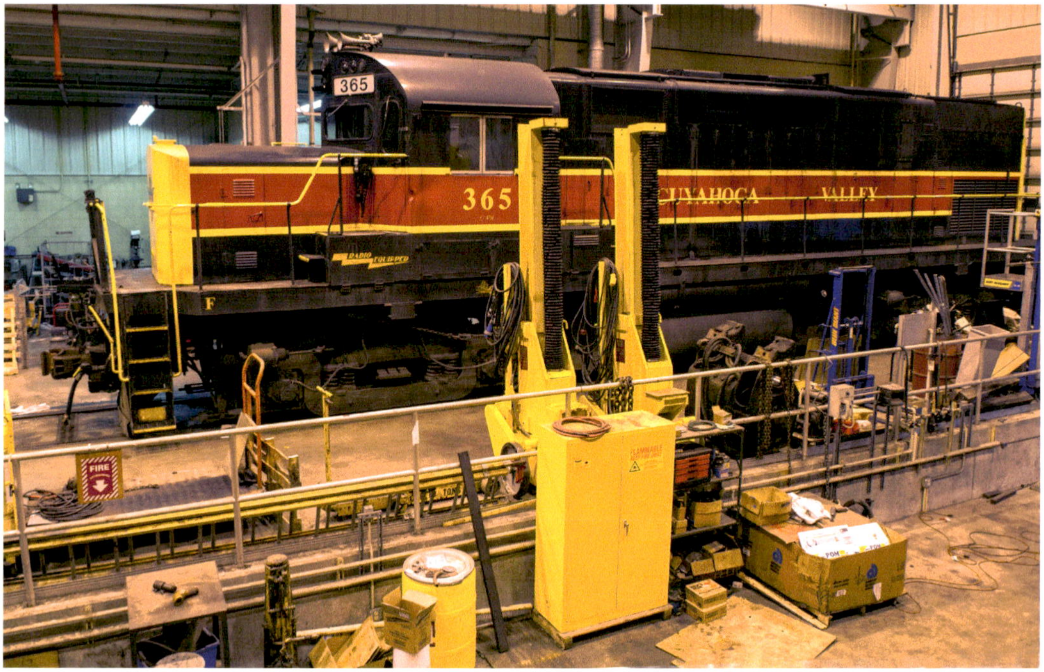

INSIDE THE SHOPS: The repair shop at Fitzwater Shops and Yard has two run-through tracks that can each accommodate two locomotives or two passenger cars. The shop operates five days a week with a combination of paid staff and volunteers. It can perform most repairs, but some work, such as changing a traction motor or wheel work, is done under contract by another railroad's shop. Above, No. 365 awaits repairs inside the shop in December 2009. Below, FPA-4 No. 14 sits atop a special set of rails that enables mechanics to work beneath the locomotive. (*Above, Peter Bowler photo; below, Tom Fritsch photo*)

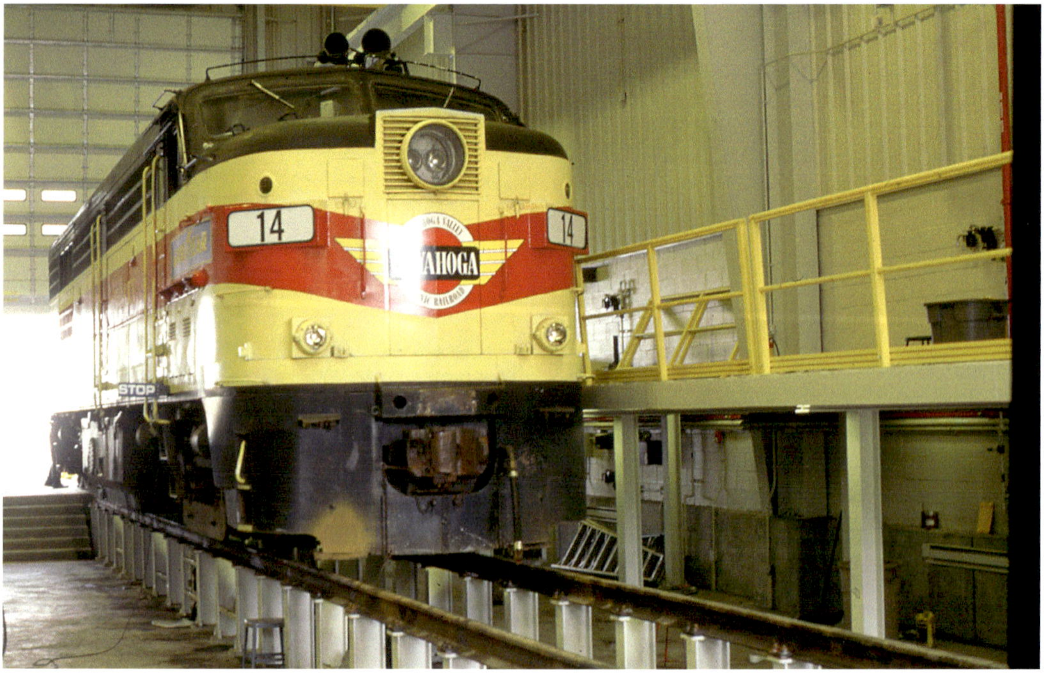

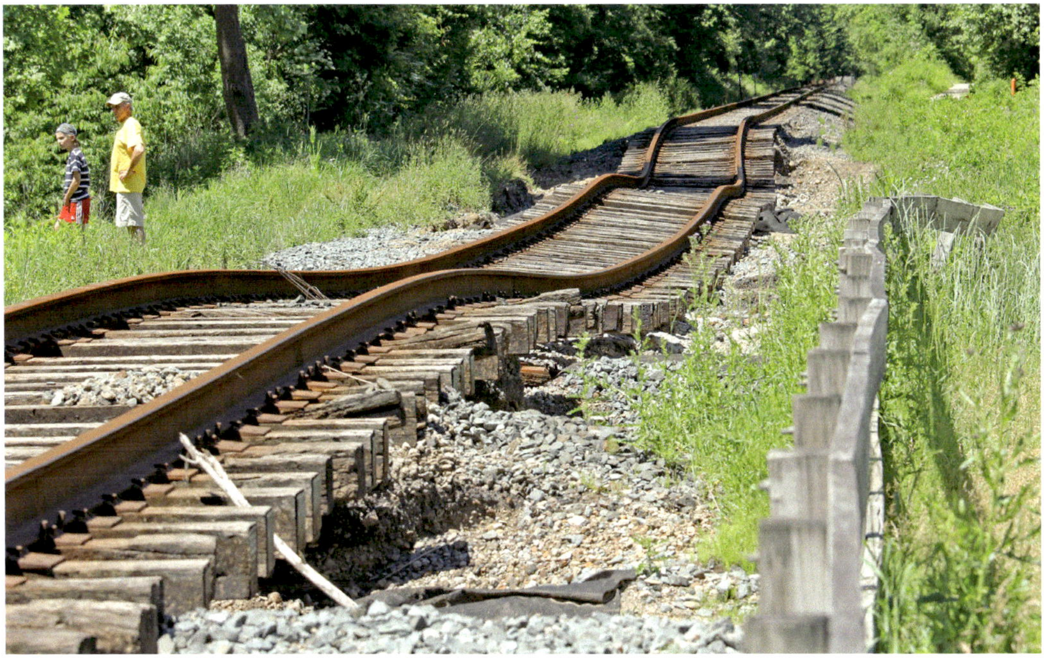

TRACK REPAIRS: Washouts caused by flooding have plagued the Valley Line since 1880. Washouts in 2003, 2006, 2011 and 2014 knocked the CVSR out of service for several weeks and cost it ridership and revenue. Above, one of the more washout-prone spots is where the tracks cross Yellow Creek near Bath Road. A storm on May 12, 2014, left the tracks resembling a roller coaster ride. Service did not resume until a month later. Above, Park Service funding helps the CVSR keep its track in good condition. Although the track doesn't take the pounding that freight railroads rails do, the track used by the CVSR still must be maintained and repaired. *(Above, Craig Sanders photo; below, Peter Bowler photo)*

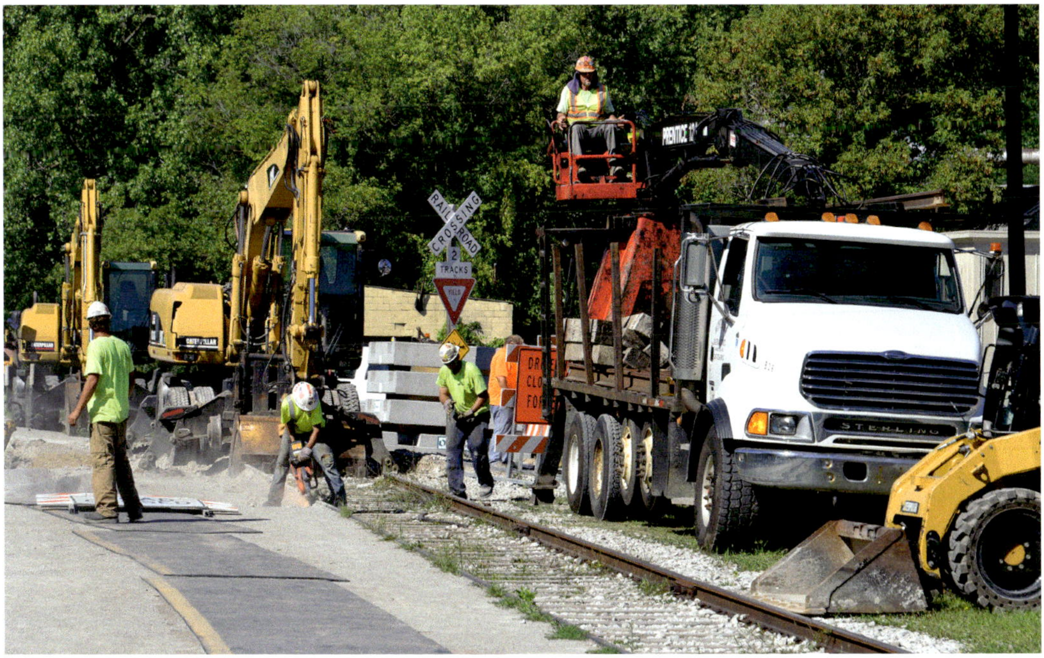

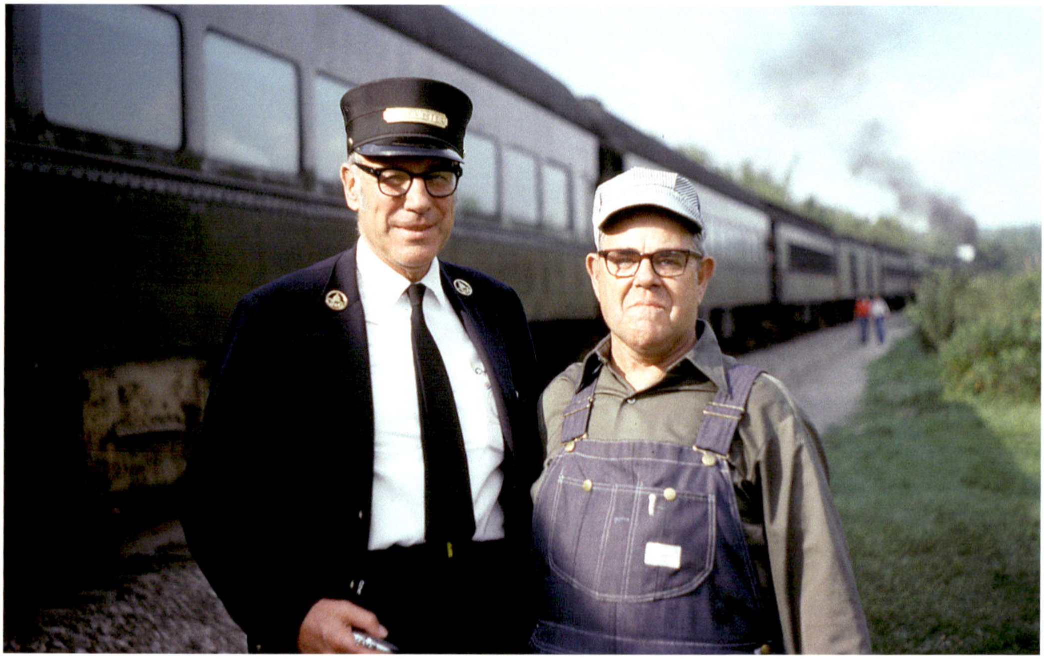

WORKING ON THE RAILROAD: In CVL's early years, Chessie System engineers operated No. 4070 alongside Midwest Railway Historical Foundation volunteers. Some Chessie engineers had operated B&O steam locomotives, including Joe Seaman (right), shown in the top photo with conductor Francis Sage in August 1977. After the Park Service purchased the railroad, CVL crews were volunteers from the MRHS or, in the case of the car hosts, the Midwest Chapter of the National Railway Historical Society. For many volunteers, working on the CVL was the opportunity of a lifetime. Below, brakeman Al Lacey (left) and engineer Bob Lods pose in the cab of No. 4070 on October 14, 1989. *(Above, Paul Woodring photo; below, Edward Ribinskas photo)*

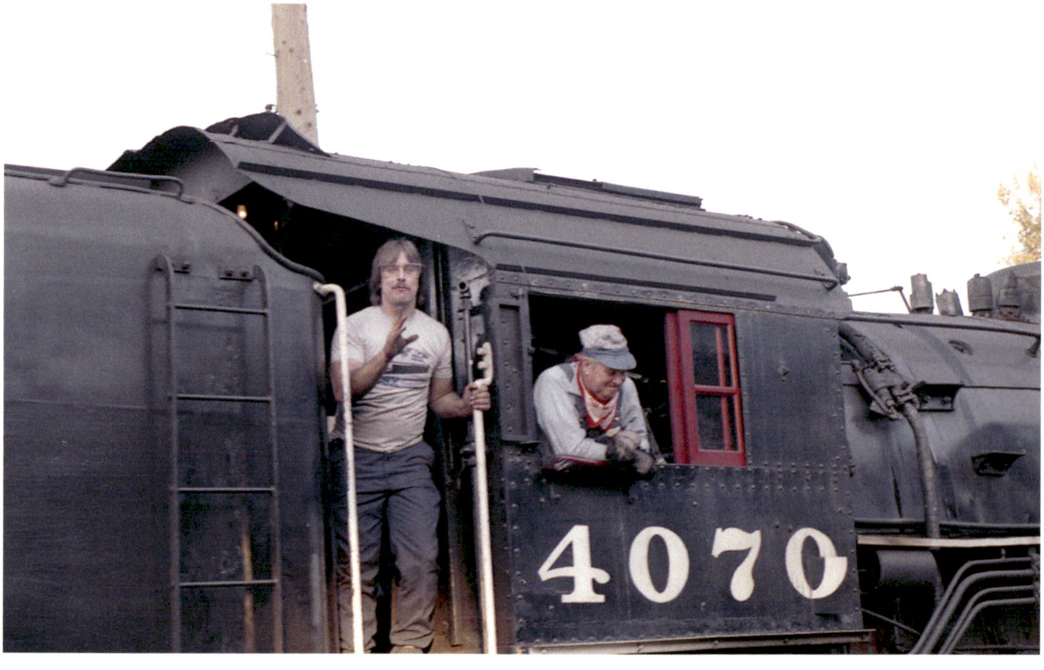

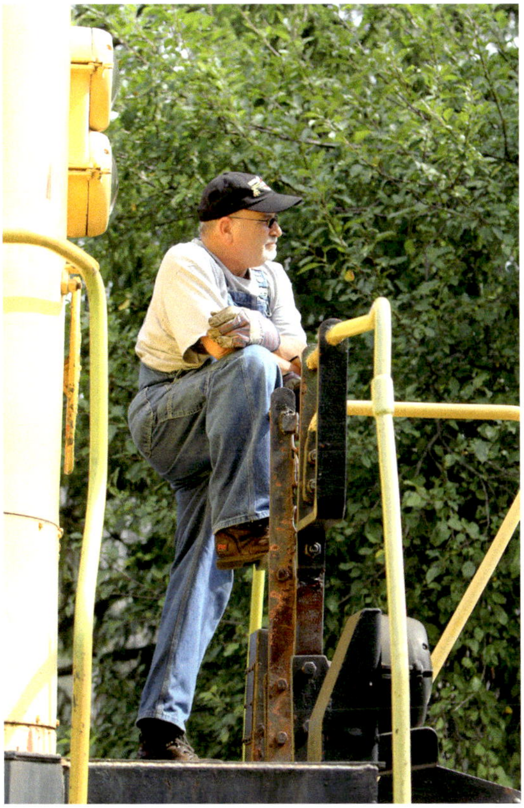

CRITICAL ROLE OF VOLUNTEERS:
Former CVSR President Steven W. Wait once said that his organization couldn't run without its volunteers, who fulfill a variety of tasks on and off the train. Although many CVSR volunteers have a passion for railroading, they come from all walks of life. Many say the camaraderie of the volunteer corps and interaction with passengers keeps them coming back. In 2015, volunteers contributed 90,848 hours of service, and every year the CVSR recognizes a volunteer of the year. Above, an engineer watches from the front porch of a locomotive for a meet with another train in Peninsula on September 18, 2016. Below, car host Gary Spencer looks out a vestibule window. (*Craig Sanders photos*)

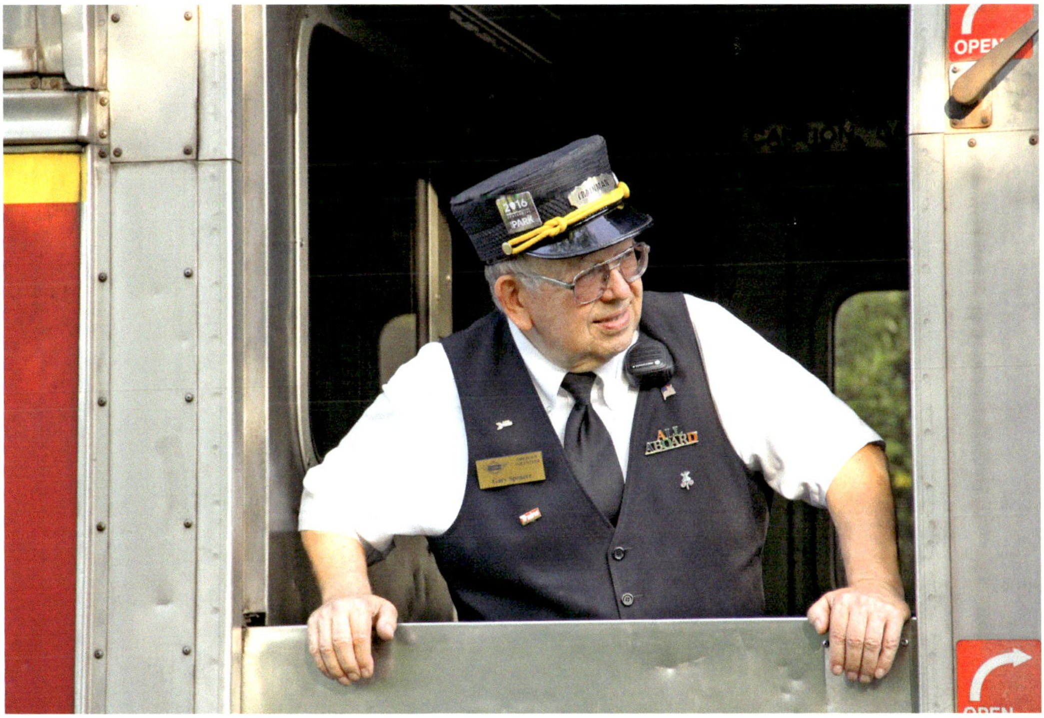

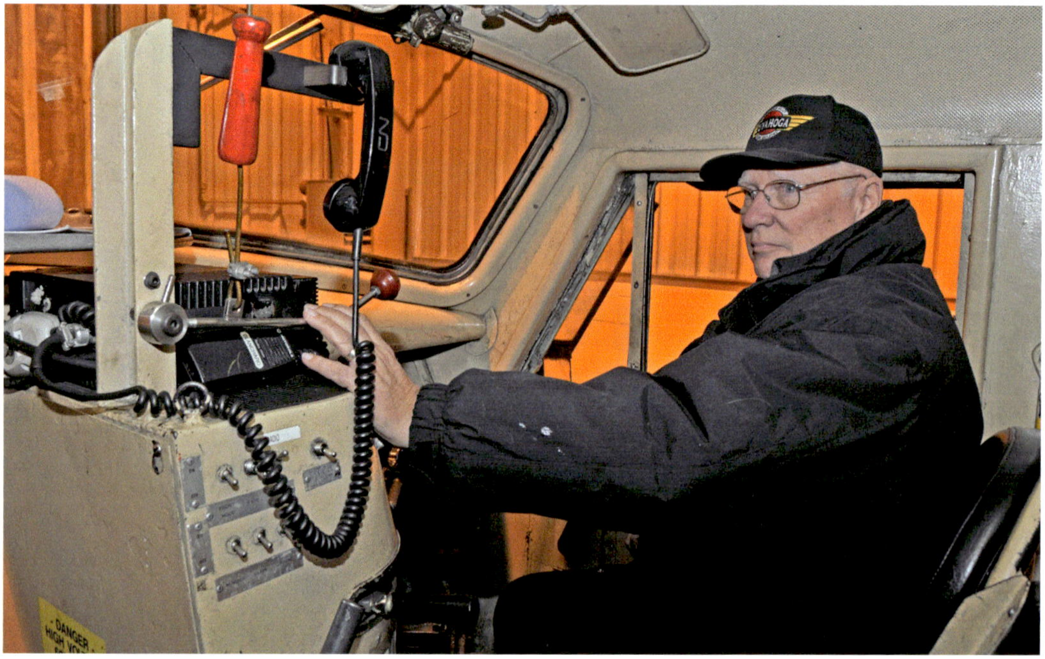

BEHIND THE SCENES: Engineers, conductors and car hosts may be among the most visible people in the eyes of passengers, but keeping the equipment functioning smoothly is the job of a corps of workers at Fitzwater Maintenance Yard and Shops. The CVSR also has a handful of supervisory positions. Above, Larry Blanchard, who is a retired CSX Transportation trainmaster who has served the CVSR as a trainmaster and director of operations, guides an FPA-4 into the shop. Below, Don Balmut (left) and Larry Drotar work inside the Fitzwater shop in December 2009. Both are qualified as CVSR operating personnel. (*Peter Bowler photos*)

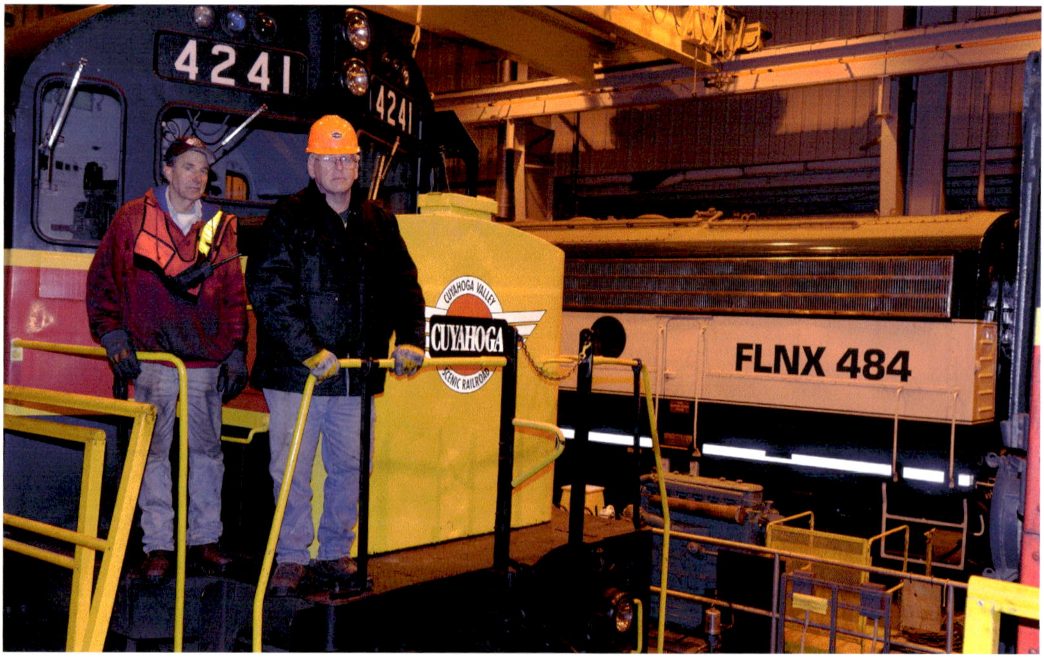

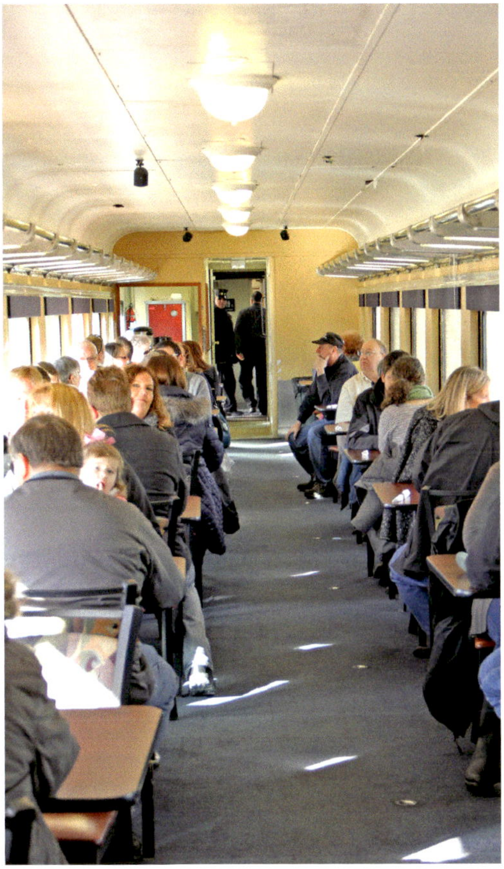

DINING ALONG THE CUYAHOGA: In 2012 CVSR renovated the *Lone Star* (above) and *Cuyahoga Inn* (below) for use as food service cars. Breakfast, brunch or dinner are provided by a caterer and served during a round trip originating in Akron or Independence. *Lone Star* was built by Pullman for the B&O as a sleeper and sold in 1970 to Ringling Bros. and Barnum & Bailey for its circus train. The *Cuyahoga Inn* was a parlor car built by Budd in 1951 for the Pennsylvania Railroad. Both are shown in Akron on February 4, 2017, and also are used for wine- and beer-tasting trains. Sandwiches and snacks are sold in concession cars. (*Craig Sanders photos*)

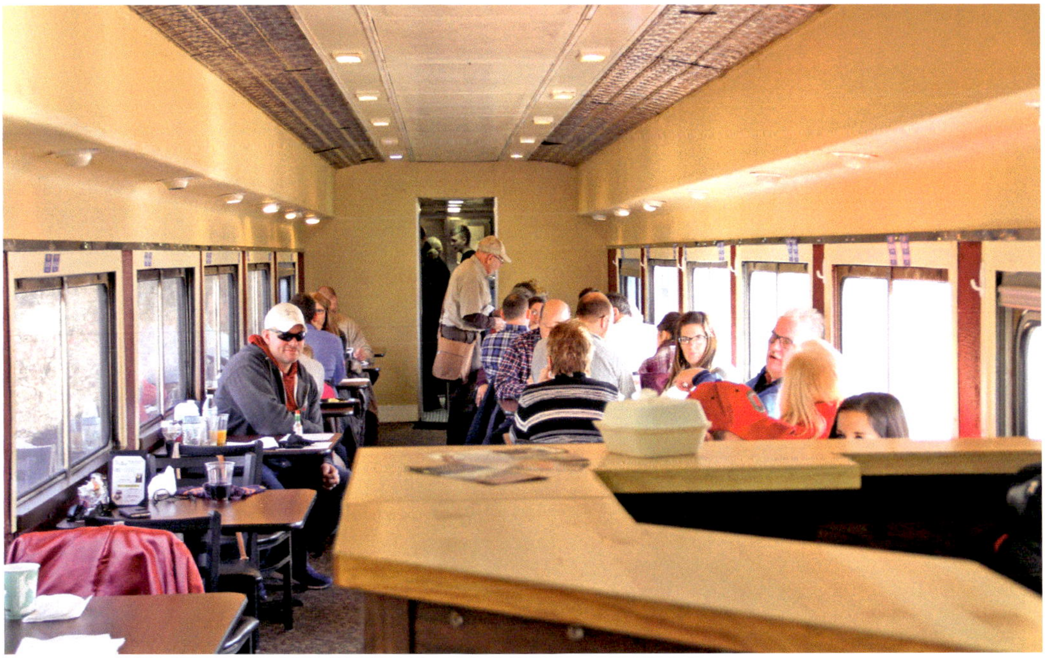

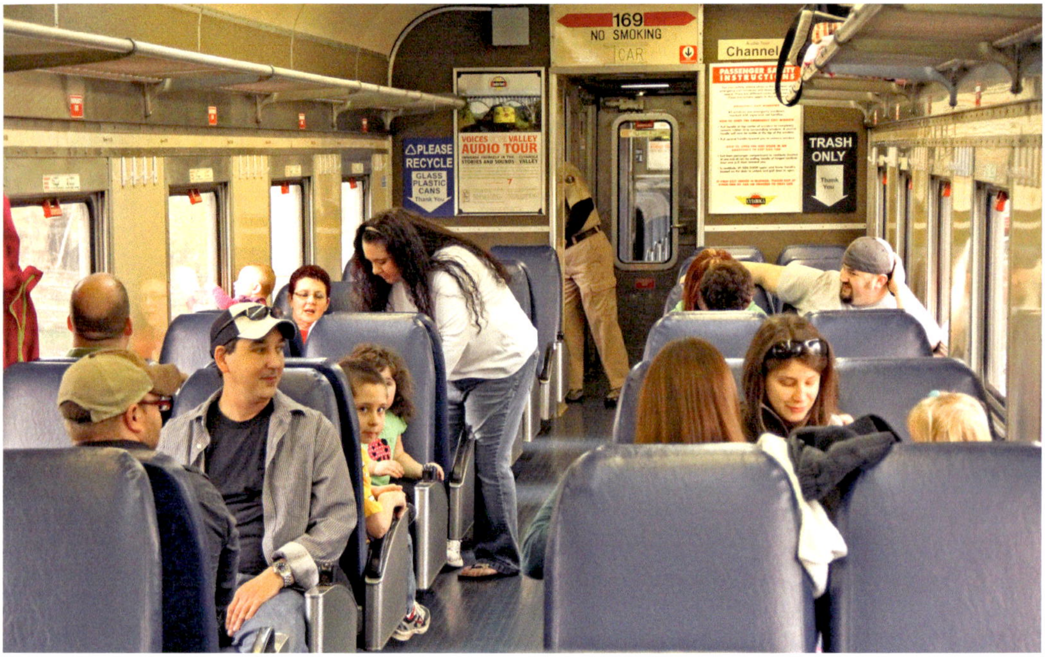

INSIDE LOOK: The CVSR has never purchased new passenger cars. In its early years the fleet resembled a rolling museum with the oldest car having been built in 1914 by Norfolk & Western Railway. Most CVSR cars today were built after the end of World War II. Above, Coach No. 169, *Spirit of Summit*, is shown in March 2012. Below, CVSR used a $373,000 grant to rebuild a coach in 2009-2010 to comply with the Americans With Disabilities Act standards. The 60-passenger car received a specially designed floor and lifts to accommodate wheelchairs. It was the CVSR's second ADA-accessible car. The first, *Invacare*, was a 36-seat car rebuilt in 2002 from coach-baggage car *Fort Mitchell*. (*Craig Sanders photos*)

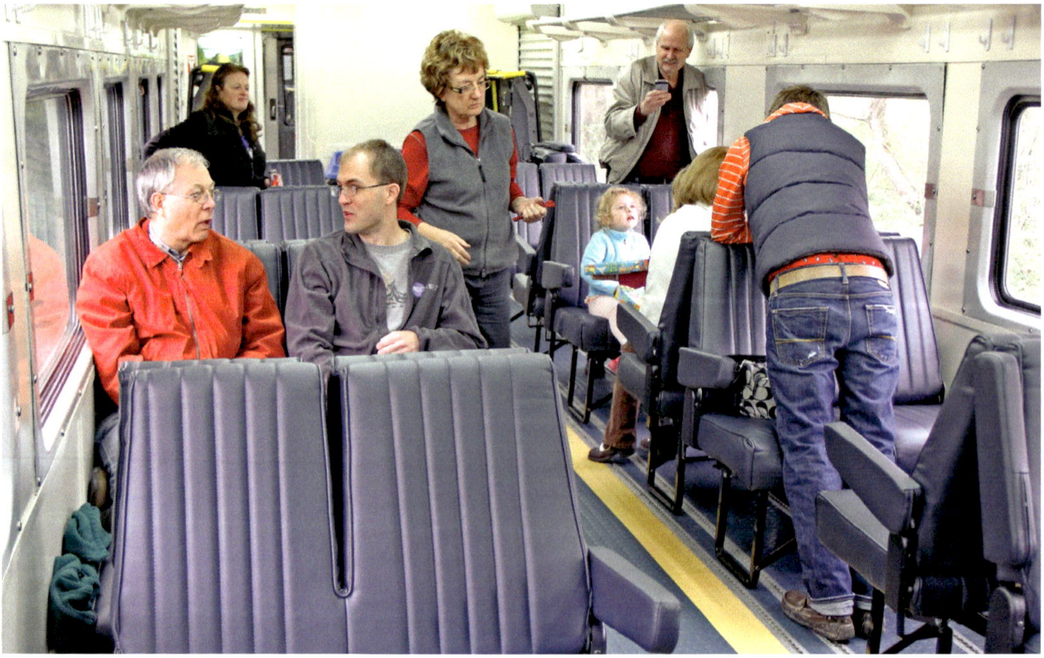

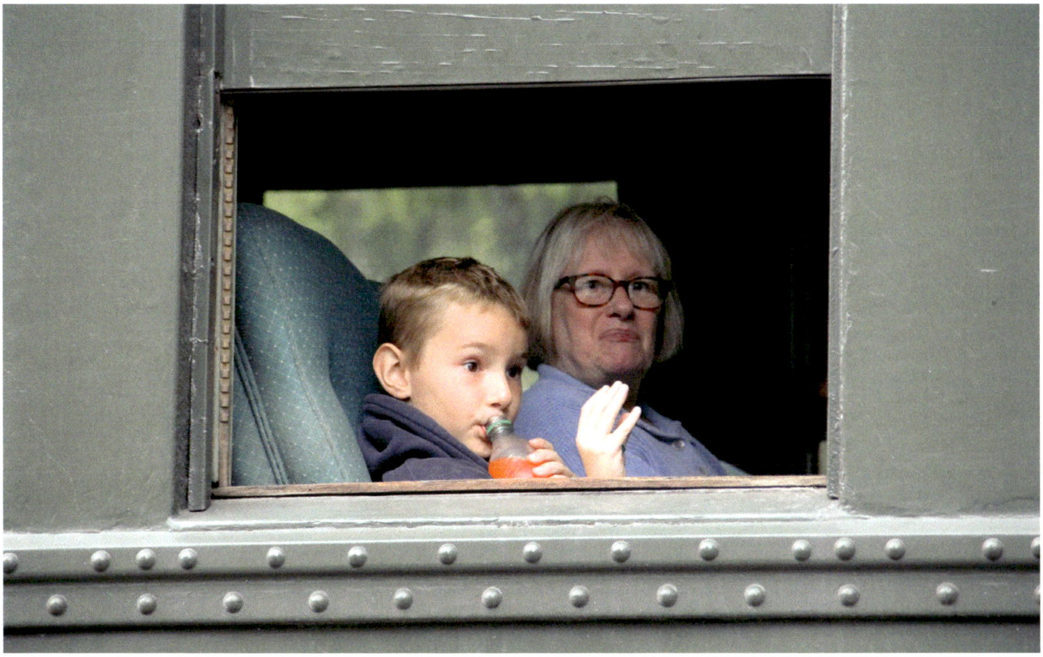

YOUNG RIDERS: Aside from its *Polar Express* and *Day Out With Thomas* trains, the CVSR offers other programs designed for children. The railroad works with schools and offers stand-alone educational programs. In 2013, CVSR served 15,289 students from 249 schools. The *Read Aboard* program, launched in June 2016, was designed to enable children ages three to seven to learn about the train and the Cuyahoga Valley National Park, and encourage summer reading while taking a three-hour train ride. Above, a boy and his grandmother enjoy the view from an open window car pulled by a steam locomotive in September 2016. Below, a trainman helps a young passenger disembark at Boston Mill. (*Craig Sanders photos*)

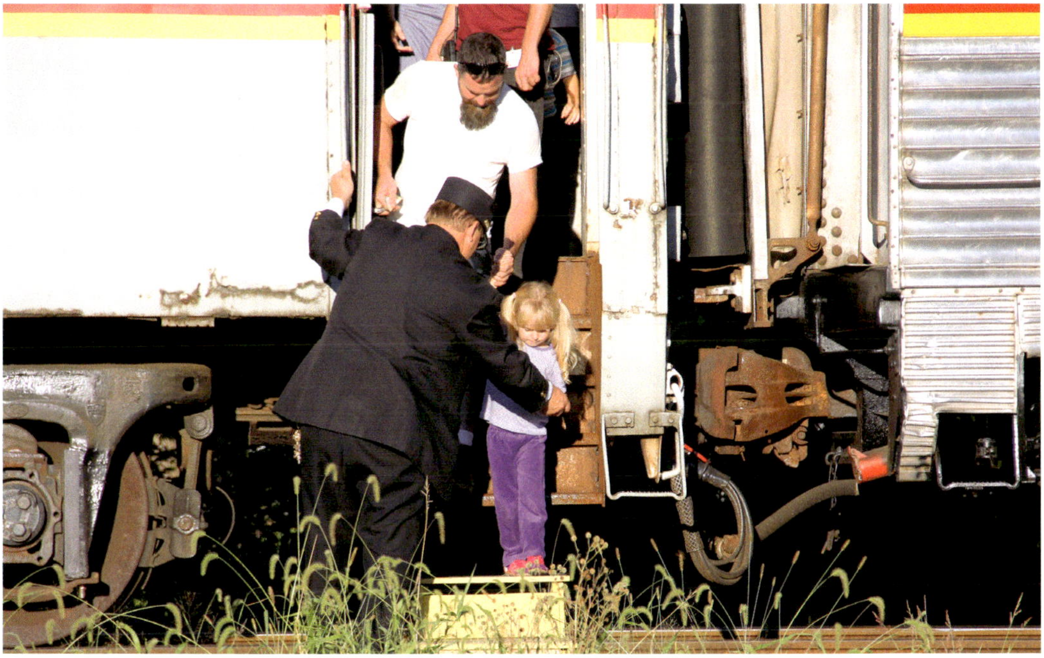

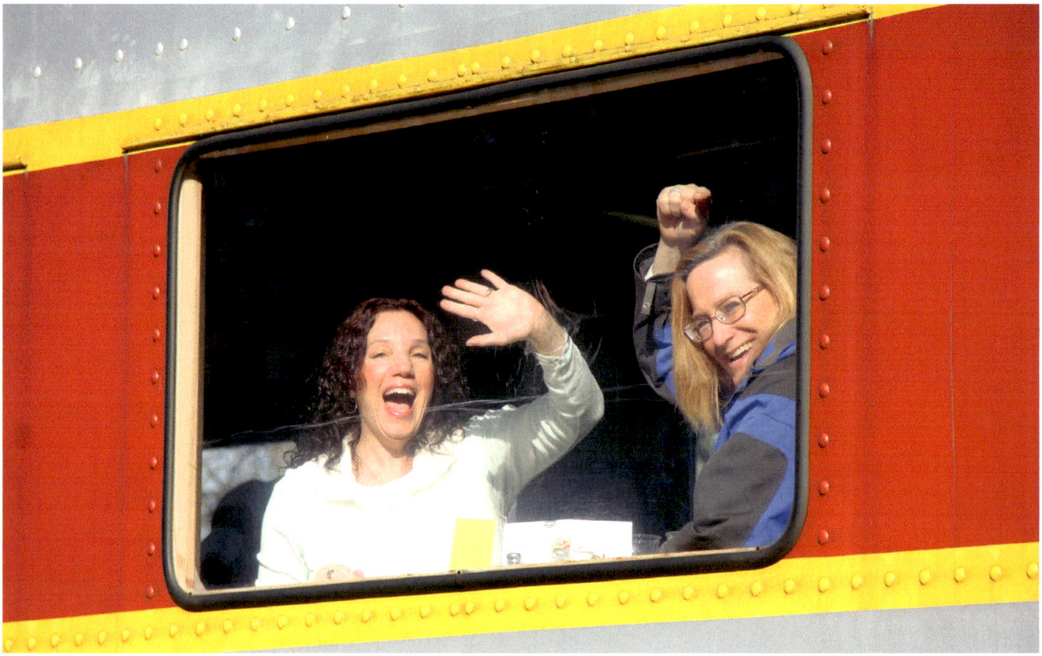

RIDERSHIP RECORDS: CVSR trains carried a record 214,063 passengers in 2016, breaking the high water mark of 210,347 set in 2012. Since topping triple digits for the first time with 100,130 passengers in 2000, the CVSR has handled more than 100,000 patrons every year except during 2003 when flooding damaged fourteen miles of track and service was cancelled for three weeks. Ridership data for the 1970s and 1980s is scarce, but the Cuyahoga Valley Line reported carrying 7,000 in its first season in 1975. Ridership can be depressed by various factors. It fell by 24,000 in 2013 when a federal government budget showdown closed national parks for about a week in October during the foliage season. (*Craig Sanders photos*)

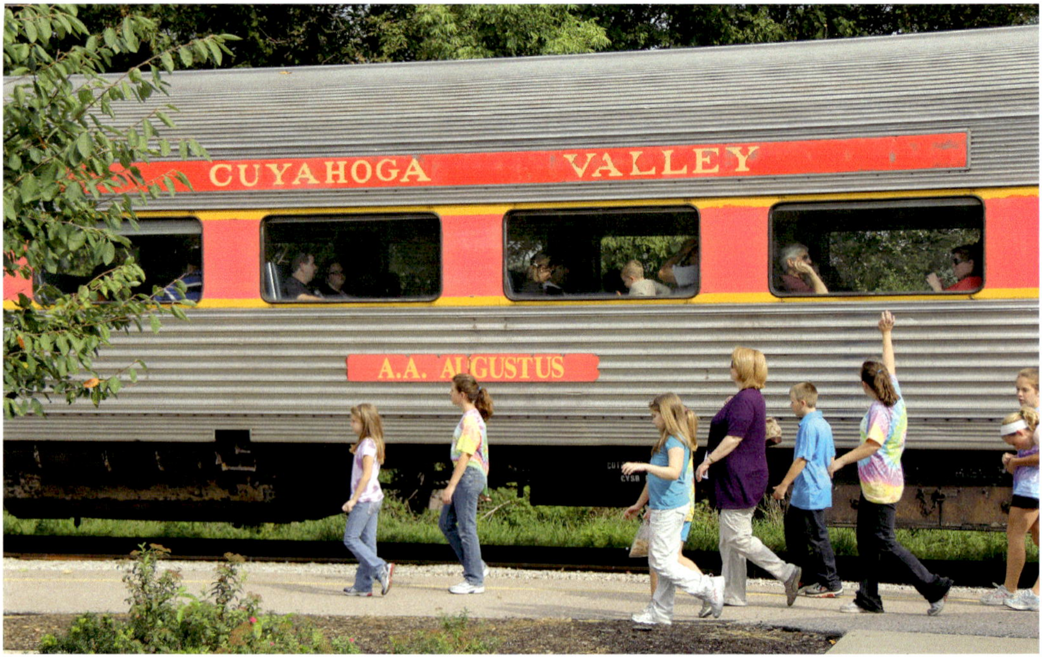

5 A NOBLE EXPERIMENT

Cuyahoga Valley Line officials talked about serving Canton in 1989, but the idea remained dormant until planning began in 1994 for a Cleveland-Akron-Canton rail commuter service. The Baltimore & Ohio Railroad's last Canton passenger service had been a Rail Diesel Car that operated to Valley Junction through September 30, 1934.

A study put the cost of establishing commuter service at $100 million with annual operating costs of $8 million. The commuter rail idea faltered, but Congressman Ralph Regula of Navarre helped secure $9.6 million in federal funds to purchase and rehabilitate the Canton route for CVSR service. Akron Metro Regional Transit Authority purchased the line on June 16, 2000, for $6.2 million. CSX had not used the tracks between Akron and Aultman since 1993, and trees were growing between the rails.

A $3 million federal grant awarded in 2003 funded track rehabilitation, and a $100,000 grant paid for construction of the Canton station. CVSR received $71,000 for locomotives and rolling stock. In all, it cost $27 million to get the Canton service started.

Workers repaired four bridges, improved thirteen grade crossings and replaced more than 15,000 cross ties. The top speed was 25 mph, and the Akron-Canton running time was 90 minutes.

CVSR President Douglas Cooper described the Canton extension as "a noble experiment ... with real potential." Operating on Saturday and Sunday during the summer, trains fed passengers to such Canton cultural institutions as the Pro Football Hall of Fame, National First Ladies' Library, McKinley Monument, Canton Art Institute and the Canton Classic Car Museum. There was no convenient connection from Canton with trains to the Cuyahoga Valley National Park.

In 2004, Canton trains operated on ten weekends between June and August and averaged 200 passengers per train. The following year the CVSR received a $20,000 state grant to promote the service.

Service was reduced to ten Saturdays between June and August in 2007. However, there were six *Polar Express* trips that year from Canton between December 12 and 14.

Canton service expanded in 2008 to Wednesday through Sunday operation and it was now possible to connect in Akron with trains to the CVNP. Aside from the *Polar Express* trains, Canton service operated only between June and August.

The *Polar Express* trains were canceled in 2011. In 2012 Canton trains operated on Fridays and Saturdays. Further retrenchment occurred in 2013 when service was reduced to one Saturday a month. However, for the first time, trains originating in Canton ran through Akron to the CVNP.

In August 2013, the CVSR suspended Canton service because a maintenance agreement with Akron Metro to maintain the tracks had expired. CVSR service to Canton has yet to resume.

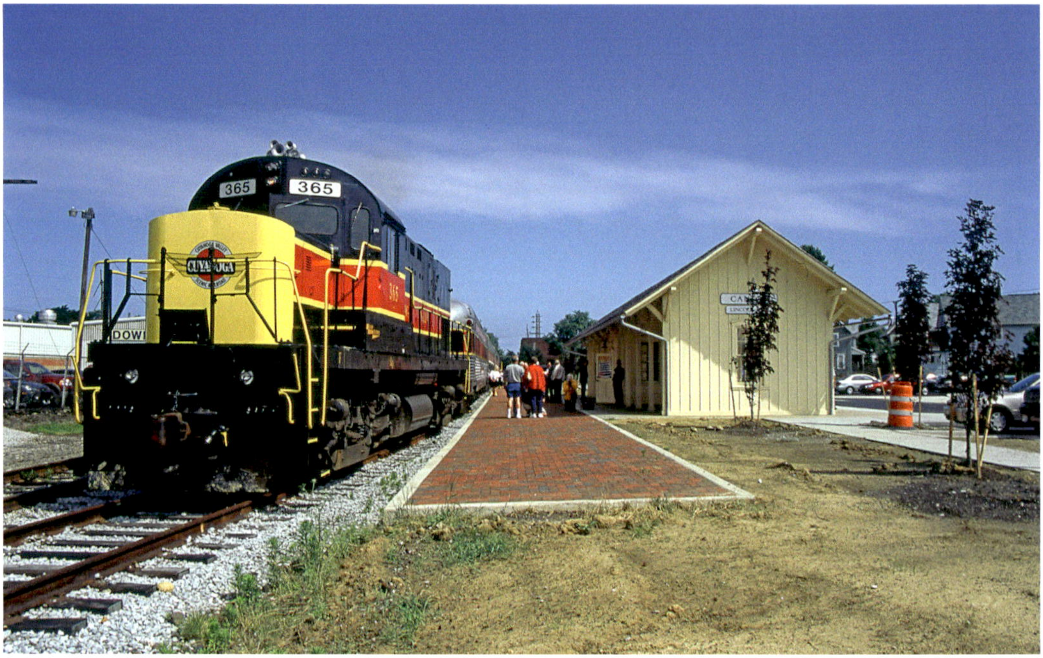

CANTON STATION: The CVSR Canton station was located on Tuscarawas Street West. A $100,000 federal grant helped fund the station, which was built in spring 2003 by the National Park Service and then turned over to the city. The first Canton train was a publicity special that ran on July 2, 2003. Regular service began on July 12, a week later than planned due to the need for track repairs. Above, a train waits in the station in June 2004 before departing for Akron. Below, CVSR engineer Mark Perri arranged for the lighting, including flash bulbs, and helped the photographer make this image of a train at the Canton station. (*Above, Craig Sanders photo; below, Paul Woodring photo*)

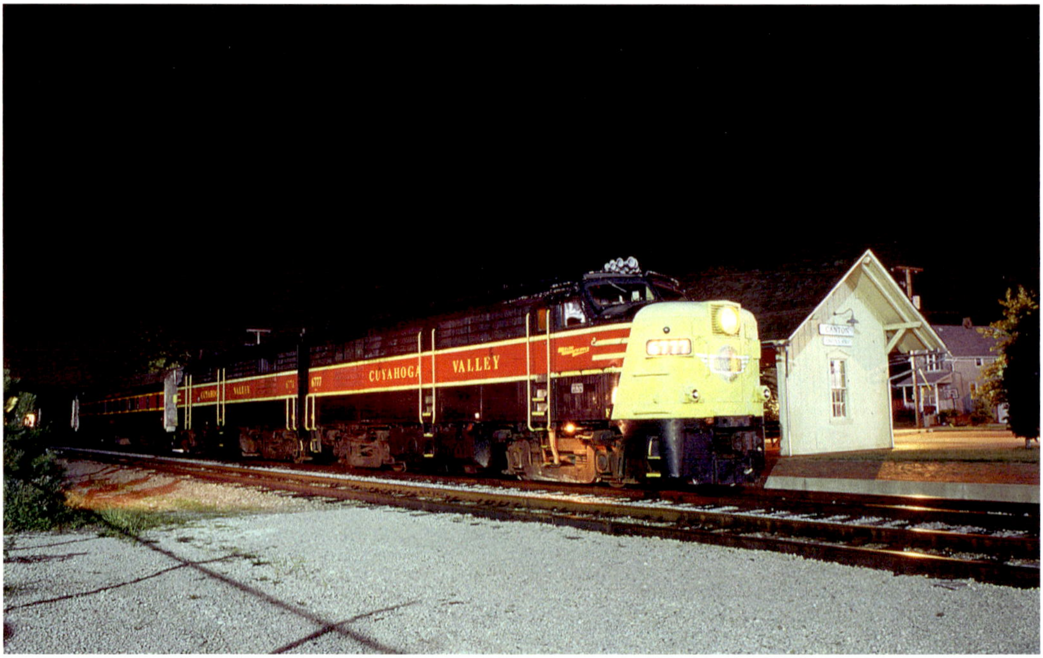

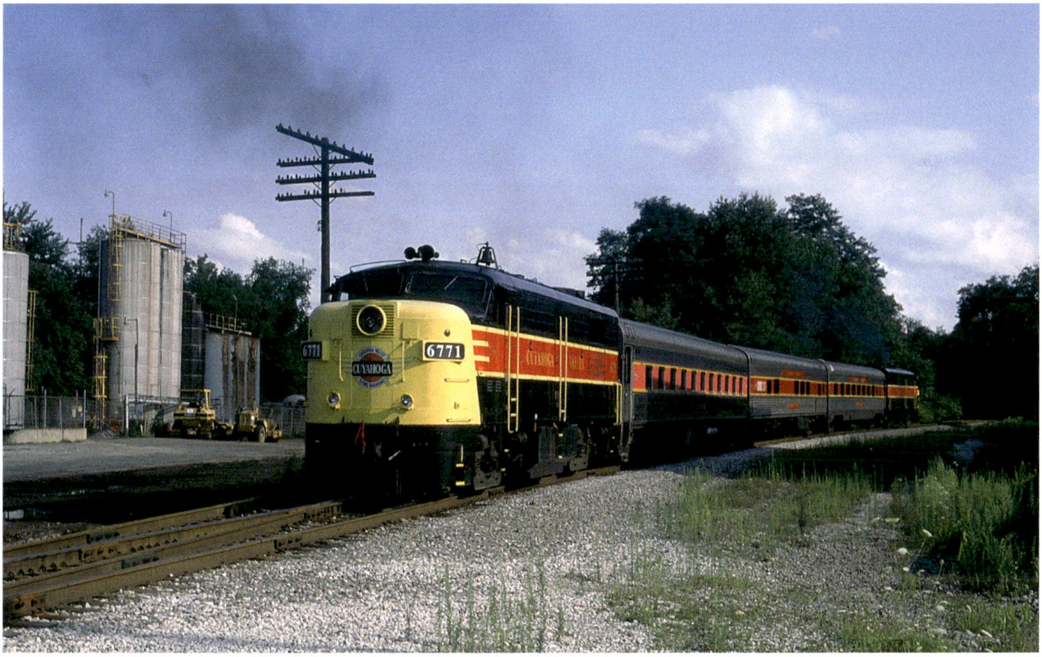

CANTON TRAINS IN AKRON: The 2003 schedule was two roundtrips of 90 minutes each way on Saturdays and Sundays between Akron and Canton. Shuttle buses took passengers to cultural sites in both cities, including the Pro Football Hall of Fame in Canton. Service was to operate through late August, but was suspended after just two weekends due to flood damage to the tracks. Service did not resume until June 2004. Canton trains operated on ten weekends and averaged 200 passengers per train in 2004. Above, a Canton train is northbound at Hazel Street in Akron. Below, a Canton train crosses North Case Avenue in Akron in a view from the East Market Street Bridge. (*Jim Mastromatteo photos*)

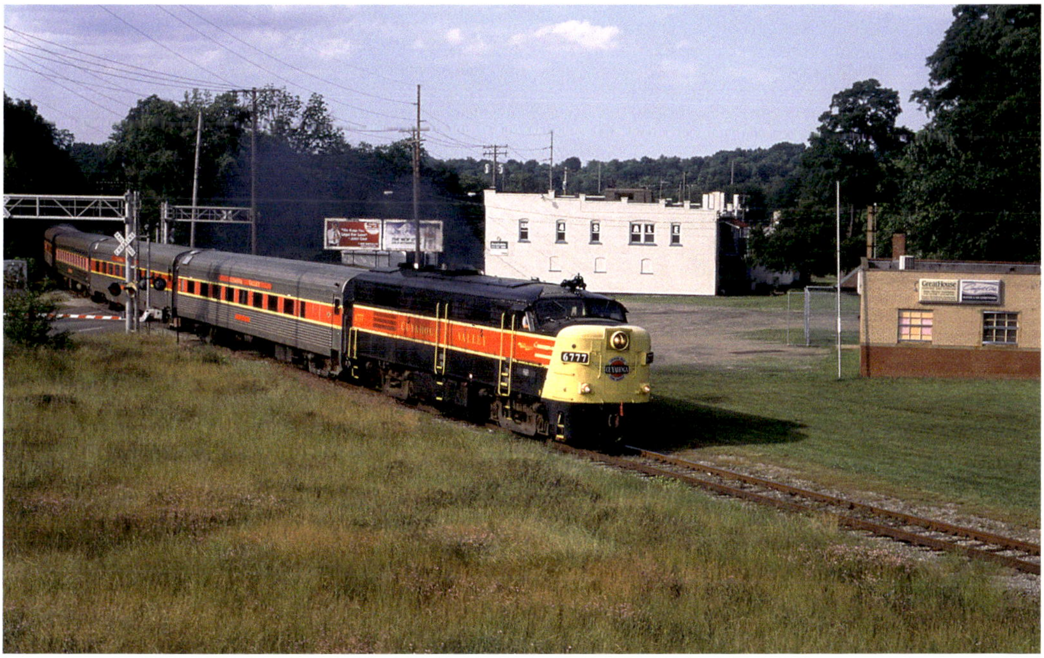

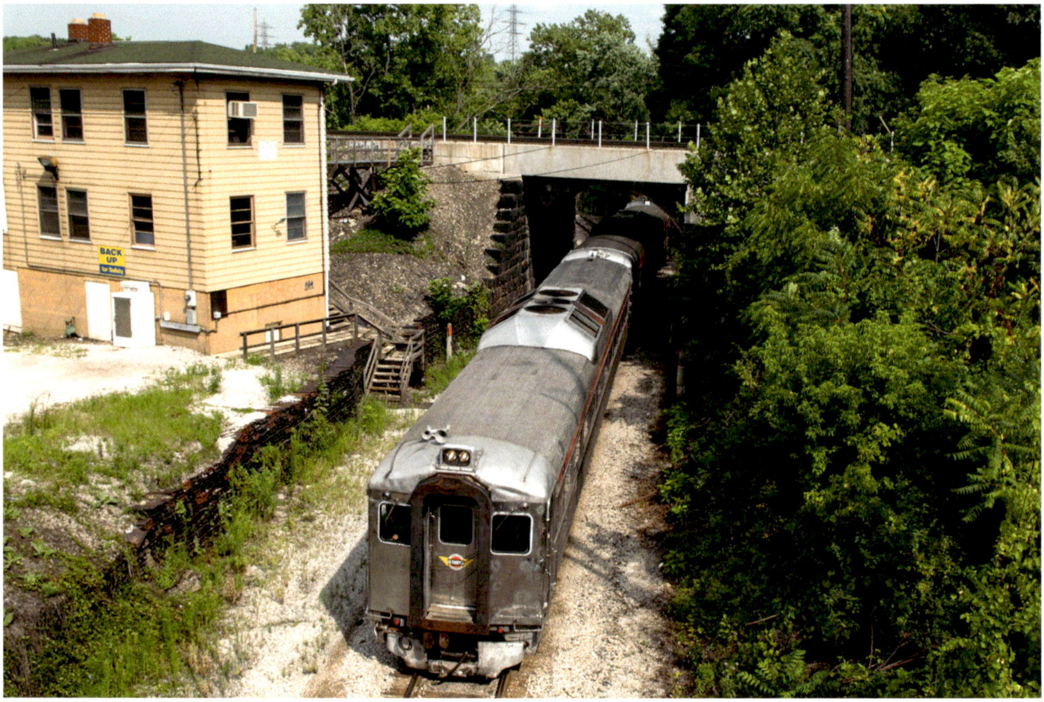

RDCS ON CANTON LINE: CVSR acquired its first rail diesel car, M-3, in fall 2003 from the Corydon Scenic Railroad in Indiana. Built by the Budd Company in 1950 for the New York, Susquehanna & Western Railway, the CVSR envisioned using its RDC for small group charters. It acquired three more RDCs, using the equipment on the Canton line in 2007. Above, RDCs pass the CSX Transportation yard office east of Arlington Street in Akron. Below, three-quarters of the CVSR RDC fleet passes a Goodyear Tire and Rubber Company plant in southeast Akron. The bridge in the distance once carried tracks of the Akron & Barberton Belt Railroad. (*Above, Peter Bowler photo; below, Craig Sanders photo*)

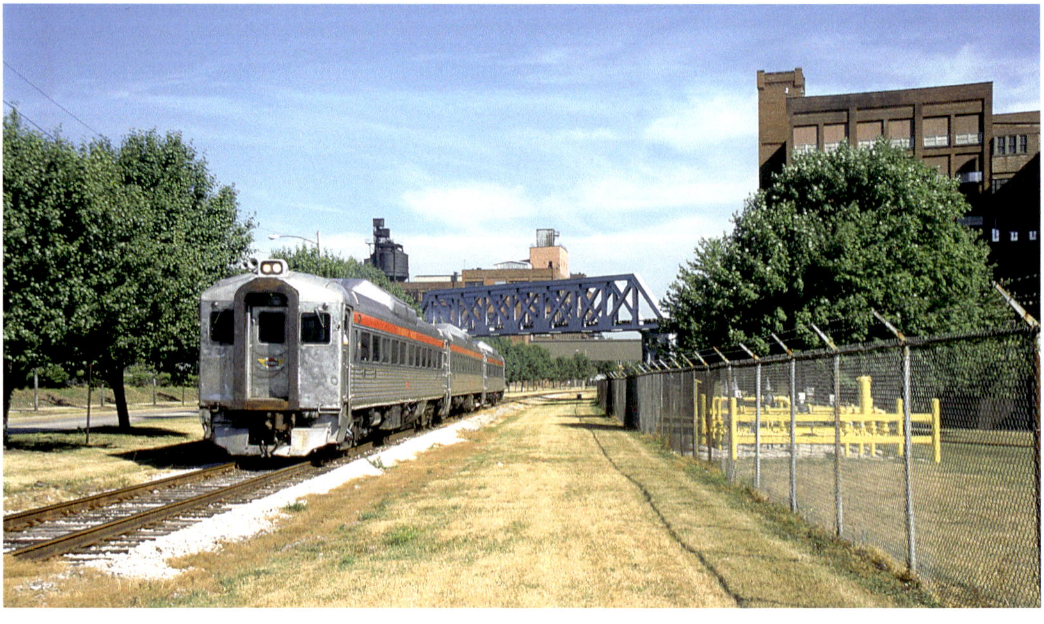

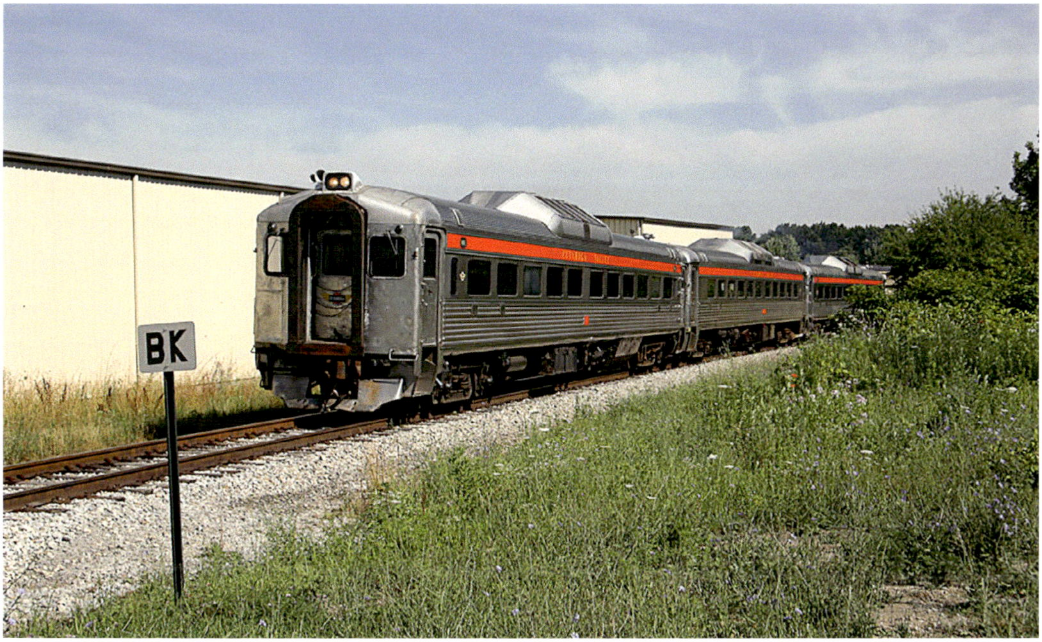

SHARED WITH FREIGHT RAILROADS: Although CVSR shared parts of the Canton line with Wheeling & Lake Erie Railway in Canton and the Akron Barberton Cluster Railway in Akron, the freight railroads worked around the CVSR schedule. The village of Uniontown expressed interest in creating a station west of town with passengers being shuttled to Hartville. A proposed North Canton station never materialized. During the eleven seasons the Canton trains ran, no intermediate stations were established between Akron and Canton. Above, a deadhead move to Canton passes Krumroy Road on the south edge of Akron. Below, a total track tour train passes through Aultman, which is east of the Akron-Canton Airport, on September 29, 2007. *(Jerry Jordak photos)*

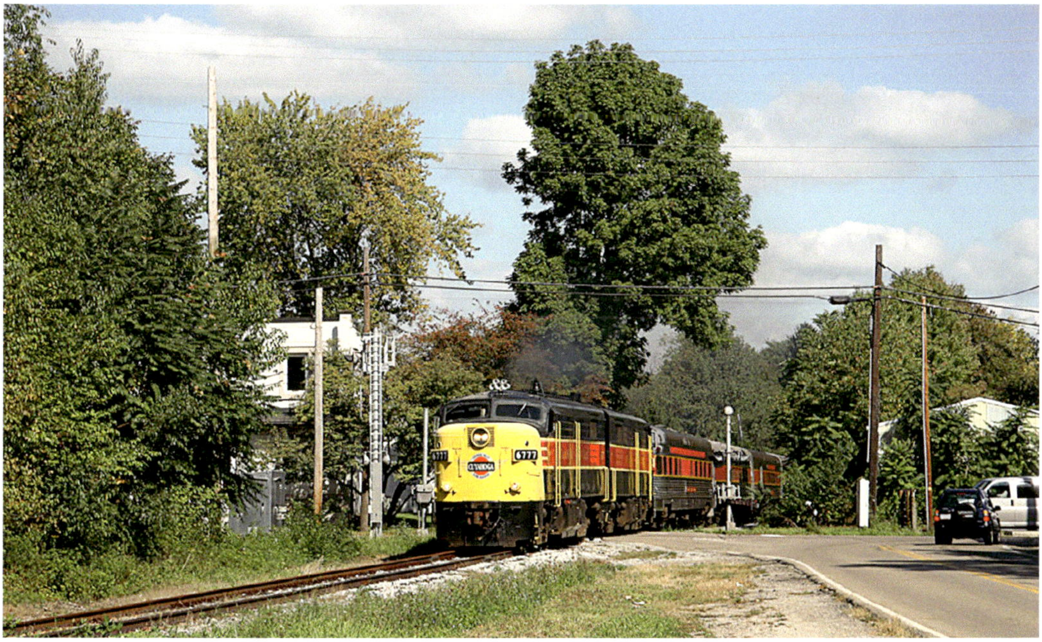

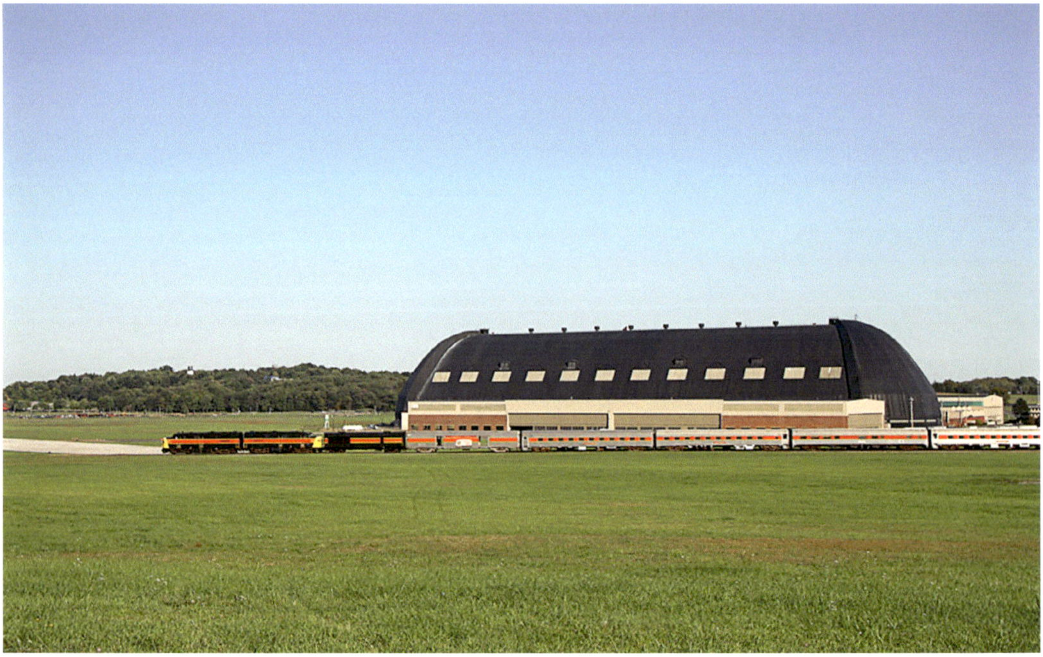

CANTON LINE HIGHLIGHT: Above, the Goodyear Air Dock at Akron Fulton International Airport was one of the scenic highlights along the 23-mile Akron-Canton route. Completed in 1929, the Goodyear-Zeppelin Corporation built airships there, the last of which was built in 1960. The Cuyahoga Valley Line envisioned making the air dock the southern terminus for trips pulled by steam locomotive 4070 when the CVL began operations in 1975, but the B&O would not allow that. Below, Canton's Monument Park is just north of the CVSR station and a popular place to photograph trains. The last CVSR train to Canton ran in August 2013. (*Jerry Jordak photos*)

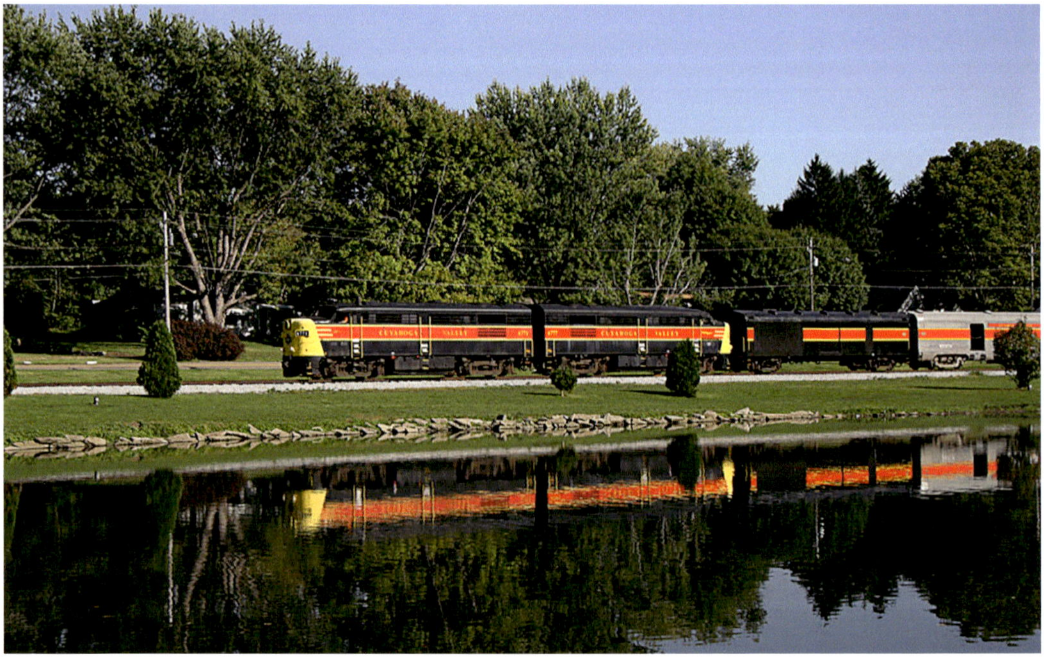

6 STEAM RETURNS TO THE VALLEY

Aside from a pair of faux steam locomotives that appealed to children—Thomas the Tank Engine and The Little Engine That Could—steam motive power was absent from the Cuyahoga Valley Scenic Railroad for seventeen years after former Grand Trunk Western 2-8-2 No. 4070 made its last run in September 1990.

Steam returned in September 2007 when Ohio Central No. 1293 pulled four trips. The 4-6-2 Pacific-type locomotive was built in 1948 by the Canadian Locomotive Company for the Canadian Pacific Railway. It had been a mainstay of OC steam excursions until the program ended after the 2004 season. Hundreds lined the tracks to catch a glimpse of No. 1293 in action.

No. 1293 returned to the CVSR in September 2008 and was featured at a steam festival held at Howe Meadow. By now Cuyahoga Valley National Park officials had recognized that a steam locomotive pulling excursion trains would attract visitors to the park.

No steam locomotives ran on the CVSR in 2009, but in September 2010 Nickel Plate Road No. 765, a 2-8-4 Berkshire-type locomotive built in 1944 by Lima Locomotive Works, in Lima, Ohio, made a two-week visit. The Howe Meadow festival was reprised.

Nearly all excursions behind No. 1293 or No. 765 featured a photo runby whereby the train backed up and charged past the crowd of passengers with smoke billowing and the whistle sounding. Other 2010 events involving No. 765 included a dinner train from Brecksville and a night photo session at Fitzwater Shops. No. 765 also led a "total track tour" covering the 51 miles from Independence to Canton.

When No. 765 returned in 2011 it spent most of September pulling trips from Akron, Independence and Brecksville. These included a wine-tasting trip and a dinner train. It participated in a night photograph session at Fitzwater. The photo runbys were moved from Indigo Lake to Boston Mill, where they have remained for subsequent steam locomotive visits.

No. 1293 came to the CVSR in September 2012, and No. 765 returned in September 2013, 2014, 2015 and 2016 to engage in activities similar to those of previous years, although some changes were made in trip lengths. Neither No. 1293 nor No. 765 have been used to pull regularly scheduled CVSR trains. All excursions and events involving steam motive power have been held between the end of the summer season and the beginning of the fall foliage season.

Some steam excursions have featured a connection to the era when No. 4070 steamed through the Valley. Two Nickel Plate Road open-window coaches owned by the Midwest Railway Preservation Society have been run behind No. 765 just as they once ran behind No. 4070.

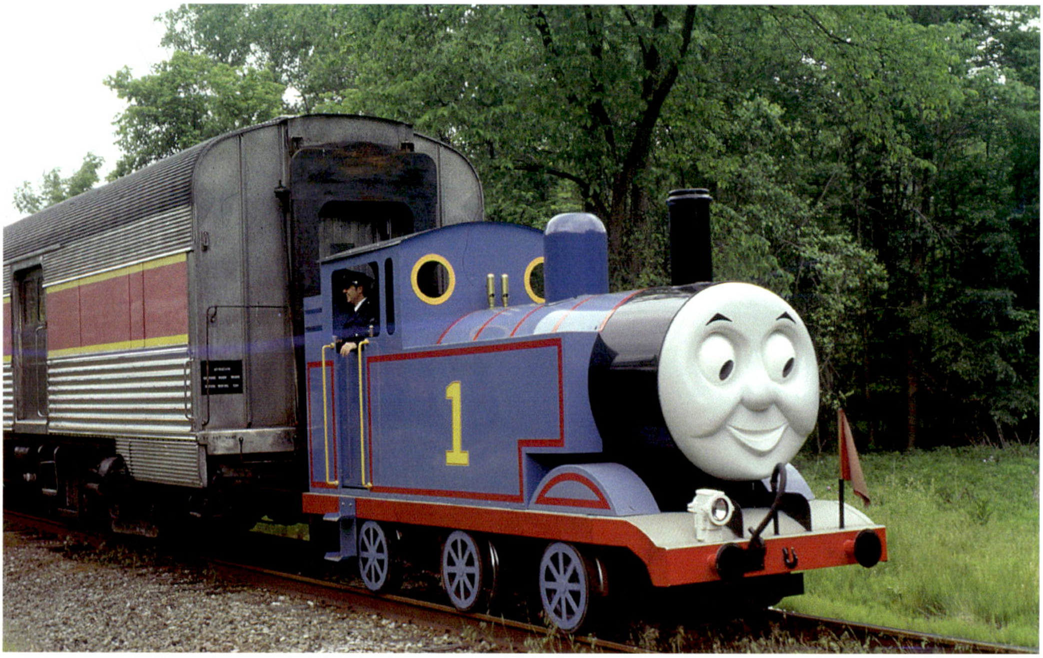

NO DOUBTING THOMAS: Since making its first CVSR appearance in May 1998, *Thomas the Tank Engine* has become the second most popular special event behind the *Polar Express*. The fictional steam locomotive first appeared in *The Railway Series* books by British authors Wilbert and Christopher Awdry and attracts 25,000 to 26,000 passengers on the CVSR. One of the four Thomas prototypes was converted from a 1916 steam locomotive used by the Brooklyn Dock & Terminal in New York City. Thomas is based on a British E2 Class locomotive. CVSR's *Thomas* trains leave from Boston Mill station for 20-minute trips with a CVSR diesel on the other end of the train. (*Above, Tom Fritsch photo; below, Mark Demaline photo*)

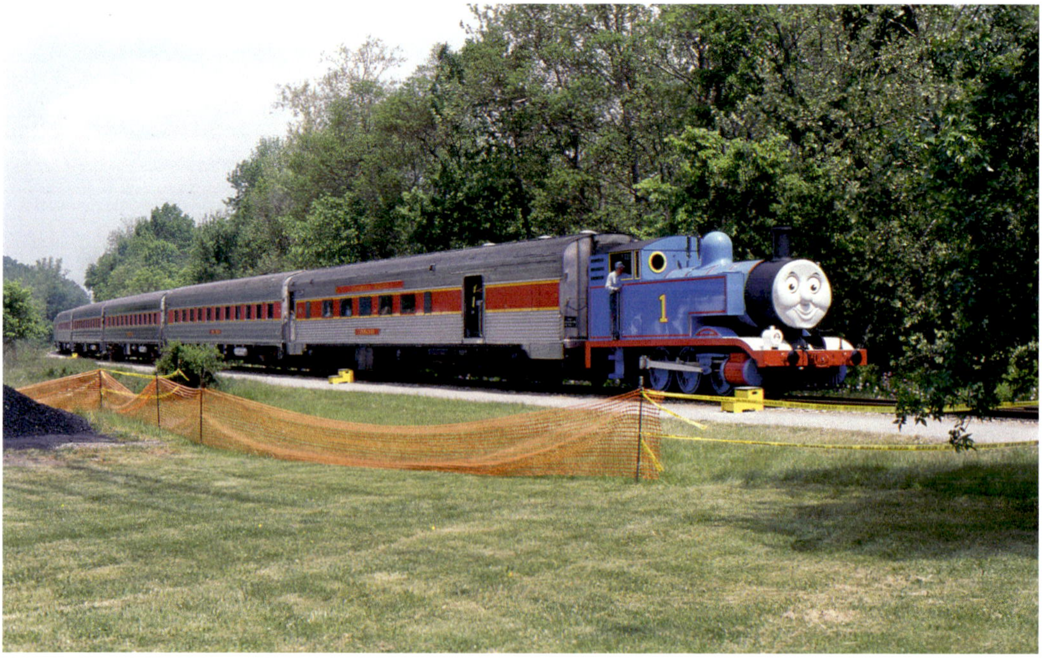

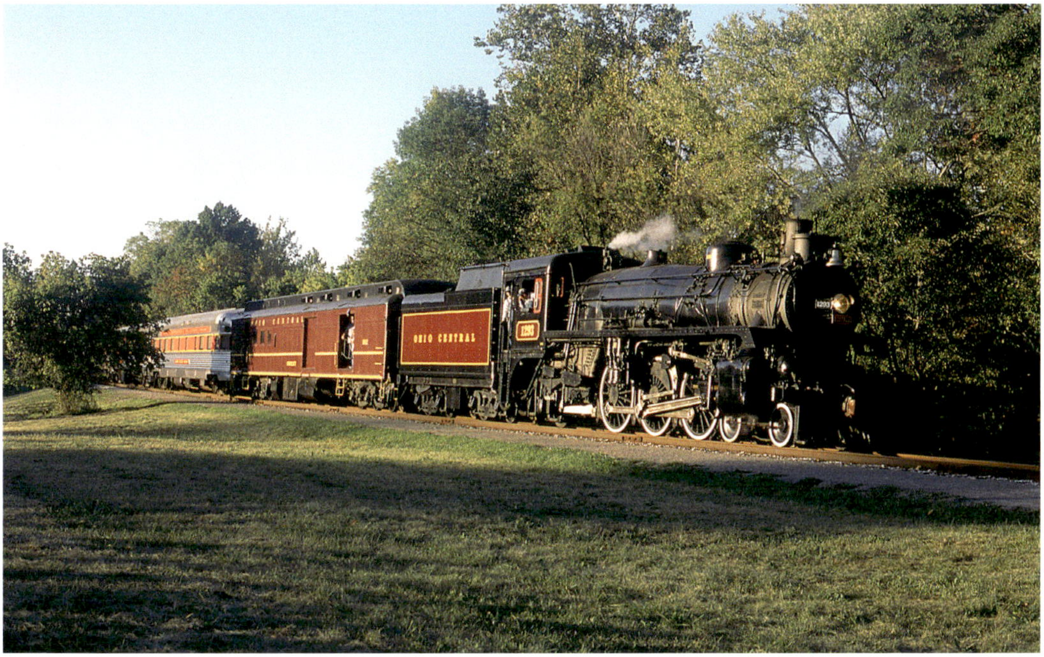

STEAM RETURNS: Steam locomotive power returned to the Cuyahoga Valley in September 2007 with the visit of Ohio Central System 4-6-2 No. 1293. The Pacific-type locomotive pulled four excursions between September 20 and 22, all departing from Independence. It had been seventeen years almost to the day since steam locomotive No. 4020 had pulled its last train on the Cuyahoga Valley Line. No. 1293 returned to the CVSR in 2008 and pulled trips between September 24 and 28. A steam festival held at Howe Meadow featured short train rides. Above, No. 1293 backs up at Boston Mill before executing a photo runby. Below, No. 1293 passes the Indigo Lake station. (*Above, Jim Mastromatteo photo; below, Peter Bowler photo*)

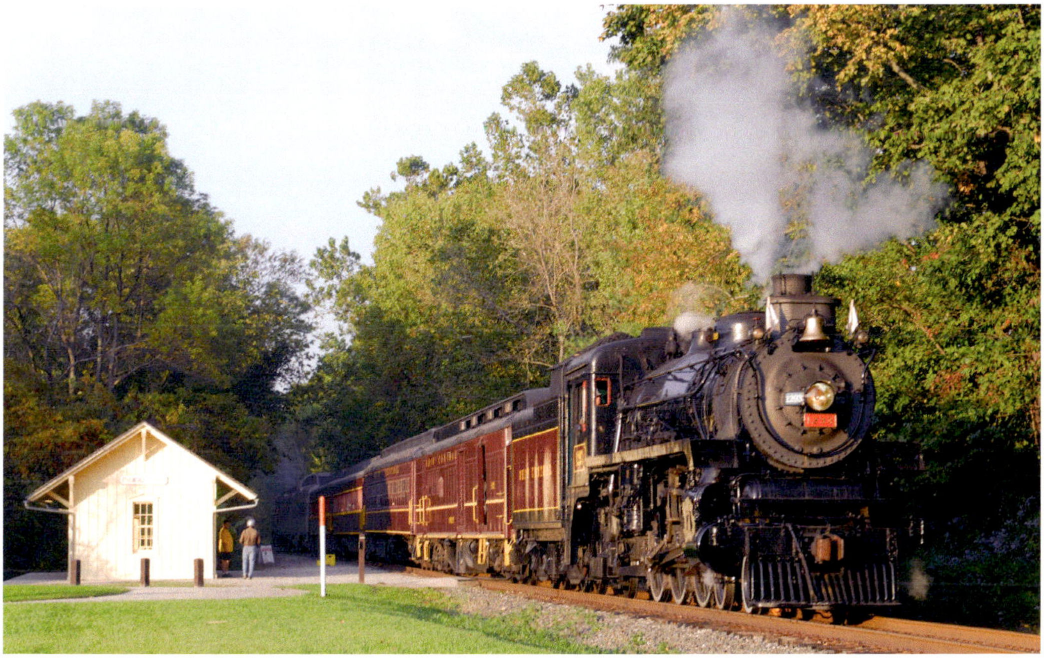

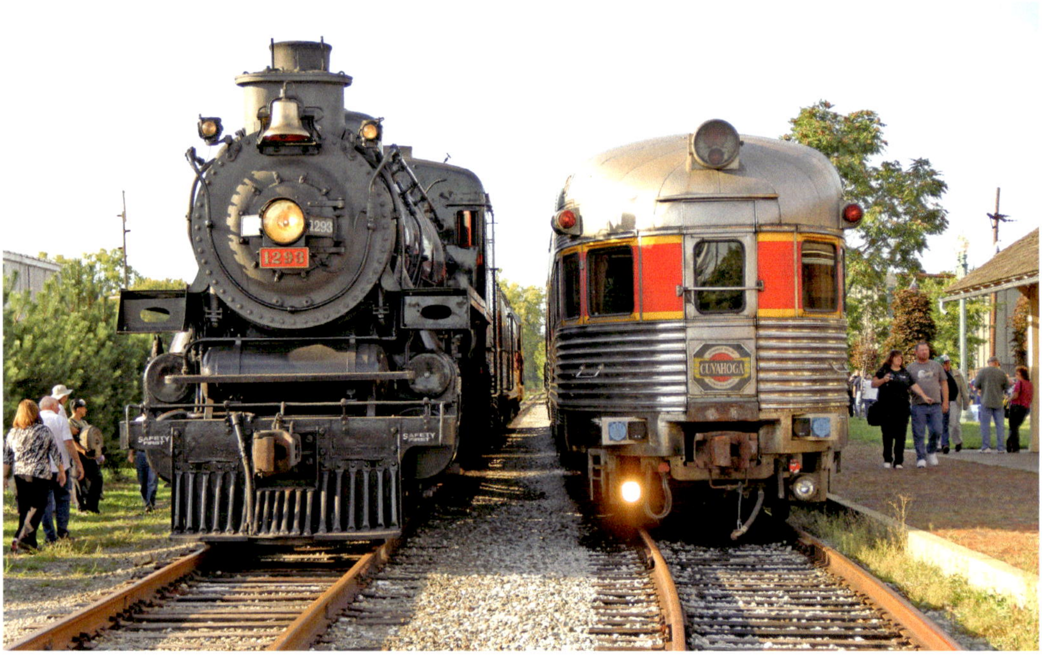

ENCORE PERFORMANCE: No. 1293 returned to the CVSR in September 2012 and pulled excursions over three weekends. Unlike during past visits, No. 1293 operated trips that covered the length of the CVSR, including a trip on September 15 that operated from Brecksville to Canton. Other trips operated between Akron and Indigo Lake, and between Independence and Boston Mill. Above, after arriving at Canton, No. 1293 moved to a siding and stood next to observation-lounge car *Saint Lucie Sound* in a pose reminiscent of railroad publicity photographs from the early streamliner era. Below, No. 1293 stands at the Akron station the night before it left the CVSR in September 2012. (*Above, Craig Sanders photo; below, Paul Woodring photo*)

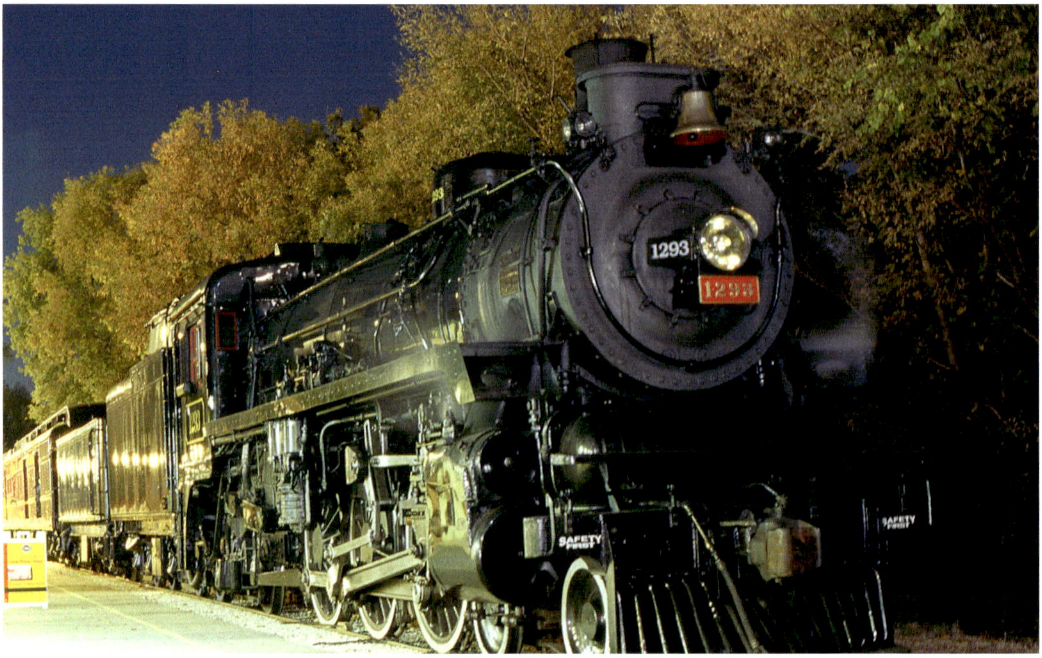

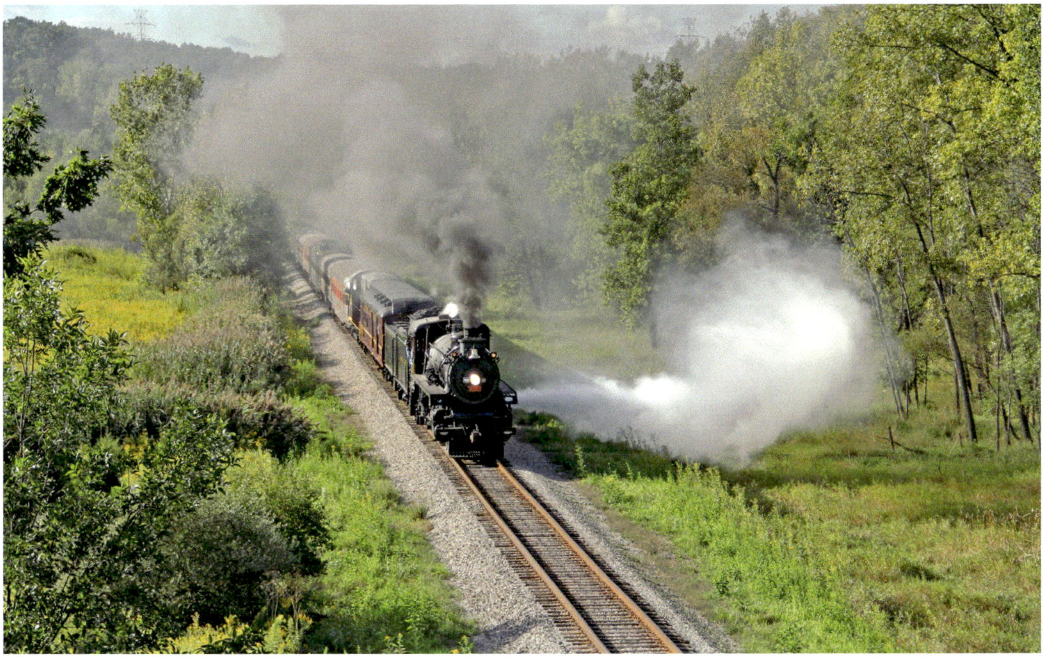

CELEBRATING AN ANNIVERSARY: No. 1293 pulled a September 8, 2012, trip that took passengers to a gala event at Hale Farm and Village to celebrate the 40th anniversary of the founding of the Cuyahoga Valley Preservation and Steam Railroad Association. The trip left from Independence and ended at Indigo Lake. Above, the anniversary celebration trip has just gotten under way and is approaching East Pleasant Valley Road. Below, the train has unloaded its passengers at Indigo Lake where a stuck throttle on No. 1293 caused its driver wheels to spin wildly. The locomotive was unable to make a scheduled run the next day but was repaired in time for a trip to Canton on September 15. (*Craig Sanders photos*)

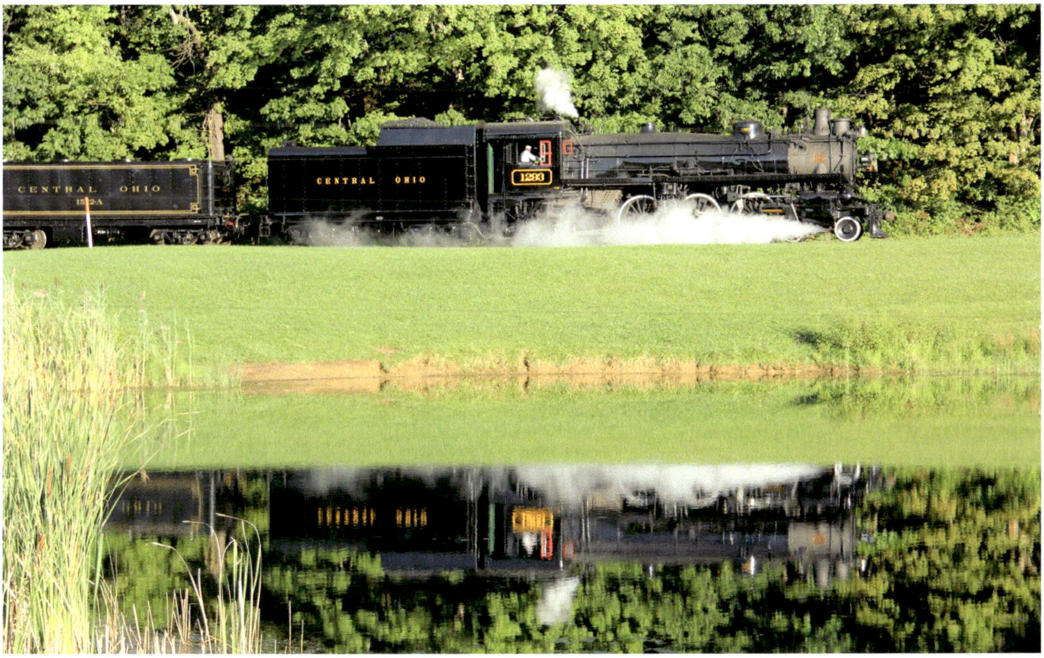

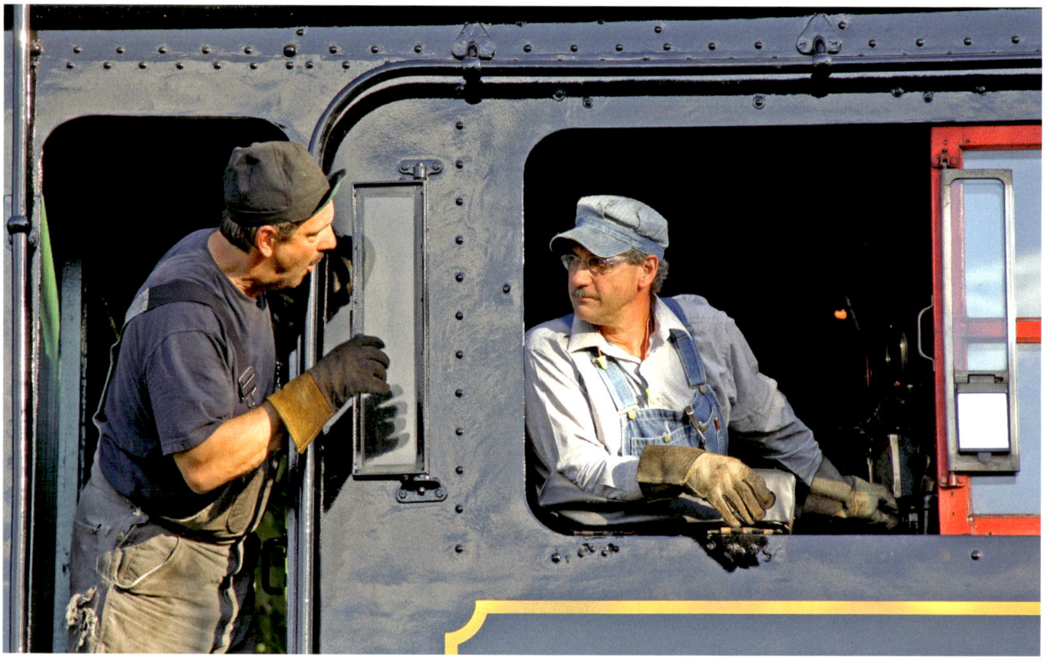

STEAMING IN THE VALLEY: When No. 1293 returned to the CVSR in 2012 it was owned by the Age of Steam Roundhouse, which was established by Jerry Joe Jacobson, the founder of the Ohio Central. Jacobson had sold the Ohio Central to the Genesee & Wyoming Inc. in September 2008 but retained ownership of the OC's steam locomotives and passenger cars. The 1293 crew members were AOS employees or volunteers and the tender carried the name "Central Ohio." Above, Engineer Tim Sposato (right) talks with crew member Mark Perri, who is also a CVSR locomotive engineer. Below, No. 1293 puts out a smoke trail as it performs a photo runby at Boston Mill on September 29, 2012. (*Craig Sanders photos*)

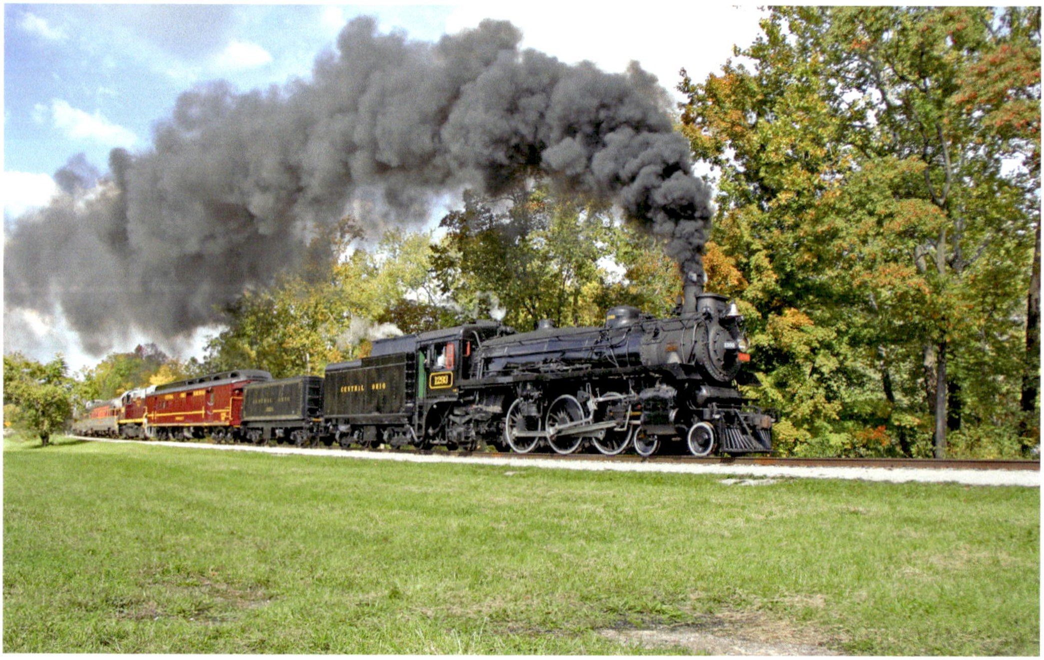

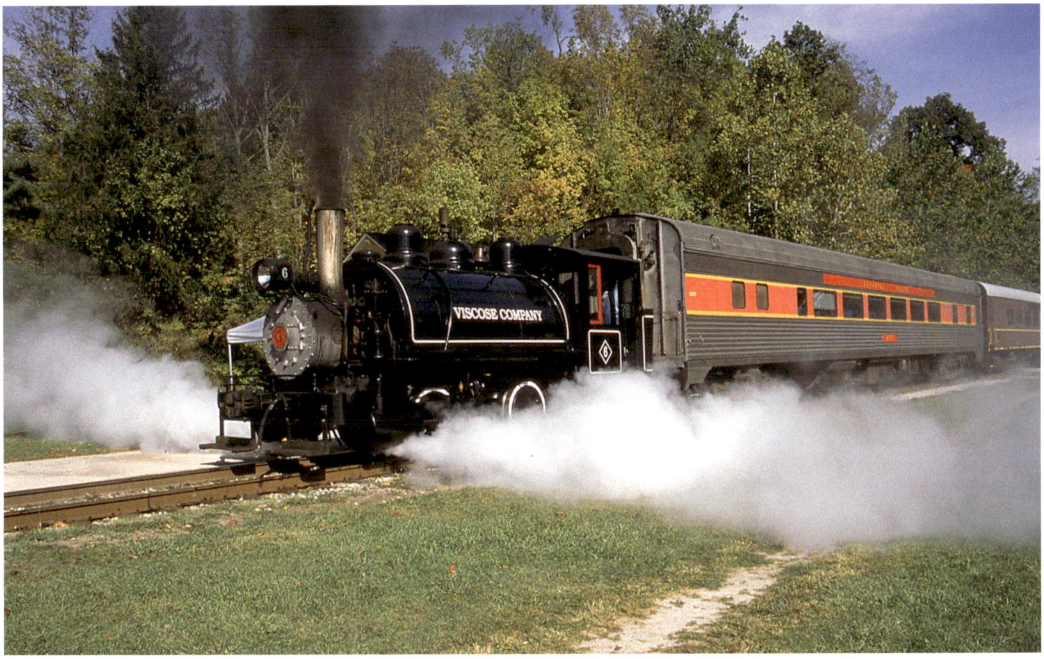

PINT SIZE STEAM ENGINE: Viscose Company No. 6, a Baldwin-built tank engine, appeared on the CVSR in September 2010 in conjunction with the first appearance of Nickel Plate Road 2-8-4 No. 765. It was the only time that two steam engines have appeared on the railroad at the same time. Shown in Brecksville in both photos, the 0-4-0 pulled trips between Brecksville station and the Fitzwater Maintenance Yard. Owner Scott Symans of Dunkirk, New York, acquired No. 6 from a Virginia scrap dealer in September 2004 and restored it to operating condition. No. 6 was built in September 1924 for American Viscose Company of Roanoke, Virginia. *(Craig Sanders photos)*

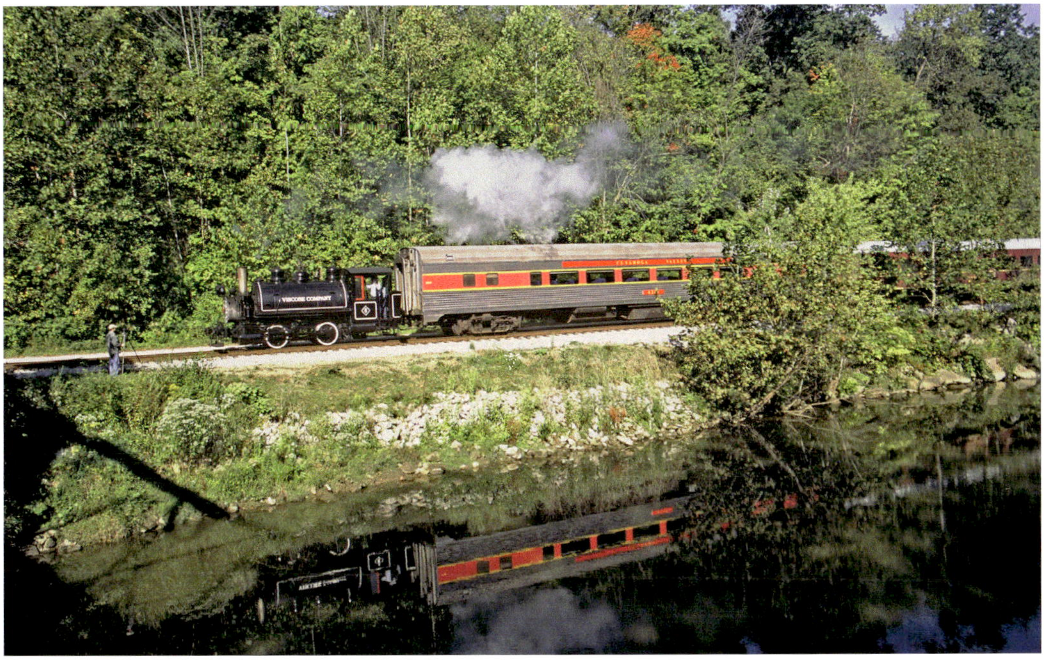

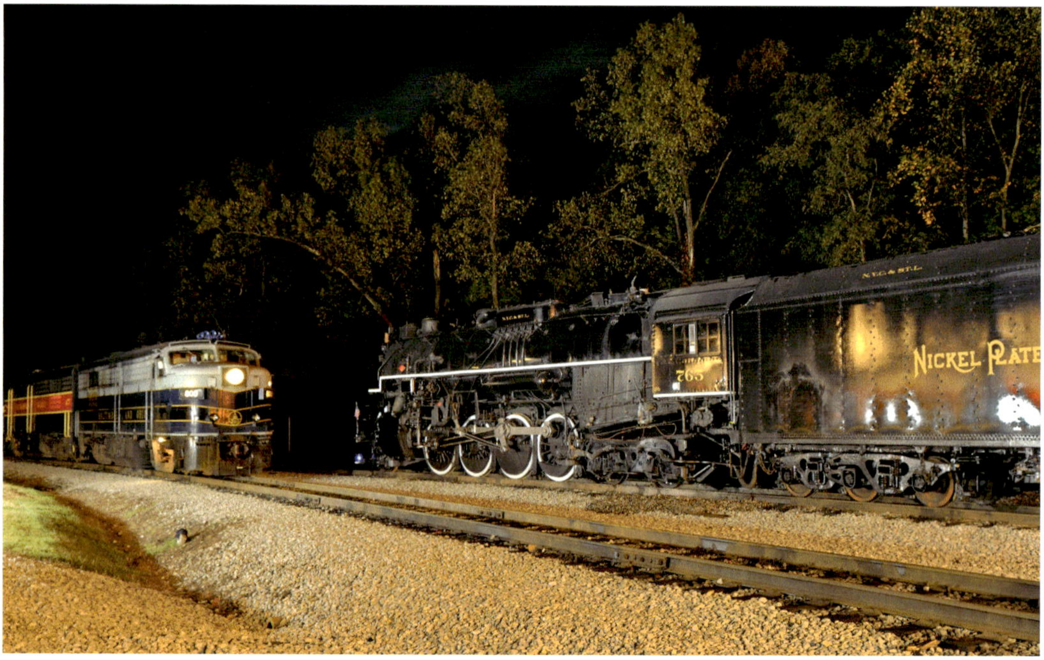

INDIANA VISITOR: No. 765 is based in Fort Wayne, Indiana, and owned by the Fort Wayne Railroad Historical Society. The Berkshire-type engine was built in 1944 by the Lima Locomotive Works in Lima, Ohio. It often pulled freight trains through Northeast Ohio and made its last revenue run on June 14, 1958. It has pulled numerous excursions throughout the eastern United States after being removed from a Fort Wayne park and restored to operating condition in 1979. Above, No. 765 poses with FPA-4 No. 800 at Fitzwater Shops during a night photo shoot on September 16, 2010. Below, the steamer pulls a train to Akron as it cruises along Riverview Road south of Peninsula. (*Peter Bowler photos*)

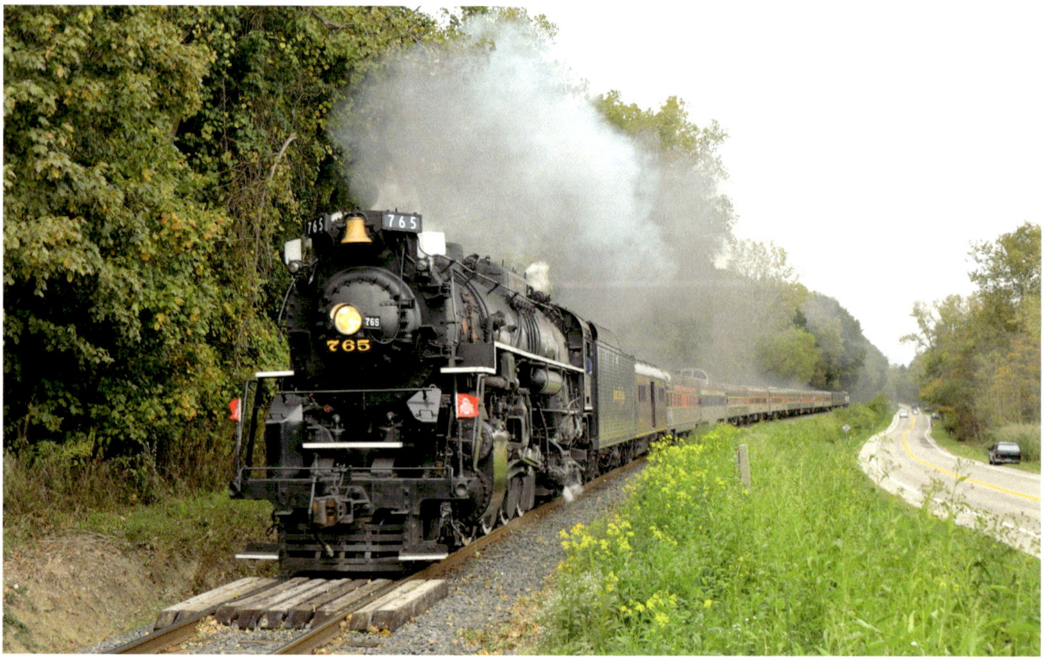

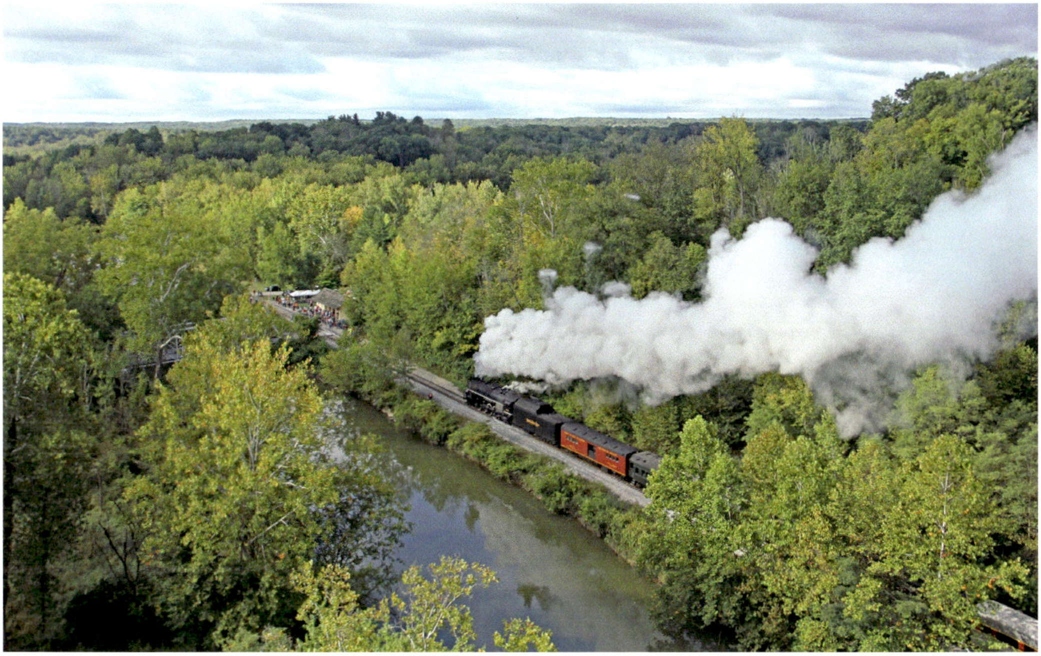

STEAM IN BRECKSVILLE: A popular place to photograph No. 765 on the CVSR is Brecksville. The cool morning temperatures of mid-to-late September are conducive to the locomotive putting out a lot of steam and smoke. Brecksville station often was used as a boarding site for excursions pulled by the locomotive. Trips also originated at Akron, Boston Mill and Independence. Above, a crowd in Brecksville awaits the arrival of the train as it rolls along the Cuyahoga River on September 20, 2015. Most trips featured photo runbys at Boston Mill. Below, No. 765 puts on a show as it cruises through Brecksville en route to Canton during a total track tour excursion on September 17, 2011. (*Craig Sanders photos*)

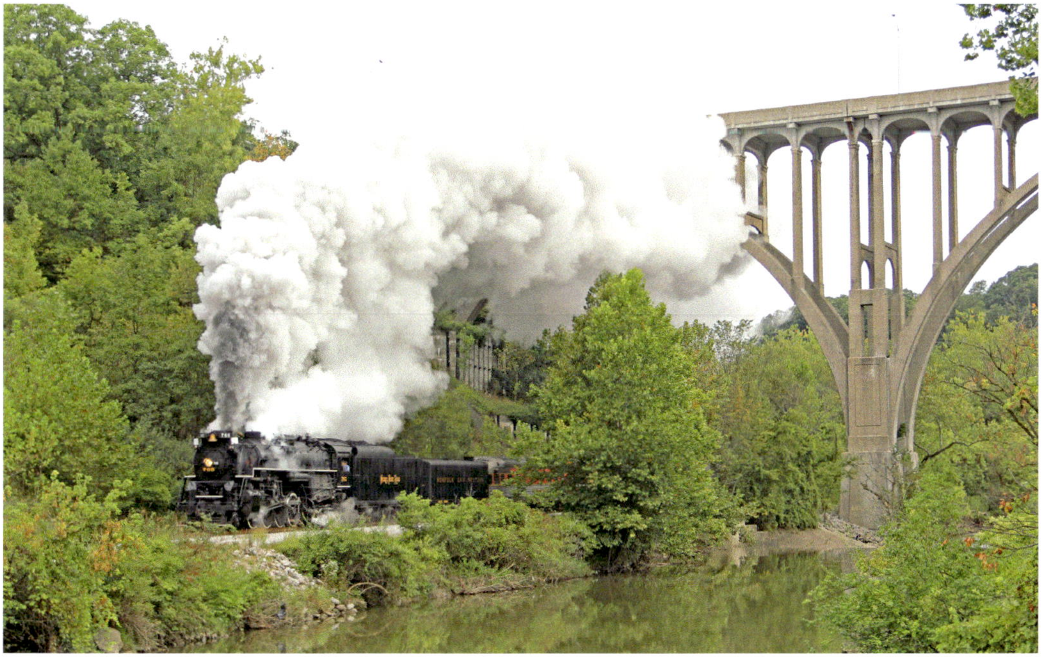

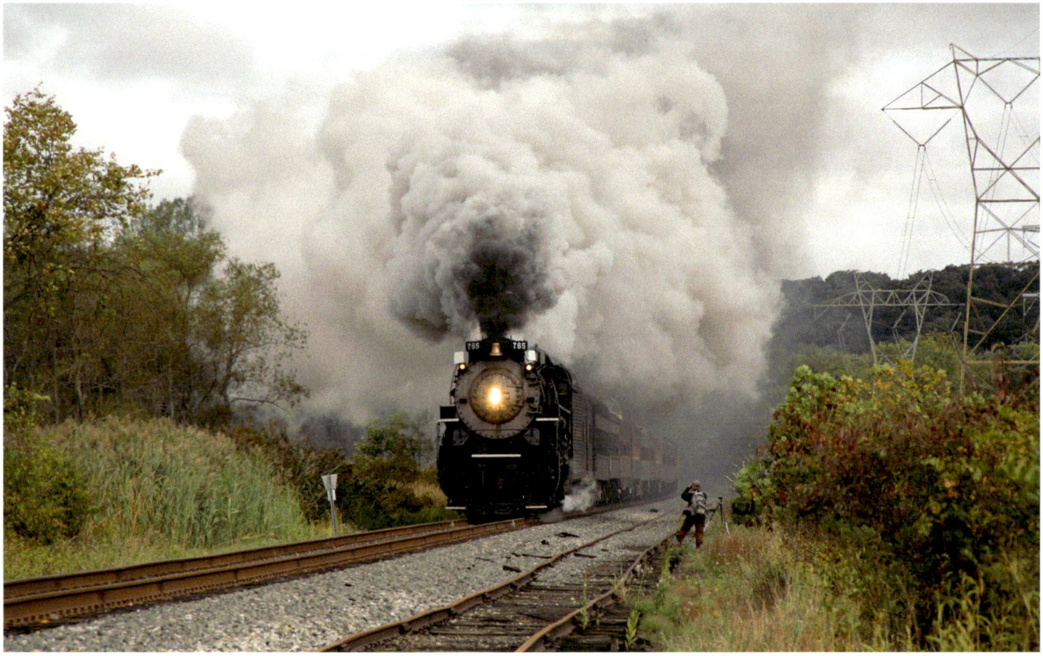

ALWAYS PHOTOGRAPHERS AROUND: Every trip pulled by No. 765 on the CVSR was assured of being photographed, whether by photographers lugging expensive camera gear or park visitors photographing it with their smartphones. Some photographers came from several states away to photograph the locomotive. Excursions behind No. 765 usually were scheduled to last three hours and operated as extra trains scheduled to avoid the CVSR's *Scenic*. In some years, No. 765 would pass the *Scenic* as it sat in the Peninsula siding. Above, No. 765 is working hard as it nears Jaite on October 4, 2015, the only time it ran on the CVSR outside of September. Below, cameras are out in Peninsula on September 7, 2014. (Craig Sanders photos)

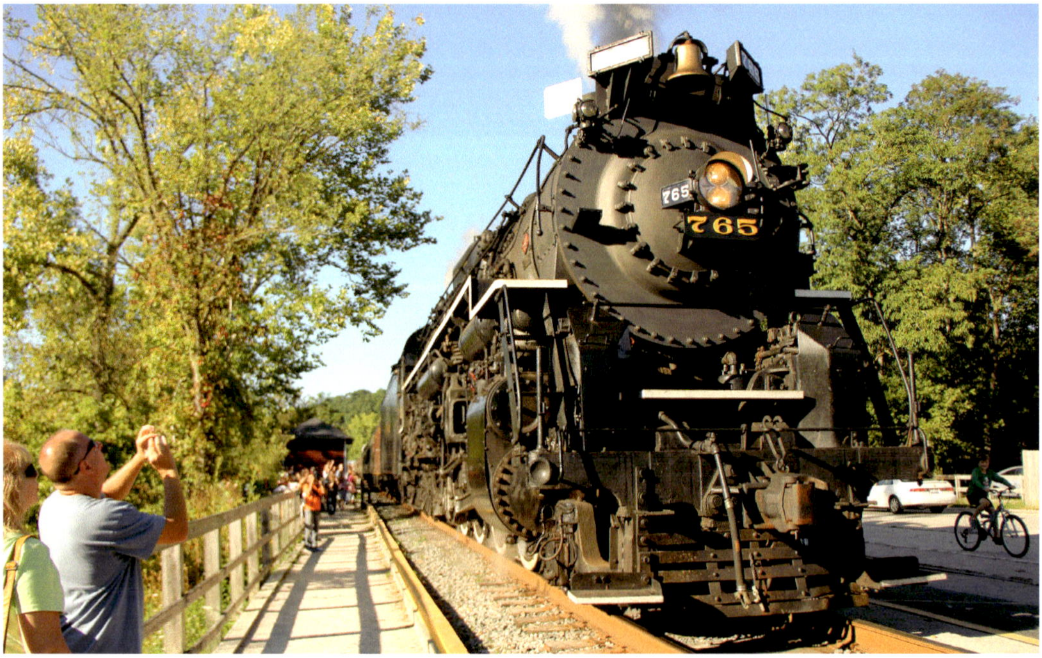

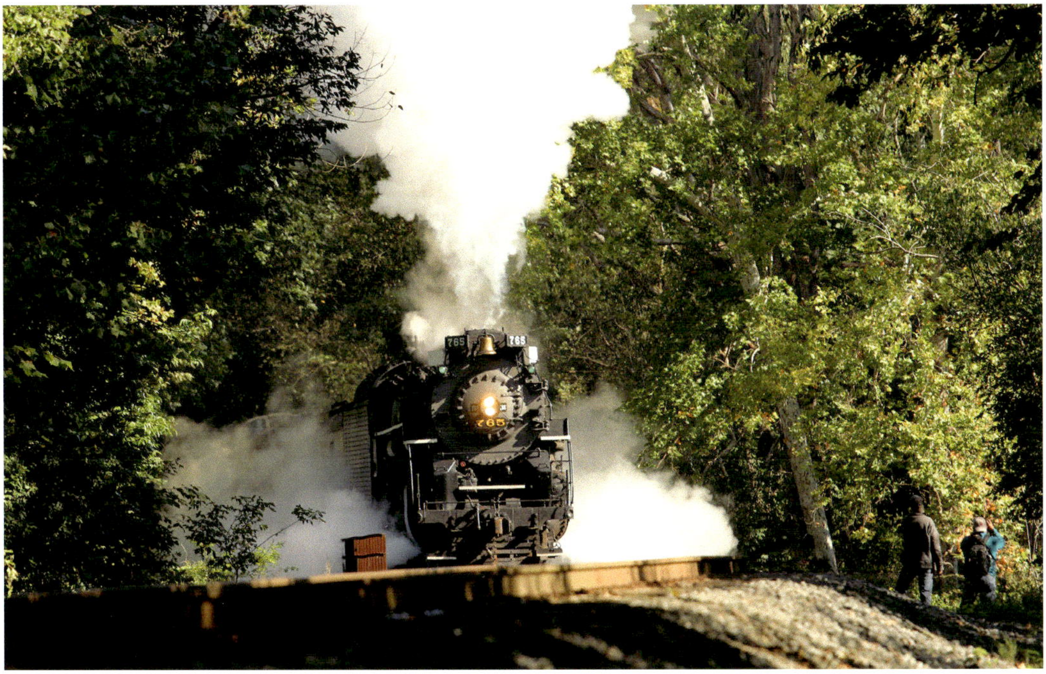

ATTRACTING PASSENGERS: The CVSR steam trains drew 3,899 passengers in 2014 and 4,525 in 2015. All of the 2016 trips were sold out in advance. By comparison, the steam trips of 2012 behind No. 1293 drew 1,500 passengers. Above, a good place to watch No. 765 at work is south of Peninsula as it climbs a 0.7 percent grade out of town. It is an ideal location to listen to the locomotive at work. The train is about to cross the Cuyahoga River on September 14, 2014. Below, No. 765 crosses the Cuyahoga River north of Peninsula on October 4, 2015. (*Craig Sanders photos*)

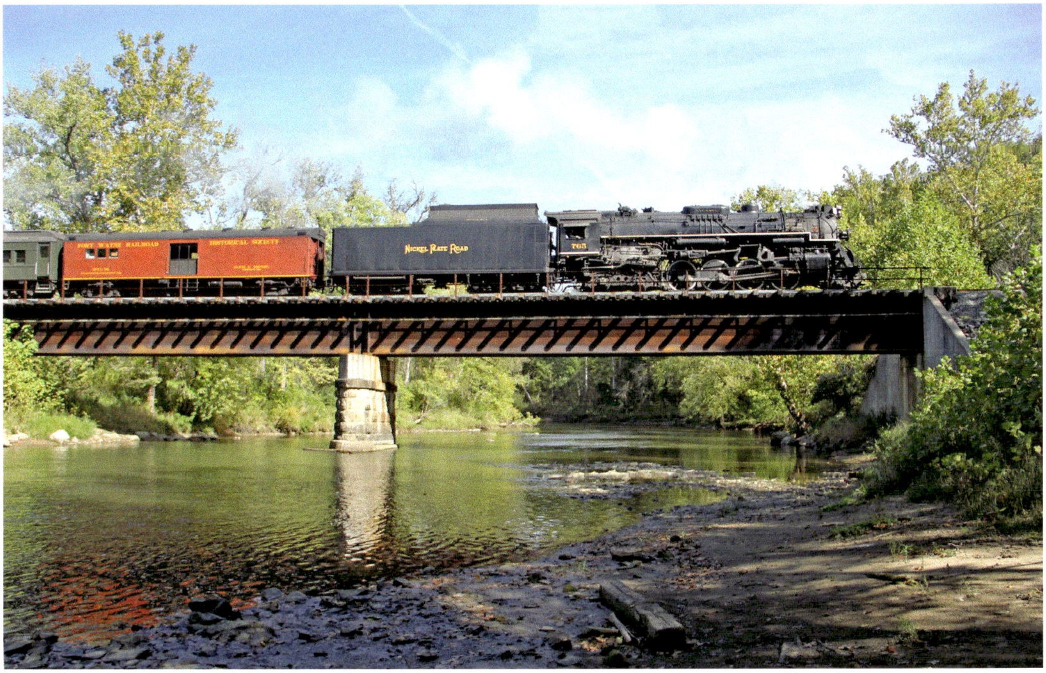

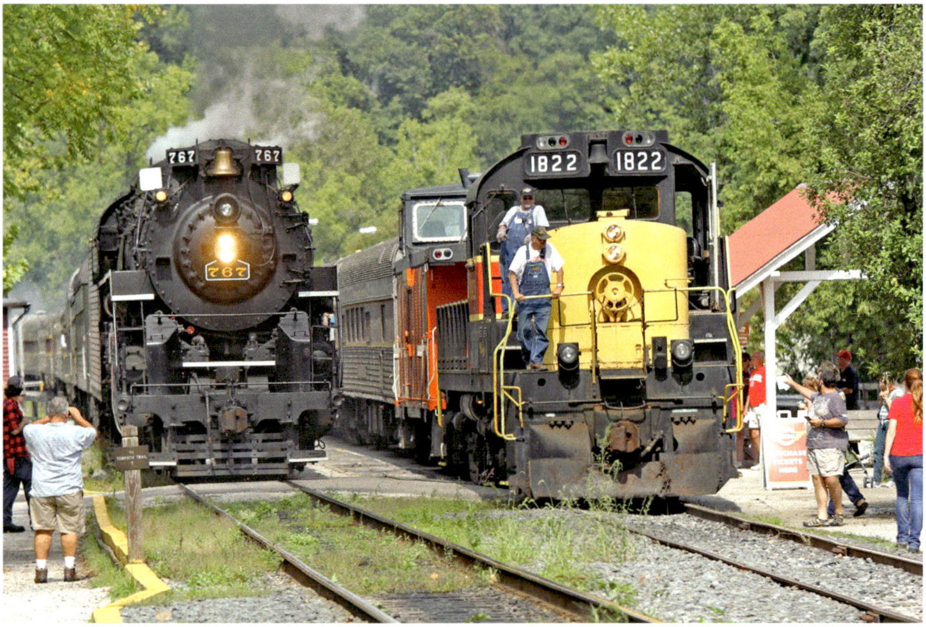

NEW NUMBER, SAME ENGINE: For its September 2016 CVSR excursions, No. 765 wore number 767, which it had worn while displayed in the 1960s in Fort Wayne's Lawton Park. City officials had asked the Nickel Plate to donate No. 767 because it had participated in a 1955 ribbon breaking ceremony to mark the completion of the elevation of the NKP tracks through downtown Fort Wayne. The railroad actually sent locomotive 765, but with number 767. The ruse was discovered when the engine was restored. Above, No. 767 meets a CVSR *Scenic* in Peninsula. Below, the locomotive is working hard as it climbs Merriman Hill in Akron. (*Above, Craig Sanders photo; below, Peter Bowler photo*)

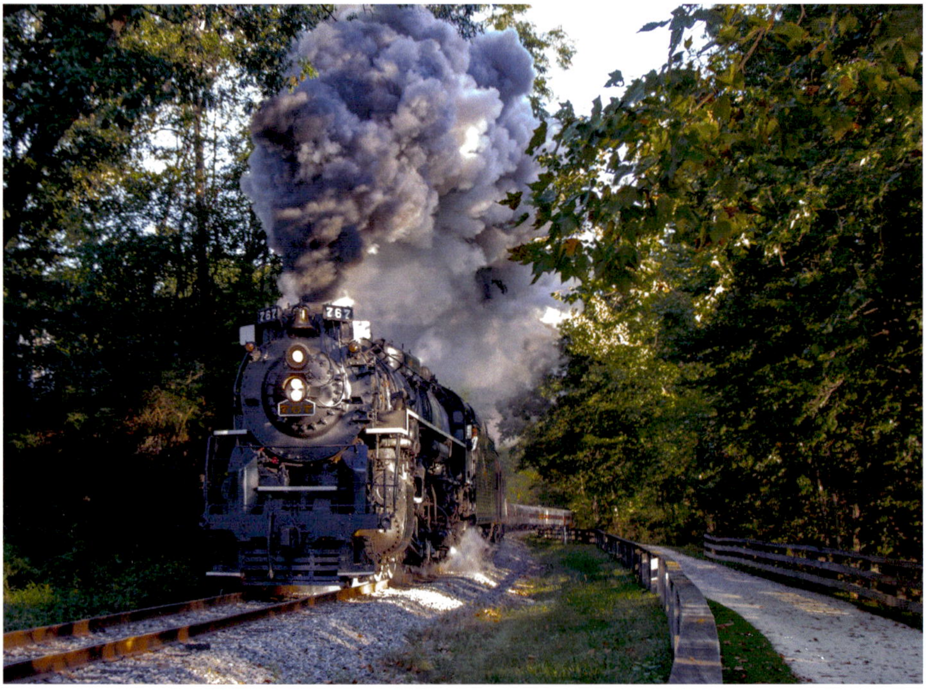